Culture and Disability

MULTICULTURAL ASPECTS OF COUNSELING SERIES

SERIES EDITOR

Paul B. Pedersen, Ph.D., Professor Emeritus, Syracuse University
Visiting Professor, Department of Psychology, University of Hawaii

VOLUMES IN THIS SERIES

Culture and Disability

Providing Culturally Competent Services

John H. Stone
The State University of New York

Editor

Multicultural Aspects of Counseling Series 21

SAGE Publications
Thousand Oaks ▪ London ▪ New Delhi

For information:

Sage Publications, Inc.
2455 Teller Road
Thousand Oaks, California 91320
E-mail: order@sagepub.com

Sage Publications Ltd.
1 Oliver's Yard
55 City Road
London EC1Y 1SP
United Kingdom

Sage Publications India Pvt. Ltd.
B-42, Panchsheel Enclave
Post Box 4109
New Delhi 110 017 India

Printed in the United States of America

Library of Congress Cataloging-in-Publication data

Culture and disability : providing culturally competent services/
edited by John H. Stone.
　　　p. cm.
Includes bibliographical references and index.
ISBN 0-7619-3083-3 (hardcover)—ISBN 0-7619-3084-1 (pbk.)
　　1. Minority people with disabilities—Services for—United States. 2. People with disabilities—Services for—United States. 3. Social work with minorities—United States. 4. Minorities—Services for—United States.
5. Ethnic attitudes—United States. I. Stone, John H. (John Henry), 1943-
HV1569.M55C85 2005
362.4'0453'08900973—dc22

　　　　　　　　　　　　　　　　2004011473

04　05　06　07　08　10　9　8　7　6　5　4　3　2　1

Acquiring Editor:	Arthur T. Pomponio
Editorial Assistant:	Veronica Novak
Production Editor:	Sanford Robinson
Typesetter:	C&M Digitals (P) Ltd.
Copy Editor:	A. J. Sobczak
Indexer:	Molly Hall
Cover Designer:	Michelle Kenny

Contents

List of Figures, Tables, Appendixes, and Charts

Series Editor's Foreword

The Multicultural Aspects of Counseling series prides itself on demonstrating the generic importance of a "multicultural" perspective as the first step in developing competence as a service provider. John Stone's book fits wonderfully into that tradition by presenting a valuable discussion and analysis of disability for the benefit of service providers who work with clients who are disabled or who are perceived by others as being disabled, whether they share that perception or not.

When I brought a team of two resource persons representing the perspective of people with disabilities into my classroom, they demanded from the beginning that the other students avoid using any term to describe persons with a disability other than *inconvenienced,* to emphasize the pejorative meanings society has attached to the alternative terms. Although we are forced to use the term *disability,* it is important to acknowledge the profoundly important feelings and emotions that society has attached to that and other similar terms. Stone's book is sensitive to the meanings of words and to the importance of relationships in serving persons with a disability. Having a good relationship has emerged in the research literature as the single most important necessary—but not sufficient—condition for competence in counseling and human services. There is a consistent focus on the process variables as well as the content variables in a dynamic interdependent balance.

On one hand, there is the "culture of disability," in which persons with a disability share a unique perspective with one another, acknowledge implicit rules for interaction, use a preferred vocabulary to express meanings, and have other markers of a cultural group that are perhaps unfamiliar to persons who do not have a disability. This unique perspective is celebrated and acknowledged by the community of persons with disabilities as a legitimate group in its own right, without reference to or judgment by those groups who do not belong. On the other hand, there is a treasure of information about similarities and differences in how disability is viewed and managed across the country-cultures of China, Jamaica, Korea, Haiti, Mexico, the Dominican Republic, and Vietnam. Stone's book takes a global perspective of the topic, providing the reader with both an in-depth/narrow view of disability as a culture and a broad/comprehensive view of different ways disability has been interpreted across cultures.

There are many new ideas in Stone's book. Although the book is primarily focused on the "new immigrant," that construct shares many features with minorities in a society shaped by a unimodal dominant culture. Many of the same problems of language, housing, employment, understanding, and being fairly understood by service providers come up repeatedly. This problem is magnified when so few service providers are themselves from minority groups or are persons with a disability, including physical, occupational, and speech language therapists; vocational rehabilitation personnel; rehabilitation-technology specialists; rehabilitation physicians and nurses; special educators; staff of centers for independent living; and community service providers, in addition to those family members and friends who care for and about the person with a disability. Stone's book will help all service providers develop a competent and meaningful level of service to their clients generally as well as to persons with a disability.

The emphasis is on providing an educational process, but the target reader is not referred to as a "patient" or "client" but more likely as a "student" or as a "consumer," emphasizing the person's role as a user of services. Another important distinction is in the use of the term *culture brokering* as the process of facilitating and mediating between the culture of the consumer and the host-culture of the provider. The importance of service providers becoming directly involved in the helping process, rather than maintaining objectivity and distance in the pretense of neutrality, is rapidly gaining credibility as service providers become more activist and less passive when confronted by injustice.

We are proud to include Stone's excellent book among the library of books in the Multicultural Aspects of Counseling series. When I first read this proposal and later the book, my first thought was "This book will make a difference!" Stone's book will have an influence on those who read it, and there will be a ripple effect throughout the profession, moving the way human services are provided toward a better understanding of the consumer's cultural context.

Paul Pedersen

Preface

The theme of cultural competence has assumed an increasingly important role in the delivery of human services in the United States as well as in other countries with large immigrant populations. Disability services are no exception. Although there may be no universally accepted definition of the term *cultural competence,* the delivery of effective services to persons from other cultures requires an understanding of the ways in which culture may affect one's views of disability, as well as information about specific cultures.

This book attempts to contribute to both of these types of knowledge. The first three chapters describe the relationship between culture and disability as well as the role of service providers in communicating across cultures, whatever those cultures may be. The following seven chapters provide information about the specific cultures of groups that account for large proportions of recent immigration to the United States.

Portions of this book originally appeared as monographs written for disability and rehabilitation service providers. It soon became apparent, however, that many university programs were beginning to include cultural topics within courses that prepare professionals to work with persons with disabilities. This book, therefore, attempts to contribute to meeting the needs of both audiences—persons already working in disability services and students preparing for such careers.

I would like to acknowledge and thank the National Institute on Disability and Rehabilitation Research of the U.S. Department of Education for its support of the work of the Center for International Rehabilitation Research Information and Exchange (CIRRIE), through which much of the original material for this book was prepared. Special thanks are also due to Ms. Kathleen Wisniewski of the CIRRIE project for her dedication during the development of the original monograph series and during the preparation of this book. Ms. Wisniewski performed many tasks during that time, from tracking submissions, to incorporating editorial corrections, to occasionally cajoling procrastinating authors.

Far from intending to be the last word on this subject, I hope that this book will stimulate the generation and dissemination of further resources that will enable us to find better ways to meet the needs of persons with disabilities who have come from other countries.

John Stone, PhD, Director,
Center for International Rehabilitation
Research Information and Exchange (CIRRIE)

Introduction and Overview

Since the early 1980s, approximately a million persons have immigrated to the United States every year from other countries. Thirty years ago, approximately 1 in 20 Americans was born outside the United States. Today, the ratio is more than 1 in 10. Many of us can remember a time when contact with other cultures was considered the domain of diplomats, missionaries, and Peace Corps volunteers. Today, nearly everyone in the United States has a cross-cultural story to tell, and those who provide services to persons with disabilities are no exception.

Disability can be a challenge no matter where one is born. For a recent immigrant, the challenge is often magnified. In addition to difficulties with language, housing, and employment, the person with disabilities may also have difficulty understanding and accessing rehabilitation and other disability services. Most service providers recognize this but often experience frustration that arises from miscommunication and differing cultural perspectives. Providers can mitigate such problems, however, by recognizing obstacles that pose difficulties for the foreign-born consumer and identifying ways to overcome them.

Leavitt (1999) pointed out that although ethnic minorities constitute approximately 25–30% of the U.S. population, they make up less than 8% of the population of health and rehabilitation professionals. Although efforts are being made to recruit more service providers from other cultures, within the foreseeable future most foreign-born consumers will be served by professionals whose cultural backgrounds are very different from their own. Therefore, it is critical that all service providers understand how such differences can affect their services.

According to Groce (1999):

Understanding sociocultural models of disability is of more than academic interest. Unless programs for individuals with disabilities are designed in a culturally appropriate way, the opportunity to make real and effective change is often lost.

[The intent is not] to catalogue every known variation in disability beliefs, but rather to alert the practitioners to the fact that the ways in which disability and rehabilitation are conceptualized will have an impact on the manner in which rehabilitation professionals are received, regarded and able to serve their patients. (p. 38)

There are two types of understanding that are useful in providing effective services to persons from other cultures. One is knowledge about the specific culture of the persons with whom we are working. To provide practitioners with information about specific cultures and their perspectives on disability and rehabilitation, CIRRIE—the Center for International Rehabilitation Research Information and Exchange at the State University of New York at Buffalo—developed a series of monographs on the cultures of 11 of the countries from which most immigrants to the United States originate. Material from several of these monographs has provided the basis for the chapters in this book on the cultures of China, Jamaica, Korea, Haiti, Mexico, the Dominican Republic, and Vietnam.

The second type of understanding useful to those working in cross-cultural rehabilitation settings relates not to specific cultures but to the general process of working with persons with disabilities from different cultures, whatever those cultures may be. Several chapters offer insights and meanings that expand the reader's understanding of this process and help develop stronger and more effective cross-cultural skills. Although the focus of this book is on persons who have recently immigrated to the United States, many of the concepts also apply to persons who were born in the United States but are from a culture other than the dominant one.

Included in the term *disability service providers* are physical, occupational, and speech language therapists; vocational rehabilitation personnel; rehabilitation technology specialists; rehabilitation physicians and nurses; special educators; staff of centers for independent living; and community service providers. While providing examples from several fields, the authors of the chapters have attempted to avoid technical terminology specific to any one of them.

Throughout this book, we have generally used the term *consumer* to describe a person with a disability who uses the service system. We recognize that the term *patient* is commonly used in the context of medical rehabilitation and that *client* is often used in other rehabilitation fields. *Student* is the preferred term within special education. *Consumer,* however, is a generic term, and besides being the term preferred within the disability community, it expresses the notion that the person is a user of services and therefore is empowered to make the same kinds of choices and decisions as those who use other kinds of services.

The first chapter, "Immigrants, Disability, and Rehabilitation," is by Nora Groce, one of the prominent scholars of cultural aspects of disability. A medical anthropologist specializing in disability beliefs and practices, Dr. Groce has identified many variations in disability beliefs among the cultures of the world. Her historical perspective of this field and her comprehensive vision of disability in a cross-cultural context provide useful starting points to a book such as this.

The second chapter, "Culture and the Disability Services," examines the rehabilitation system in the United States and describes its cultural under-pinnings. It also shows why some consumers from immigrant groups may find it difficult to identify with many of the cultural values and practices that they encounter when interacting with disability service providers. The authors of this chapter are uniquely prepared to write on this subject. Paula Sotnik has worked for many years with foreign-born persons from diverse cultures in the context of rehabilitation services. She has also been the lead trainer in the CIRRIE workshop series *Culture Brokering: Providing Culturally Competent Disability Services.*

The coauthor of the second chapter is Mary Ann Jezewski, an anthro-pologist who developed a model of culture brokering and adapted it for reha-bilitation service providers. She defines culture brokering as the process of facilitating and mediating between the culture of the foreign-born person and the culture of the host country as well as the culture of the rehabilitation service system itself. It is this concept that forms the core of the third chapter, "Disability Service Providers as Culture Brokers," also coauthored by Jezewski and Sotnik.

In speaking of a therapist's role, Miles (1999) has written:

> It is hardly the therapist's job to try to change a client's fundamental beliefs—to do so might be seen as unprofessional conduct. Yet for most therapists, their work is more than a bag of techniques and gadgets. The therapist cannot avoid some engagement with clients' efforts to make sense of their disabilities, or those of their relatives. To listen attentively and with understanding requires the compe-tent therapist to have some broad awareness of the range of human beliefs in the disability area, and at least an outward tolerance of some that may seem person-ally repugnant. One benefit of studying a little further is that it may be possible to hint at paths that would take clients toward a more positive position within their own belief system. (p. 55)

It is usually not possible for busy service providers to learn several new languages or develop a deep knowledge of all cultures. Nevertheless, if providers understand some of the basic principles and common themes of a culture, they will have a better sense of how their clients perceive disability and what they consider to be appropriate goals and methods of rehabilitation. The next several chapters of this book examine cultural and disability from the perspectives of the cultures of seven prominent immigrant groups: China, Jamaica, Korea, Haiti, Mexico, the Dominican Republic, and Vietnam.

Although **China** is the most populous nation on our planet, historically, due to strict immigration quotas, Chinese immigration to the United States was limited compared with immigration from Europe. In recent decades, however, that has been reversed. Currently, China, including Hong Kong and Taiwan, is one of the principal countries of origin of immigrants to the United States.

Despite the large numbers of Chinese in the United States, most Americans have a very limited knowledge of Chinese language and culture. Therefore, like other recent immigrants, persons born in China may have difficulty using rehabilitation services in this country. The goal of the chapter "Best Practices: Developing Cross-Cultural Competence From a Chinese Perspective" is to provide an introduction to Chinese culture, focusing on information that may help rehabilitation service providers to better serve this population.

The author is very well qualified to write on this subject. A first-generation immigrant from the People's Republic of China, Gloria Zhang Liu has worked with people with disabilities in various capacities, including those of counselor and bilingual case manager. These activities have given her a keen insight into the difficulties in bridging the cultural gap between the rehabilitation service provider and persons from China, as well as strategies for overcoming these difficulties. Most of the case examples presented in this chapter are derived from the author's own experience.

Among the 10 principal countries of origin for immigration to the United States, **Jamaica** is the only one in which English is the principal language. Partly for this reason, Jamaicans in the United States are not always thought of as a distinct cultural group. They are often identified with African Americans, and it is sometimes assumed that they share similar values and perspectives. Jamaicans, however, have a distinct history and culture. Professionals providing human services to Jamaicans in the United States may benefit from an introduction to some of the basic themes that run through Jamaican culture.

Jamaicans are often stereotyped as carefree and fun loving. Although most Jamaicans do value a sense of humor, as well as music and dance, they also have a tradition of hard work and a strong respect for education. A history of slavery and resistance to it has resulted in an independent spirit that sometimes is manifested in a distrust of establishment organizations if these are perceived as intrusive. Health and other human services are sometimes not sought until there is a dire need.

The history of slavery, as well as poverty, has had an impact on family structure and gender roles. The need to seek employment in locations distant from their families, both within Jamaica and abroad, has frequently resulted in households run by mothers or grandmothers.

The chapter "An Introduction to Jamaican Culture for Rehabilitation Service Providers" reviews some of the historical influences on Jamaican culture and examines the cultural implications for the delivery of disability services to Jamaicans in the United States. The author of this chapter, Doreen Miller, was born in Jamaica and lived in both urban and rural Jamaican communities. She holds a doctorate in rehabilitation counseling and has been a faculty member in the United States for many years.

In 1997, 591,000 Korean-born persons were living in the United States (Schmidley & Campbell, 1999), making **Korea** one of the top 10 countries of origin for immigrants to this country. Despite various obstacles, many Koreans have been quite successful in the United States. The average American's knowledge of Korean culture is very limited, however, and some first-generation Koreans do not have strong English language skills. The result is the possibility of miscommunication between the newly arrived and native-born Americans. Cultural and language barriers can arise between disability service providers and their Korean-born clients that may hamper the progress of rehabilitation.

The author of the chapter "Disability and Korean Culture" is well qualified to help American service providers understand Korean culture and the perceptions of disability and rehabilitation that prevail within that culture. Weol Soon Kim-Rupnow was born in Korea and is a faculty member and service provider. She also directs the National Technical Assistance Center for Asians and Pacific Islanders with Disabilities at the University of Hawaii.

Many persons have come to the United States from **Haiti** for economic reasons, to escape one of the poorest economies in the Western Hemisphere. Others have fled for political reasons. Haitian culture is quite distinct and less familiar to most Americans than many other cultures (Latino cultures, for example). Haitian culture and language are also quite distinct from those of other Caribbean peoples. Often, these distinctions are not recognized. Most persons in the United States have very little information about Haitian culture and history. Perceptions often are influenced by simplistic Hollywood depictions.

For disability service providers who work with Haitians, it is imperative to become familiar with the Haitian understanding of the nature of disability and the shame and social stigma that often are attached to those individuals in the Haitian community who have disabilities. These attitudes prevent Haitian families from seeking support and social inclusion of their sons and daughters in community activities and programs, and families may never take advantage of social programs and services that are available. Many children with disabilities become socially isolated, and the families live a life apart from their community. Educators and health specialists who have an understanding of Haitian beliefs about disabilities will be in a better position to build bridges for Haitian families and to shape programs and services that account for their belief system. A better understanding of the nature of the social stigma that parents and children live with will also allow non-Haitian professionals to join forces with Haitian colleagues who are attempting to change their community's attitudes toward disability. Erik Jacobson, the author of the chapter "An Introduction to Haitian Culture for Rehabilitation Service Providers," is a literacy and community-based education specialist who has worked with the Haitian community of Boston for 9 years in a variety of capacities.

Mexico is by far the leading country of origin of immigrants to the United States. In 1997, more than 7 million Mexican-born persons lived in the United States, representing 28% of its foreign-born population. The immigrant population from Mexico is nearly six times that of the next highest country. The Mexican-born population in the United States increased from 0.8 million in 1970, to 2.2 million in 1980, to 4.3 million in 1990, to 7.0 million in 1997. (Schmidley & Campbell, 1999). In light of the large number of Mexican-born persons in the United States, it is surprising that Mexican culture is not well understood by many Americans.

The Mexican-born population differs from other foreign-born groups in the United States in several ways. Only 15% of U.S. residents born in Mexico are U.S. citizens. This contrasts sharply with the U.S. citizenship rates for persons born in Europe (53%) and Asia (44%), and even for those from other parts of Latin America.

Mexican-born persons in the United States tend to differ from other Latino groups in other ways as well. Forty-seven percent of all Latin American–born U.S. residents have a high school diploma. Among Mexican-born residents, the rate is 31%. Only 6% of the Mexican-born persons in the United States are employed in managerial and professional specialty occupations, compared to 23% of those from South America. The median annual earnings of U.S. workers born in Mexico were below those of workers born in the Caribbean or South America. The poverty rate for those born in Mexico is 34%, while for those born in South America it is 15%. Only 46% of the U.S. population that is Mexican-born has health insurance, compared to 69% for the Caribbean-born and 66% for South American–born. The average size of household was also larger for the Mexican-born (4.38 per household) than for those born in South America (3.17) (Schmidley & Campbell, 1999).

This profile indicates that many Mexican-born persons in the United States are poor, are not highly educated and lack access to many important services, even when compared to those from other parts of Latin America.

Individuals in such circumstances may experience difficulty accessing and using health, rehabilitation, and human services. It is particularly important that professionals in these fields develop at least some familiarity with Mexican culture if they are to provide effective services to this vast population in need of their services.

The authors of the chapter "An Introduction to Mexican Culture for Service Providers" are well qualified to interpret Mexican culture for rehabilitation service providers in the United States. Sandra Santana-Martin is a clinical psychologist who works with the Mexican farmworking community in a community health center in California. Felipe O. Santana is a clinical psychologist with 38 years of experience, including extensive experience with clients of Mexican origin.

Immigrants from the **Dominican Republic** are also among the 10 largest immigrant groups in the United States. Dominicans have settled largely on the East Coast of the United States. They are the second largest Hispanic/Latino group in New York City, with Puerto Ricans being the largest. Many persons in the United States identify the Dominican Republic as a land that produces great baseball players and as a country with tropical beaches. Few persons in the United States understand well the nature of the Dominican culture, the reasons for Dominican immigration to this country, or the difficulties encountered there. Rehabilitation service providers in the United States might be better equipped to work with Dominicans with disabilities if they were provided more information about Dominican views of the nature and origin of disabilities, the role of families, and other factors that can influence the success of disability services. The authors of the chapter "An Introduction to the Culture of the Dominican Republic for Disability Service Providers" are themselves immigrants from the Dominican Republic. Ana López-De Fede teaches and conducts research on the relationship between health and family well-being. She is actively involved in consulting on the development of programs that address the needs of individuals from the Caribbean basin. The second author, Dulce Haeussler-Fiore, came to the United States at the age of 37 and was surprised to see persons with disabilities working. She eventually worked as a case manager for 4 years and as a service coordinator for 6 years, as well as a clinician in a mental health clinic in Lawrence, Massachusetts.

In this chapter, the authors trace the history of Dominican emigration to the United States and its causes. Through numerous case studies, they demonstrate the impact of cultural variables on the experience of disability by Dominicans. They explain certain traits of Dominican families that have children with disabilities: the fear of children being removed from the home, shame over disability, and the tendency to hide children with disability. The authors also describe the great support and assistance provided by the families to providers of disability services, once the families understand the system and the purpose of the services.

Since the second half of the 20th century, **Vietnam** has been a country very much in the American consciousness. Despite the fact that many Americans have been to Vietnam and despite the large number of immigrants who have come to the United States from Vietnam since the war, Vietnamese culture is not widely understood in the United States. Vietnamese culture is complex, having been influenced by many foreign invaders over the centuries. It has foundations in Confucian and Buddhist philosophies. Its collectivist world-view values group harmony over individual goals. Because Vietnamese patterns of respect differ from many American behavioral patterns, recent immigrants from Vietnam may often misunderstand American behavior and speech.

The purpose of the chapter "An Introduction to Vietnamese Culture for Rehabilitation Service Providers in the United States" is to help rehabilitation service providers to understand some of the main elements in Vietnamese culture, especially those that relate to disability. The author of this monograph, Peter Cody Hunt, is of Chinese origin but was born in Vietnam. He came to the United States when he was 9 years of age. His interest in disability stems from his own personal experiences as a person with an acquired disability. Over the years, he took the responsibility for arranging services for two other family members with disabilities. As a result, he became aware of the deficits and shortcomings in the health care delivery system and rehabilitation services, especially for persons with disabilities from cultural minorities.

The concluding chapter, "Understanding Immigrants With Disabilities," discusses some of the multiple factors that may simultaneously affect the immigrant with disabilities. One of these is the phases of culture shock through which most persons pass when they find themselves surrounded by a new culture. Another is the phases of adaptation to disability. The chapter also summarizes some of the values and perceptions related to disability and rehabilitation that seem to be common to many of the cultures of recent U.S. immigrant groups.

The author of this chapter is John Stone, who is also the editor of this volume. A member of the Rehabilitation Science faculty at the State University of New York at Buffalo, he is the Director of the Center for International Rehabilitation Research Information and Exchange (CIRRIE) and editor of the 12-volume CIRRIE monograph series on culture and disability. His interest in other cultures began as a Peace Corps volunteer in India in the late 1960s. It was further developed through a sojourn in Greece with the Experiment in International Living and through 17 years in Brazil as a faculty member in Brazilian universities. In those countries, he received guidance on several occasions from certain local individuals who instinctively understood that a person from another land might need help in understanding and adapting to the local culture. These "culture brokers" served him as examples for understanding the need for similar guidance for recent immigrants in the United States.

The contributors share my hope that this book will be useful to service providers in their work with individuals from diverse cultures, especially those who are foreign-born. We are becoming an increasingly global community. It is our hope that the concepts presented in this book will help make all of us better citizens of that community, particularly in our ability to adapt services to meet the needs of foreign-born persons with disabilities.

References

Groce, N. (1999). Health beliefs and behavior towards individuals with disability cross-culturally. In R. Leavitt (Ed.), *Cross-cultural rehabilitation: An international perspective* (pp. 37–47). London: W. B. Saunders.

Leavitt, R. (1999). Introduction. In R. Leavitt (Ed.), *Cross-cultural rehabilitation: An international perspective* (pp. 1–7). London: W. B. Saunders.

Miles, M. (1999). Some influences of religions on attitudes towards disabilities and people with disabilities. In R. Leavitt (Ed.), *Cross-cultural rehabilitation: An international perspective* (pp. 49–57). London: W. B. Saunders.

Schmidley, D., & Campbell, G. (1999). *Profile of the foreign born population in the United States: 1997* (U.S. Census Bureau, Current Population Reports, Series P23–195). Washington, DC: Government Printing Office.

1

Immigrants, Disability, and Rehabilitation

Nora Groce

Introduction

In 1909, Israel Zangwill published a popular melodrama titled *The Melting-Pot*. Although the plot of Zangwill's play has long been forgotten by most, the title, for many, came to represent an assumption about cultural assimilation that has characterized much American social policy—including rehabilitation and disability policy—over the intervening decades.

This assumption, common well into the 1970s and 1980s, was that it was incumbent on immigrants to America to take on a new, national identity while rapidly abandoning their own ethnic identity or heritage in the process. Actually, even in its heyday, the concept of a "melting pot" was never applied equally within American society. Immigrants from Puerto Rico or Italy or Japan were criticized if they did not quickly abandon dearly held cultural beliefs and values, whereas immigrants whose ancestors had come over on the *Mayflower* were praised for keeping alive the values and practices their ancestors had carried with them in 1620.

A generation of ethnic studies has made us keenly aware of the fact that cultural heritages are more complex and more durable than originally thought. Increasingly, we have come not simply to recognize but to value ethnic diversity. Only recently, however, have we begun to better understand that this diversity also has implications for the disability and rehabilitation community. An individual with a disability does not exist in isolation but is a member of a family and of a social universe. When this individual is a member of an immigrant family or a family that holds firmly to an ethnic or minority heritage distinct from that of "mainstream" American society, this must be taken into consideration if appropriate rehabilitation services and supports are to be provided.

In response to this growing awareness of cultural diversity, there have been increasing calls for programs and services for individuals with disability to become "culturally sensitive" and be "culturally appropriate" (Coleridge, 1993; UNICEF, 1999). Simply labeling something "culturally sensitive" or "culturally appropriate," however, does not automatically make it so. This chapter will explore these concepts and discuss some of the issues that must be considered in designing and implementing workable, culturally relevant interventions for children and adults who live with a disability in ethnic and minority communities. Subsequent chapters will provide more in-depth discussion and definitions of some of the issues broached here.

A Few Notes of Caution

Before discussing the issue of cultural competence in relation to disability, it is perhaps wise to introduce a few notes of caution. To begin, this is a new field—so new, in fact, that an entire chapter could be devoted simply to identifying what we still do *not* know regarding disability in ethnic and minority communities within the United States, both from theoretical perspectives and from field studies that would better document beliefs, practices, and needs in specific ethnic and minority communities. What we do know at this point is that, as a consequence of immigration, millions of individuals with disability and their families throughout the United States find themselves balancing cultural roles and expectations against the social, economic, medical, and rehabilitation resources available through the dominant national "norms" and practices.

It is also important to note the following:

a. **Ethnic Heritage Is Not a Diagnostic Category.** No ethnic background wholly explains the way any individual or family will think or act. It can help professionals *anticipate* and *understand* how and why individuals, families, or communities make certain decisions, but it is not predictive at the individual level. Just because a person is Senegalese or Mexican or Canadian, we can not assume we know how he or she will think or behave in any given situation. If not used with caution, assumptions about an individual based on his or her cultural background can veer toward stereotyping and, in the worst cases, toward racism.

b. **Variations Exist Within Groups.** Too often, different cultural belief systems are approached by dominant society and by professionals in an oversimplified manner. All but the smallest cultural groups are further subdivided along socioeconomic, educational, caste, and class lines. We encounter examples of this on a daily basis. The Jamaican mother of a disabled child might be a married lawyer from the suburbs or a single teenager from a poor, urban area.

A Hispanic young man with a disability can come from a wealthy family from Puerto Rico, a poor Indian family from the highlands of Guatemala (someone for whom Spanish language and culture itself is a foreign system), or a middle-class family from New Mexico whose ancestors have lived in the same community for the last 400 years. The term "Asian," as it is currently used in the United States, includes almost a third of the world's population and refers to geographical areas that are home to several dozen major nation-states and hundreds of smaller ethnic and minority groups. Assuming that one can predict cultural heritage and understanding based on whether someone is from Thailand or Peru often glosses over those very cultural details that provide real understanding and insight when trying to provide culturally appropriate services.

c. **The Rehabilitation System Is Not "Culture-Free."** A great deal of the literature on cultural sensitivity and cultural competency assumes that the ethnic or minority community studied are variables, necessitating deviations from the "right approach" to programs or services that are professionally agreed upon as culture-free "norms" or "standards." However, this is misleading. In fact, rehabilitation laws and services for individuals with disabilities and their families that exist today in the United States (or in Japan or Sweden or Canada, for that matter), are not "culture-free." These systems are unique products of specific historic, political, social, and economic developments in each country. Given that, it is vitally important to keep in mind that when dealing with the interface between immigrant populations and the rehabilitation system, we are dealing with not one but two culturally defined and culturally bounded systems.

Ethnicity, Disability, and Globalization

In many ways, the growing interest in ethnic and minority issues in relation to rehabilitation is a by-product of the growing process of globalization. Although the term *globalization* is new, the phenomenon itself is as old as humankind. For thousands of years, trade routes have stretched across hundreds or thousands of miles, and people have used them to cross continents exchanging goods and ideas. Armies have marched across continents, disrupting whole populations that have, in turn, sought refuge in other kingdoms and principalities. Although globalization may not be new, the nature of the phenomenon today is markedly different. The pace of the exchange of ideas, peoples, and goods is greatly increased; modern technology makes the communication of ideas almost instantaneous; and there are few places on the globe to which the average person cannot travel within 24 hours.

These changes, in turn, have had significant impacts on patterns of immigration. Where once a family would come to the United States—whether by choice or in response to political, economic, or environmental upheaval—with little expectation that they would see their home or family again, today, many families have circular patterns of settlement. Individuals and families come to settle in the United States but return home on a regular basis. Relatives and friends will arrive from an immigrant's country of origin, staying for short or extended periods and bringing with them (and helping to reinforce) traditional beliefs about the nature of family, the role of the community, and expectations for individuals with disability. Individuals anywhere can sort through the mass of information from around the world that is available on the Internet, seeking new ideas about rehabilitation and disability and identifying innovative advocacy strategies.

Blending traditional beliefs and practices with new ideas and resources available in the United States is often all the more difficult because immigrant status itself is a factor that can increase tension between the traditional and new cultural systems of belief and practice. Even for individuals and families who have planned and waited for years to come to the United States, reality may differ significantly from expectations. Psychological stressors ("culture shock") such as linguistic differences, changing personal and family values, changing role expectations, and lower economic and social status all have the potential to have negative effects on families. For those who are in the United States not because they have planned for a new life here but because they have fled as a result of war or natural disasters or political upheavals, these stressors and their effects may be intensified.

For those who have a disability (or for families who have a member with a disability) who are here as political refugees or illegal aliens, there is often an additional stressor: the fear of being sent back to a country of origin that has no rehabilitation or disability support services, or where individuals with disability are routinely institutionalized. In response to all of this, recognition for the need for rehabilitation professionals to become culturally competent has become increasingly widespread, and responses to cultural differences have— or at least we can hope that they have—become more sophisticated.

Cultural Competence

This need to understand and respond to the needs of immigrant populations has given rise to calls for increased "cultural sensitivity" and "cultural competence." Both terms are a bit misleading. "Sensitivity," in and of itself, means little to the individuals and communities that rehabilitation professionals hope to serve. One can be exquisitely *sensitive* to cultural differences—being aware that they exist, noting their presence when encountered—and still not be able to competently address issues of real importance to individuals and their families in these communities.

Competence is perhaps a better goal toward which to strive. Competence is defined by the Oxford English dictionary (*The Illustrated Oxford English Dictionary*, 1998) as being "properly qualified or skilled; adequately capable." In the case of cultural competency, this implies the ability to adequately understand and respond to the needs and concerns of individuals with disability and their families from ethnic and minority communities, with responses based on an accurate understanding of their specific cultural practices.

Cultures are immensely complex, however, and no individual—no matter how well versed in cultures—can realistically expect to become competent in all cultures, particularly around an issue as complex as disability. Many rehabilitation professionals who work specifically with one or two ethnic groups will broaden and deepen their knowledge of specific beliefs and practices over time, and many will reach a level of real proficiency and understanding of the specific cultures with which they work. Less proficiency usually is possible when a rehabilitation professional, social service provider, or other expert must divide his or her time and work among members of many different immigrant communities at once, as is often the case in large urban centers.

Even anthropologists, who specialize in cultures, do not claim to be universally competent in all cultures. What they do, and what will be recommended here for rehabilitation professionals to do, is understand that there are categories of human endeavor—among them, family, education, community, and employment—that are universal. By anticipating that all communities, including all immigrant communities, will respond to these categories in culturally defined ways, the rehabilitation professional is able to better assess and address the needs of individuals with disability from immigrant communities, in systematic and rigorous ways.

Cultural Categories

Much of the discussion of disability in society, within the extensive professional literature, is embedded in sweeping stereotypes that provide relatively little information about disability at the individual or the community level. In fact, disability as a unified concept is not universal. Indeed, many languages lack a single word for disability. Rather, societies around the world have tended to group together individuals with specific types of impairments (e.g., those who are blind, those who have a physical disability) and often have very different ways of responding to individuals depending upon what kind of social interpretation underlies their specific disability. Although traditionally there may be broad categories (e.g., the unfortunate, the infirm), the idea of disability as a single category—into which individuals with all types of physical, emotional, sensory, and intellectual impairments are routinely placed—has come into more prominent usage as a by-product of broad social insurance and social security schemes that have grouped previously distinct categories of individuals together in order to provide benefit packages within nation-states (Groce & Zola, 1993).

Conceptual frameworks of disability also affect the ways in which individuals with disability see themselves and the world around them (Blancher, 2001; Das, 2001; Helander, 1993). They influence the manner in which people in their worlds—members of their families and their communities—interact with them (Ingstad & Whyte, 1995), and they are the basis upon which societies implement policies and programs that directly and indirectly affect many, if not most, aspects of their lives. These conceptual frameworks, whether positive or negative, are important to understand in order to effect changes, either by addressing negative models or by building upon positive ones.

There have been a number of successful adaptations to disability, and there are without doubt many more as-yet-undocumented ones, that represent real strengths and provide decided advantages for disabled members of the community. In some communities, strong and supportive family structures, special roles, and specific types of disabilities may provide a solid foundation upon which individuals with disability should build. Some of these adaptations may provide models that should be considered far more carefully and instituted far more widely.

In all societies, individuals with disability are not only recognized as distinct from the general population, but value and meaning also are attached to their condition. Moreover, the same ethnic or minority community may attach very different significance and grant different status and rights to individuals with different types of disability. For example, individuals who are blind may be included and supported, whereas those with mental health disabilities may be ignored or shunned. Although dozens of different examples exist, for the purposes of this discussion, these social beliefs will be grouped together in three categories that regularly appear cross-culturally. Although specific adaptations to these different categories will vary from one ethnic community to another, cross-culturally, some variant of these categories seems to be found regularly in all societies. Moreover, consistently, people's expectations and demands for services and support seem to regularly reflect the expectations delineated by such categorizations. These categories will effect both individuals' ability to participate in family and community and society's willingness to integrate these individuals into daily life. Although there are many variations, these issues can be roughly divided as follows: beliefs about causality, valued and devalued attributes, and anticipated role.

BELIEFS ABOUT CAUSALITY

Cultural explanations concerning why a disability occurs help to determine how well or poorly individuals with disability are treated in many societies. For example, the birth of a child with a disability is often considered a sign of divine displeasure with the child's parents, evidence of incest or "bad blood" in a family, marital infidelity on the part of the father, or bad luck or fate (Groce & Zola, 1993; Ingstad, 1990). Disability that occurs later in life may also be considered divine punishment of the individual or the community. Even when a disability is believed to be caused by the misdeeds of others, disabled individuals may not always be seen as innocent victims. It is often believed that they may have done something to antagonize a spirit, and the individual who is disabled is often avoided for fear that close association with such a person will put others at risk. The belief in reincarnation often leaves individuals who are disabled in a particularly difficult situation. Their current status is seen as earned, and there may be less sympathy and less willingness to expend resources on their behalf. Moreover, improving their present lives, some in the immigrant community believe, lessens the amount of suffering they must endure, thus compromising the possibility of future rebirth at a higher level of existence.

The cause of disability is not always believed to be divine or supernatural. The idea that a disability can be "caught"—transmitted either by touch or by sight—is found widely. Pregnant women in particular are discouraged from seeing, hearing, or touching someone with a disability, for fear that they may give birth to a similarly disabled child. In some immigrant and ethnic communities, this idea of "contagion" remains strong. For example, Thomason (1994) reports that some Native American parents continue to discourage their children from even touching assistive technology devices, such as wheelchairs, for fear that they will acquire a disability through this contact.

Modern science has redefined disability causation, seeking explanations in the natural world: genetic disorders, viruses, and accidents are now commonly accepted as explanations for why one is born with a disability or becomes disabled. If modern medicine has replaced older causation concepts, however, it has often not done so completely. The idea of blame, inherent in most cultures for centuries, often reappears in more "scientific" forms. Both professionals and lay people are quick to question whether the mother of the disabled newborn smoked, drank, or took drugs. Many are anxious to know if the young man injured in a driving accident was going too fast, or whether drugs or alcohol were involved.

What seems to exist is a need to determine whether the individuals thus affected are in some way responsible for their current condition or the condition of their children. It has been hypothesized that part of this interest may be a psychological distancing: individuals try to establish a logical reason why a disability has occurred to someone else, thus reassuring themselves that something similar will not happen to them. Another reason why there is such widespread attention to causality may be society's attempt to determine what demands the individual with a disability (and that individual's family) may justifiably make on existing social support networks and community resources.

Beliefs that link disability to intentional causality are not always negative. For example, a study of Mexican American parents found a common belief that it is God's will that a certain number of disabled children be born. God, however, being kind, chooses parents who will be kind to and protective of these "special" children (Madiros, 1989).

VALUED AND DEVALUED ATTRIBUTES

Specific physical or intellectual attributes are valued or devalued in a particular society. In predicting how well an individual with a disability will fare in a given society, including immigrant communities, beliefs about how a disability is caused are important, but even more important are what personal attributes a society finds important. Those individuals who are able to manifest or master these attributes will be able to play a broader role in their societies than those who cannot or who can do so only with difficulty (Wolfensberger, 1983). This, in turn, will be reflected both in the manner in which these individuals are treated and in the society's willingness or reluctance to allocate resources to meet their needs.

There are other issues as well. For example, in some Asian societies and groups from Central America, calling attention to oneself is considered improper. A valued attribute is to blend into the larger community rather than to stand out. Having a disability that automatically makes one stand out from one's peers is considered, in such a community, to be particularly stressful.

Finally, in a cultural context, disability also intersects with other practices and beliefs, and a combination of factors will determine what are considered desirable attributes. This is nowhere more apparent than in the case of gender. In immigrant communities in which boys are preferred, the willingness of families to expend scarce resources—whether for job training, school, or greater social inclusion—on a girl with a disability might be substantially less than for a comparably disabled boy.

ANTICIPATED ROLES: THE INDIVIDUAL, THE FAMILY, THE COMMUNITY, AND THE PROFESSIONAL

The Role of the Individual

The role an individual with a disability is expected to play as an adult in a community is important. The willingness of any society to integrate individuals with disability into the surrounding society, including willingness to expend resources for education and health care, will also depend in large measure on the role(s) it is anticipated that individuals with disability will play in the community as adults.

Some have argued that in many immigrant societies, the relative ability of an individual with disability to contribute to the family's economic needs is the deciding factor in what status he or she maintains in the household and in the community. However, calculating a person's contribution in terms of formal employment, even marginal employment outside the home, may be misleading. Many individuals with a disability who do not work outside their own homes or family units do make significant contributions to their families' economic well-being. In some cases, although individuals with disability are valued within their own homes, they can anticipate no outside role in the community. They will be cared for by relatives, but there is no provision made for their participation in society. Indeed, it is assumed that they will not want to or be able to participate.

A full adult role in any community implies not simply employment but also the ability to marry and have a family of one's own, to decide where one will live, with whom one will associate, and how one will participate in the civic, religious, and recreational life of the community. Although ethnic communities differ as to where, when, and how individuals carry out these roles, the issue is whether individuals with disability are participating in such activities at rates comparable to those of their nondisabled peers (i.e., individuals from comparable socioeconomic and ethnic/minority backgrounds).

It is important to note that beliefs about causation and appropriate role do not exist in isolation. Rather, they are manifested within a matrix of broader cultural ideas and interpretations. Although space limitations make it impossible to cover all these variables in depth here, three merit brief comment as precursors to issues that will be raised in the following chapters: (a) the role of the family; (b) the role of the community; and (c) the role of the professional in a cultural context.

The Role of the Family

Both in law and in practice in most Western societies, the nuclear family is the norm. However, cross-culturally, in 94% of all the world's societies the extended family, not the nuclear family, is the norm. In few societies are families as isolated as they are in the United States. In most countries and in many immigrant communities in the United States, extended families still determine where you live, with whom you live, where you work and at what occupation, whom you marry, and where and from whom you seek health care.

This is distinctly at odds with much of the rehabilitation training and services delivered to individuals in the United States, where the goal is to foster and maintain independence and self-sufficiency for individuals with disability. There may be inherent conflicts between the rights of individuals with disabilities, on one hand, and what the immigrant family feels are its needs and rights to make decisions, on the other.

The Role of the Community

Closely knit immigrant communities will be there not only to provide support and services but also to oversee—and often comment upon—how individuals with disability are doing and how families are responding. Oversight by family, friends, and neighbors, can be a significant influence, guiding decisions and actions throughout the life cycle. For example, Gannotti and Handwerker (2002) report an early example of this in their study of disabled Puerto Rican children. They found that the Puerto Rican mothers with whom they worked continued to spoon-feed their toddlers and help them dress long after the mothers of similarly disabled non–Puerto Rican children had begun to foster skills of self-sufficiency in their children. As Gannotti and Handwerker insightfully note, this practice is continued because the Puerto Rican definition of what it means to be a good and caring mother incorporates this ongoing assistance for younger children, and both the family and the community watch and discuss a mother's behavior toward her disabled child with this in mind.

This is also seen in other arenas. For example, the right and the ability of an individual with a disability to obtain and maintain employment are primary goals in the United States toward which much of our rehabilitation system is geared. In many immigrant communities, however, sending a disabled family member out into the workforce is considered a sign of neglect and abuse by the family. The role of the family, it is believed, is to provide and care for this individual. Even if the family of an individual with disability understands the importance of fostering self-sufficiency, they must often endure the criticism and oversight of the surrounding ethnic community, where making individuals with disability work outside the home is considered "cruel" (Ingstad, 1990).

Traditional responses to disability issues can have profound implications for other family members as well. For example, in families worldwide, much of the responsibility for assisting individuals with disability, both children and adults, falls on the mothers and grandmothers of the household. In the United States, these immigrant women may be expected to continue this role of caretaking, with little or no outside support. At the same time, responding to both financial strains in the family and to assumptions about the role of women in American society, these women are often also expected to take a job outside the household. The multiple strain on mothers in these households has yet to be closely examined, but is significant and needs further investigation.

As noted, tension between cultural heritage and participation in modern American life may also be felt strongly by the individuals with a disability themselves. Balancing the needs, expectations, and concerns of family and community against the plans and hopes they themselves carry for their lives now and in the future may present real and significant conflicts that must be addressed.

The Role of the Professional

Culture may affect not only the way disability is conceptualized and responded to but also the manner in which individuals, families, and communities interact with rehabilitation professionals. In many societies that are structured hierarchically, professionals are considered to be members of the upper social and economic ranks of society, and their word carries great weight. In such hierarchies, professionals asking a client whether a particular course of action is acceptable may cause confusion—"*Why doesn't she know this?*" Any suggestion made will be responded to with a polite "yes"—no matter what the individuals or families think or feel.

Conversely, in some societies with strong social hierarchies, individuals from families of wealth and power are used to having privileges and choices, and they look down upon those who must go out and work for a living (including rehabilitation therapists, doctors, and nurses). Professionals report that such families are at times difficult to work with. When issues need to be clarified or services are needed, families from such cultural backgrounds often demand to speak to the "top man" (rarely the "top woman") and make what rehabilitation professionals can only feel are unreasonable demands.

Another aspect of the role of professionalism in America is the strong and too often unquestioned belief in the value and validity of science and its tools. In the United States, over the past 50 years, increasing stock has been placed in a complex battery of tests and evaluations—tools that often have little meaning or relevance to immigrants' priorities and concerns.

I saw an excellent example of this while observing a parent-teacher conference in Hartford, Connecticut, several years ago. A Puerto Rican mother had settled in Connecticut 6 years earlier with her three children, hoping that better schools on the mainland would enable them to become the first high school graduates in her family. The older two children had not completed high school, dropping out to take jobs and marry. The youngest, a girl of 14, was the subject of the conference. The group of professionals ringed the table and brought forth test score after test score and evaluation after evaluation, while solemnly explaining to the mother, once again, that after her daughter finished school, she should be enrolled in a good transition program for job training and support. For these professionals, the future they were predicting for this child was bleak, represented by scores and evaluations that bespoke limitations and potential struggles. For the mother, the expectation she held out for her daughter was different. Leaning over to me as the professionals filed out of the room, she asked, tentatively switching from English to Spanish, if her daughter should leave school at age 16. No, I said; I thought it would be better if she completed high school and got a degree. The mother stiffened. Her jaw dropped, and tears began to well up in her eyes. "My daughter will get a high school degree? Are you sure?" Warming to the subject, she said, "This is just wonderful. She will be the first in my entire family to get a high school degree. After that, I'm sure she'll find a nice guy and settle down, maybe get a job, have kids. And these teachers think they're experts? Don't they understand what it means to be a high school graduate? She'll be the first one in all my family. Who said the mainland isn't full of opportunities!"

Culture and Change Over Time

One final note: It is important to underscore the fact that no ethnic or minority community is frozen in time. In all societies, change is a constant, and expectations are readjusted in response to these continuing changes. This is nowhere more true than in immigrant communities, where there is often a struggle to balance and integrate the new with the old. It is not news to anyone who has come to the United States as an immigrant, or who lives in ethnic or minority communities, that things are done differently in mainstream American society.

There are a number of ways in which individuals, families, and communities react to this ongoing exposure to new ideas and new expectations. It is interesting that one way is for some societies to become more rather than less traditional about some issues. For example, studies among South Asian families in the New York metropolitan area indicate that in some families, the role that women are expected to play in the family has become more conservative. The response of families in support of a member with a disability may fall into this same category. At this point, this response warrants greater study. We simply do not know—but it is important that we find out.

Conclusion

In conclusion, it is important to stress once again that cultures are fluid systems and that members of ethnic and minority communities in particular are well aware of the fact that they are balancing traditional ideas and attitudes with new and evolving concepts. Such balancing between new and old is of particular concern and importance in discussions concerning the need to provide adequate care and intervention for an individual with disability. Ultimately, it is the individuals with disability and their families who must decide how disability will be defined and dealt with in the context of their cultural heritage, the rehabilitation services system, and the support mechanisms that exist and must be accessed.

All cultures are complex in and of themselves, and there will always be some tension when individuals, families, and communities must balance the competing expectations and limitations inherent in both systems. Ethnic and minority heritage is *not* in itself a diagnostic category, but it allows us to anticipate and to understand issues that may arise. Although none of this is easy, if we are to meaningfully reach millions of individuals and families in need, the issues discussed above must be addressed.

References

Blancher, J. (2001). Transition to adulthood: Mental retardation, families and culture. *American Journal on Mental Retardation, 106*(2), 173–188.

Coleridge, P. (1993). *Disability, liberation and development.* Oxford, UK: Oxfam.

Das, V. (2001, September). *Stigma, contagion, defect: Issues in the anthropology of public health.* Paper presented at the Stigma Conference, Bethesda, MD. Available at www.stigmaconference.nih.gov/FinalDasPaper.htm

Gannotti, M., & Handwerker, W. P. (2002). Puerto Rican understandings of child disability: Methods for the cultural validation of standardized measures of child health. *Social Science and Medicine, 55*(12), 11–23.

Groce, N., & Zola, I. K. (1993). Multiculturalism, chronic illness and disability. *Pediatrics, 91*(5), 1048–1055.

Helander, E. (1993). *Prejudice and dignity: An introduction to community-based rehabilitation.* New York: United Nations Development Programme.

The Illustrated Oxford English Dictionary. (1998). New York: Oxford University Press.

Ingstad, B. (1990). The disabled person in the community: Social and cultural aspects. *International Journal of Rehabilitation Research, 13,* 187–194.

Ingstad, B., & Whyte, S. (1995). *Disability and culture.* Berkeley: University of California Press.

Madiros, M. (1989). Conception of childhood disability among Mexican-American parents. *Medical Anthropology, 12,* 55–68.

Thomason, T. C. (1994). *Native Americans and assistive technology.* Flagstaff: Northern Arizona University, American Indian Rehabilitation Research and Training Center.

UNICEF. (1999). *An overview of young people living with disabilities: Their needs and their rights.* New York: UNICEF Inter-Divisional Working Group on Young People, Programme Division.

Wolfensberger, W. (1983). Social role valorization: A proposed new term for the principle of normalization. *Mental Retardation, 21,* 234–239.

Zangwill, I. (1909). *The melting-pot: A drama in four acts.* New York: Macmillan.

2

Culture and the Disability Services

Paula Sotnik
Mary Ann Jezewski

Introduction

This chapter presents basic information about key concepts related to cultural diversity among foreign-born persons. Examples relevant to the practice of disability service providers are provided in each section. These concepts will assist the reader in understanding the culture-brokering model presented in the next chapter. Also included in this chapter is a discussion of concepts related to foreign-born consumers and rehabilitation services.

This chapter should be viewed as a starting point for understanding and providing culturally sensitive services to foreign-born consumers. It is beyond the scope of this chapter to include all the information necessary to provide services to persons from different cultures, but it does provide some generic information necessary to move toward that goal. To truly reach the goal of providing culturally responsive services, one must take the time, despite heavy caseloads and busy schedules, to understand the people we are supporting.

Discussion of Key Concepts

Several concepts are important to understand when providing services to consumers whose culture is different from that of the provider. Knowing

Authors' Note: The authors would like to acknowledge Rooshey Hasnain, EdD, for her contribution to this chapter.

Table 2.1   Key Concepts in Understanding Cultural Diversity in Rehabilitation

Foreign-born	Activities of daily living
Refugees/immigrants	Diversity
Culture	Stereotyping
Worldview	Acculturation
Disability	Cultural competence
Rehabilitation	

the meanings of the following concepts helps service providers reflect on their values and their role in providing services to consumers. A discussion of key concepts also provides the basis for understanding the culture-brokering role and the role of rehabilitation service providers as culture brokers. The terms *disability*, *rehabilitation*, and *activities of daily living* will be discussed within a cross-cultural context. The key concepts in understanding cultural diversity in rehabilitation are listed in Table 2.1.

Who Are the Foreign-Born?

The Commerce Department's Census Bureau estimates that the foreign-born population of the United States numbered 32.5 million in 2002 (U.S. Census Bureau, 2003). This was the largest number of foreign-born persons in U.S. history and accounted for 11.5% of the total population. In 1970, persons who were foreign-born were only 4.7% of the U.S. population. The rapid increase in the foreign-born population has had an impact on all sectors of U.S. society, including rehabilitation services. Among the foreign-born population in the 2003 census, 52% were born in Latin America, 26% in Asia, 14% in Europe, and the remaining 8% in other regions of the world, such as Africa and Oceania. The rapid growth in the foreign-born population in the past generation has been due primarily to large-scale immigration from Latin America and Asia. According to the 2002 census, the largest foreign-born groups, by country of birth, included persons from Mexico, China, India, Korea, the Philippines, Cuba, Vietnam, the Dominican Republic, and El Salvador.

Persons who are foreign-born include (a) "immigrants," or nonresident aliens admitted for permanent residence; (b) "refugees" admitted to the United States outside normal quota restrictions, based on a well-founded fear of persecution; (c) "asylum seekers" applying to the United States for refugee status; and (d) "undocumented persons" entering the United States without the documents required to reside there legally (Lipson, Dibble, & Minarik, 1996). The foreign-born are those who were not U.S. citizens at birth. Native-born are those who were born in the United States or on a U.S. territory such as Puerto Rico or were born abroad of at least one parent who was a U.S. citizen (Schmidley, 2003).

According to Schmidley (2003), the foreign-born are a diverse group, with variable demographic, social, and economic characteristics depending on the region of birth. The following characteristics are important for understanding the culture-brokering model, which is described in the next chapter. Each factor can expedite or hinder the brokering process and affect the success of service provision. In 2002, 25.5% of the family households with a foreign-born house-holder included five or more people. In contrast, only 12.5% of the family households with a native householder were this large. Educational attainment among the foreign-born varies by region of birth. The highest percentages of high school graduates among the foreign-born were from Asia and Europe (86.8% and 84.0%, respectively). In sharp contrast, the proportion of high school graduates from Latin America was much lower, at 49.1%.

The foreign-born are more likely than the native-born to be unemployed, are more likely to live in poverty, and generally earn less. Data from the March 2002 survey by the U.S. Census Bureau (Schmidley, 2003) show that 31.1% of foreign-born, full- time, year-round workers earned less than $20,000, com-pared with 17.4% of native workers. High proportions of foreign-born indi-viduals are employed in labor, farming, and service jobs rather than technical or professional specialties.

Estimating the number of foreign-born individuals with disabilities is an extremely difficult task. One reason is that there are many different definitions of disability, both within and between cultures and groups. Smart and Smart (1997) point out that there is no uniform definition of disability in the United States, and different government agencies define disability differently. The National Institute on Disability and Rehabilitation Research, Office of Special Education and Rehabilitative Services (1993) compared three national surveys sponsored by three different federal agencies: the National Center on Health Statistics, the Bureau of the Census, and the Bureau of Labor Statistics. The report shows that each agency uses definitions that address its specific purpose, such as employment, health care, or social security benefits. Particular agencies define the term according to their own limited concerns. Disability rights advocates often use broader definitions.

Individuals, families, and communities also perceive and respond to disabil-ities differently. A person with a hearing loss, for example, may not consider it to be a disability, and some Southeast Asian groups view a person with blindness as one who possesses a certain valued insight, not a disability. Such great variances in the definition of disability present difficult challenges in measuring the rate of disability in a group. Additionally, changes in terms over time may affect these rates. For example, when the American Association on Mental Deficiency revised its definition of mental retardation to set the IQ cutoff at 70 instead of 85, the population defined as mentally retarded decreased by 13% (Harry, 1992).

According to the National Council on Disability (1993), "Due to a disturbing lack of hard data on minority populations with disabilities, it is not certain precisely how many members of minority groups have disabilities or how fast this population is growing" (p. 3). Furthermore, the National Council on Disability (1999) indicates that virtually every federal estimate of the incidence of disability among people from minority cultures in the United States is likely to be low. This report further indicates that these low estimates appear to have substantially affected the effectiveness of service delivery. Culturally and linguistically inappropriate assessment tools and the stigma associated in identifying oneself as a person with a disability are also among the reasons for a lack of data or inaccurate data on disability rates in certain groups. Because disability involves not only medical considerations but also social, economic, and cultural factors, estimates of the prevalence of disability can vary significantly from one segment of society to another.

However, data compiled by the U.S. Census Bureau have revealed significant differences in disability rates among Americans belonging to various racial and ethnic groups. According to the 2000 Census Bureau's brief on disability status (U.S. Census Bureau, 2003), the overall rate of disability in the U.S. population is 19.3%. The rate is highest for Native Americans and Blacks/African Americans (each at 24.3%), Native Hawaiians and other Pacific Islanders (20%), and whites (19.7%), while those of Hispanic origin have a significantly lower rate (15.3%). Unfortunately, this report does not identify the specific subsets of foreign-born individuals, within a larger ethnic population, who have disabilities (e.g., a Cambodian subgroup within the Southeast Asian population, in which posttraumatic stress syndrome affects a high percentage of adults). Such factors make it nearly impossible to extrapolate the number of individuals with disabilities from specific foreign-born groups.

Refugees and Immigrants

Also important to understand are the reasons foreign-born individuals leave their countries of birth and how the factors behind the decision might influence their lives in the United States. Refugees and immigrants arrive in the United States for many reasons. Some come voluntarily, whereas others are forced to migrate as a result of political volatility or persecution in their homelands. The need or choice to immigrate is often influenced by a number of complex and interwoven political, social, and economic factors that can change over time.

Immigrants, as defined by the Immigration and Naturalization Service, are persons admitted to the United States for lawful permanent residence. The general term *immigrant* can refer to individuals who are granted permission to reside permanently in the United States for a variety of reasons. For example, many immigrants who came voluntarily to the United States between 1820 and 1960 were Europeans wanting to attain the *American dream.* Conversely, *forced immigrants* who migrate to the United States because of persecution or fear of death are termed *refugees.* That group is defined by U.S. and international law as persons outside their own countries who are unwilling or unable to return because of persecution, or a well-founded fear of persecution, based on religion, nationality, social group membership, or political opinion. To illustrate, groups of special concern include the Bosnians who were given priority for refugee status by the United States in 1997 because they were being persecuted by their government because of ethnicity or political opinion. Since 1975, more than two million refugees have been offered permanent resettlement in the United States (U.S. Department of State, 2000).

As mentioned, some immigrant groups who were motivated by the hope of freedom and economic opportunity have voluntarily relocated to the United States. The impetus to move was the desire for access to education, good wages, property ownership, and financial assets. Thus, some individuals decide that a new country is a better option for them than their native country, positively anticipate a move, and plan accordingly. One can surmise that this group and others that share similar migration characteristics might embrace adjustment and acceptance of mainstream America more readily than individuals forced to flee their countries because of force or persecution.

Refugees abandon their countries and their former patterns of existence to relocate to a very different, sometimes unwelcoming new world in which language, culture, social structures, and community resources may be totally unfamiliar. This type of move, referred to as *displacement,* can be characterized by the loss of most of one's belongings; lack of personal, emotional, and physical preparation; and no choice of one's next destination. Frequently, this move, although necessary to escape harm or death, is not a planned or chosen option for refugees. Acceptance and adjustment can be more difficult for refugee groups than for other immigrants. This is particularly true for older refugees, who leave rooted memories, achievements, and, oftentimes, love for their abandoned homeland. It is not unusual for elders to cling to traditions and beliefs because of a strong desire to return someday to the old country.

As an illustration of the plight of one refugee group, consider the recent migration of the Somalis to the United States. Somalis are mostly Sunni Muslims with traditional Islamic values including a strong family base (usually extended family), respect for the elderly, and an ethic of caring for children, the indigent, and individuals in poor health. Many recent arrivals are widows with children who lost their husbands to war. They are both mother and father, without the support of an extended family. Many women have no prior academic or employment skills. The language difference is a major barrier, and their situation can be further aggravated by illiteracy in their own language. Children often serve as interpreters, which can result in a role reversal that diminishes the mother's influence as a revered parent.

Of special significance to disability service providers is understanding the challenge that accessing institutions and services can pose for refugees and immigrants. This challenge, coupled with the sometimes unfavorable perception of disability held by refugees and immigrants, exacerbates the lack of access to needed supports. In addition to facing language and cultural barriers, many individuals are not familiar with the existence, range, and purpose of services for individuals with disabilities. Often, similar services and programs did not exist for individuals with disabilities in their country of birth. Even if refugee groups are made aware of relevant programs, the documentation and processes required by bureaucracies further impede an individual's access to services. Additionally, some groups who fled countries that were ruled by brutal systems might be fearful of any services that might be associated with government, even indirectly, particularly those that request the identification of a physical or emotional disability. Finally, therapies and services might be contrary to the values and beliefs of some groups. Consider our system's advocacy of independence through the use of assistive technology in cases when a family believes its role is to provide total care for an individual. Also consider a mainstream culture that directs an individual to comfortably and proudly divulge his or her disability, contrasted with cultures that believe disability represents dishonor because it is caused by ancestral sins.

This snapshot of many refugees and immigrants is intended to provide the reader with the perspective of recent arrivals and the potential implications for their understanding and acceptance of our service systems. Getting to know newcomer populations by researching and visiting community refugee and immigrant organizations—for example, mutual assistance associations—is a valuable means by which to acquire understanding of the past and current experiences of these groups.

Culture

Hundreds of definitions of culture can be found in the anthropology literature. In this chapter, culture is broadly defined as a system of learned and shared standards for perceiving, interpreting, and behaving in interactions with others and with the

Table 2.2   Dominant U.S. Values

Democracy	Achieving/doing
Individualism	Working
Privacy	Materialism
Change	Cleanliness
Progress	Time
Optimal health	Directness/assertiveness
Informality	

environment (Jezewski, 1990). Two key components in this definition are that culture is learned and that it is shared. Human beings learn culture from those with whom they interact, beginning at the moment of birth (and some would say before birth). Family, as well as any others who cared for us as young children, are the formidable teachers of cultural values, beliefs, and behaviors. Values are ideas about what is normal and abnormal, proper and improper, desirable and undesirable, right and wrong. Values form the basis for our beliefs and behaviors. Some of the values held by the majority of Caucasian, middle-class Americans—often referred to as dominant U.S. values are listed in Table 2.2.

For example, many Americans believe it is important to work hard because they value *achieving and doing*; that is, it is important to accomplish tasks. This is not a universal value: Not all cultures value *doing* to this degree. In some cultures, who you are in relation to your family or community is valued more than what you do as an individual.

Culture should be viewed as a system; that is, culture is made up of discrete but interconnected components. A culture system consists of the following elements:

- Normative codes (ways of behaving) such as food practices, religious practices, child-rearing practices
- Communication codes (both verbal and nonverbal)
- Knowledge (information necessary to function as a member of a culture group)
- Problem-solving strategies (how everyday problems are resolved)
- Relationships (family and social)
- Methods of transmitting culture to the young or to new members of the culture group

Underlying and shaping these elements are the basic values and beliefs of the group. These elements function as a whole. A change in one component, or the introduction of new or unfamiliar elements, can affect other components as well as the system as a whole. For example, a recently immigrated elderly Vietnamese woman who develops a disability, and for whom an assisted living environment has been recommended, may have a difficult time adjusting to this environment because she is no longer a part of her family's household. Feelings of abandonment may be strong as a result of the culture from which she comes. The traditional Vietnamese culture is highly family oriented. Two or three generations may be living in the same household. Elders are highly respected, and adults within the family are expected to assume full responsibility for them. Traditionally, elders with disabilities are cared for at home. Institutionalizing an elder member of the family is believed to be disrespectful. The Vietnamese family may feel that it is abandoning the family member and not fulfilling its role as a good and loyal family if it institutionalizes that member. This disruption changes the configuration of the family and, in turn, violates many of the values of Vietnamese culture. In all likelihood, this recently immigrated Vietnamese family will not easily resolve the value conflict that has arisen as a result of the family member's disability. In turn, the life of the person with disabilities is vastly disrupted because of changes in her cultural system. The changes may involve inability to continue some religious practices or the loss of ability to communicate with others. Communication, because of the inability to speak English, and dietary practices are some of the components of the cultural system that could be affected by moving the member with disabilities out of the Vietnamese family. Cultural values and beliefs are continually changing, but at the same time they resist change because they serve the purpose of defining who we are within a group.

It is useful to distinguish between the terms *culture*, *ethnicity*, and *race*. Although these terms are sometimes used interchangeably in the literature, they are not the same and should not be used interchangeably.

Ethnicity refers to groups of people who are united socially, politically, and geographically and possess a common pattern of values, beliefs, and behaviors (culture) as well as language. Examples of ethnic groups are Irish, Iranian, German, Italian, and Ethiopian. *Culture* is a principal force in shaping an ethnic group.

Race, on the other hand, has to do with the biological component of being human. However, the term *race*, as it has evolved, does not help in understanding the biological component of humans. Historically, the term *race* has evolved into political, emotional, and social situations and constructs that, very often, create dissension and bias between human groups. For the purpose of understanding the diversity of culture, race has little relevance. Essentially, race does not form our values, beliefs, and behaviors, but our values and beliefs *do* influence our views on racial differences and mold our behavior toward people of different races.

Worldview

A fundamental component of culture is an individual's worldview, which includes beliefs about religion, humanity, nature, and one's existence. Worldview relates to the philosophical ideas of being (Jandt, 1995). To effectively support individuals with disabilities who are foreign-born, rehabilitation service providers should have an appreciation of the varied perceptions of one's existence in the world.

Samovar, Porter, and Jain (1981) defined three components of worldview: the individual's perception of himself or herself in relationship to nature, the individual's perceptions of science and its ability to explain the world, and attitudes toward material goods. Differing interpretations are paired with these components in the framework presented in Table 2.3.

One's worldview takes into account many beliefs that guide behavior and may have particular implications for the perceptions of disability and related services held by some foreign-born groups. One facet of worldview is an individual's relationship to science and technology (Samovar et al., 1981). People who abide by mainstream U.S. culture believe that a scientific strategy can solve problems and that technology can help in this effort. Applying this concept to rehabilitation, an individual with a disability could successfully use a communication device that was developed based on rigorous research. This example is considered commonplace in our rehabilitation service world and culture. In some cultures, however, challenges posed by a disability are conditions that should not be altered; an individual's disability is

Table 2.3   Samovar's Components of Worldview

Component	Different Views
Individual and nature	Human life is more important than nature OR Humans are part of nature; nature cannot be modified
Science and technology	Individuals can discover an explanation and solution to problems by scientific methods OR Problems are predetermined by fate and cannot be solved by human intervention
Materialism	The acquisition of material goods is important OR Self-sacrifice is valued; tangible assets are not

Table 2.4   Collectivist and Individualistic Value Systems

Cultural Orientation	Personal Characteristics	Behavioral Indicators
Individualism	• Self-expression • Assertiveness • Self-advocacy • Self-realization	• Communicating dissatisfaction with services • Holding a view of services different from that of the family unit or community • Focusing on the individual's unique set of talents and potential
Collectivism	• An individual's existence is inseparable from the family and community • Self-interests are sacrificed for those of the family or larger group • Group activities are dominant	• An individual may not accept transportation and work outside his or her community • Supports to achieve self-sufficiency are not welcomed

predetermined by fate and thus cannot be modified by an adaptive device. To further illustrate, some religions are said to be fatalistic because they require submission to the will of God, which some would argue contradicts practices for preventing or remediating disabilities (Miles, 1995).

Another major dimension to the manner in which people perceive their world and behave is an adherence to a collectivist or individualistic value system. The framework shown in Table 2.4 indicates several examples of diverse cultural values and potential implications for understanding disability and accepting disability-related supports.

Implicit in the U.S. rehabilitation system are *individualistic* values that uphold and encourage self-sufficiency, along with the use of technology or other adaptations to complete daily living tasks independently. Rehabilitation policies and practices including assessments, programs, supports, and success criteria are based on meeting these standards of independence.

For some individuals who embrace strong family interdependence rather than individual independence, these standards will most likely pose conflict with the theory and practice of rehabilitation. Many persons with disabilities want assistive technology, vocational rehabilitation, and other disability services, but—depending on their cultural values—they may want them for different reasons. For example, persons with an individualistic worldview may want assistive technology so that they will be able to live independently in their own homes and be economically self-supporting. Persons who abide by collectivist values may want assistive technology in order to continue living with their family and participating in family tasks and recreation. Thus, diverse views guide one's choice of values and goals. Before discussing possible interventions, the service provider should be aware of the consumer's values and goals. Whatever interventions are discussed should be presented in the context of the consumer's preferences as means of meeting those goals. Consider the following scenario.

A middle-aged Chinese man, Mr. Chen, attended a demonstration of assistive technology products with his wife and two adolescent children. Mr. Chen became blind, as a result of illness, about 5 years ago. Following Mr. Chen's acquired visual disability, his wife shaved him daily. However, being assisted by a female in completing such a personal and masculine task was perceived as devaluing according to his cultural beliefs. Throughout the demonstration, Mr. Chen appeared to disregard the description of products to assist individuals with disabilities. However, he became interested as the presenter explained the functions of a buzzing shaver that beeped when it touched facial stubble. This product enabled effective shaving without the need to see facial hair. He anticipated an opportunity to once again shave himself, and he became very interested in this particular device. Although he did not value many assistive technology products designed to increase overall independence, this particular device was appealing because it supported Mr. Chen's cultural values and beliefs about personal care tasks and masculinity.

Disability

To understand how other cultures understand and define disability, one should begin by examining how disability is seen and understood in the United States. Legislation signed into law to provide equal access for individuals with disabilities in the United States demonstrates an example of how disability is interpreted by Western culture. For example, the Americans with Disabilities Act (ADA) defines the term *disability* as follows:

> With respect to an individual, the term "disability" means (A) a physical or mental impairment that substantially limits one or more of the major life activities of such individual; (B) a record of such an impairment; or (C) being regarded as having such an impairment. A person must meet the requirements of at least one of these three criteria to be an individual with a disability under the Act. (Equal Employment Opportunity Commission and the U.S. Department of Justice, 1991)

The ADA stipulates various modalities of supports and accommodations, including products and environmental modifications. Self-sufficiency is often based on nonhuman assistance—for example, assistive technology or environmental interventions—although personal care assistants are also part of the equation.

Analysis of the language and intent of the law reveals significant underlying characteristics that frame the Western definition of disability. Harry (1992) describes these suppositions.

> First, it is assumed that the occurrence of the condition is located within the individual, and only in certain cases of clear genetic or biological etiology would other family members be implicated. Second, it is assumed that the condition should be treated by objectively verifiable interventions, conceived within the parameters of the scientific method. Third, the Western faith in science has tended to result in the belief that, wherever possible, biological anomalies should be corrected; there is little tolerance for deviation from the norm. (p. 22)

What constitutes having a disability in the United States often varies considerably among government agencies, public and private institutions, and consumer groups. Thus, the definition and significance of disability are contingent on the differing perceptions of individuals, communities, and institutions.

The National Institute on Disability and Rehabilitation Research (1999) has identified a new paradigm of disability that

> maintains that disability is a product of an interaction between characteristics (e.g., conditions or impairments, functional status, or personal and social qualities) of the individual and characteristics of the natural, built, cultural and social environments. The construct of disability is located on a continuum from enablement to disablement. Personal characteristics, as well as environmental ones, may be enabling or disabling, and the relative degree fluctuates, depending on condition, time and setting. Disability is a contextual variable, dynamic over time and circumstance. (p. 68578)

The meaning of disability is influenced by the cultural beliefs and values of consumers and service providers. Euro-American values of equality and individual ability as a source of social identity shape a concept of disability that may not be applicable in other groups (Ingstad & Whyte, 1995). Foreign-born populations may view a disabling condition, causal factors, and related services differently than does mainstream America. For Euro-Americans, causation may be attributed to factors such as disease or genetic disorders. Acknowledgment of having a disability is acceptable, and outside intervention is thought to be desirable in American mainstream culture. Individuals who are foreign-born may not hold these opinions about disability. Descriptions of traditional beliefs in some Latino and Asian groups have shown how differential interpretations of the meanings of a disability can become a source of dissonance between professionals and culturally different families (Chan, 1986; Harry, 1992; Leung, 1989; Sotnik & Hasnain, 1998).

For example, Southeast Asian beliefs related to disability and its causation range from those that focus on the behavior of the parents, particularly the mother, during pregnancy to sins committed by extended family members and reincarnation. Disability is sometimes attributed to the sins of the parents or ancestors. A Southeast Asian individual with a disability may be segregated from the community because the disability represents a wrongdoing by the parents or ancestors and is considered a source of disgrace. Generally, disability from birth is stigmatizing for the individual and family because of these traditional beliefs. Acquired disabilities are less stigmatizing (Sotnik & Hasnain, 1998).

The experience of an assistive technology public awareness project illustrates the miscommunication surrounding the term *disability* when used with persons from other cultures. The project disseminated multiple copies of a flyer that publicized the availability of products for people with disabilities. The project's efforts to attract individuals from diverse linguistic, ethnic, and cultural backgrounds to inquire about an assistive device strategy proved unsuccessful. Project staff inquired about the lack of interest and made significant discoveries. Most individuals did not define themselves as persons with a disability because they did not know what the word implied or because disability was considered as a condition that rendered a person helpless. Thus, a person who could not hear was not considered an individual with a disability because he could otherwise function very well at activities that did not require auditory ability. Better success was achieved when outreach materials deleted the term *disability* and described specific conditions, such as "if you have difficulty walking, hearing, seeing, etc."

A collectivist view, inherent in many foreign-born cultures, prescribes that disability reflects the totality of the family rather than just the member with the disability. Harry (1992) also indicates that families who believe that the source of a disability lies in spiritual rather than physical phenomena may be committed to spiritual rather than medical interventions. Harry further states that this finding has been documented among Mexican Americans (Adkins & Young, 1976), Native Americans (Locust, 1988), and some Southeast Asian groups (Chan, 1986).

In the Southeast Asian community, Buddhism is the predominant religion. The principles of Buddhism stipulate that each person is responsible for his or her actions. A belief in Buddhism may establish a precedent wherein Southeast Asians adhere to the concept of *karma*, a belief that one's present life is determined by what one has done, right or wrong, in a previous existence. Thus, followers will accept a perceived misfortune, such as a disability, as predestined.

Disability Service Systems

Disability service systems can be considered as entities that, similar to a country or ethnic enclave, embody a philosophy, values, policies, and practices. The United States Vocational Rehabilitation (VR) system is one example. Although each state's and region's VR program will reflect some divergence in practices, the systems share similar dominant cultural aspects. A brief review of the origin of VR will enable an understanding of the system's cultural foundation. The VR system was created in 1918 with the passage of the Soldier Rehabilitation Smith-Sears Act to enable veterans with war-related disabilities to become self-sufficient through employment. Amendments to the 1973 Rehabilitation Act launched a growing increase in consumer self-sufficiency and advocacy by initiating Individual Written Rehabilitation Plans, the independent living program concept, consumer involvement in state agency policy, and increased access by consumers to federally funded programs. A review of contemporary VR legislative content, funding processes, policies, and programmatic practices confirms the incorporation of individualism and independence. Within the last two decades, vocational rehabilitation legislation (Pub. L. No. 95-607 and Pub. L. No. 102-569) reflects the increased emphasis on consumer empowerment and overall independence. Recall our earlier discussion of individualism and collectivism. Table 2.5 provides some examples of the effects that the values of individualism have on vocational rehabilitation principles.

In a focus group conducted by this author, vocational rehabilitation counselors were asked about the culture of the rehabilitation system. The participants characterized the rehabilitation system as institutionalized and linear. They pointed out that vocational rehabilitation is regulated by legislation, so services are regulated by rules and statutes. The system is driven by outcomes, especially job placement. Success is defined as the quickest route to being placed. Services are very effective for a certain segment of the population that

Table 2.5   Effects of Values of Individualism on Vocational Rehabilitation
             Principles

Individualism	Concepts of Vocational Rehabilitation
Self-determination: individuals control personal situations	Consumers set their own rehabilitation goals and are self-advocates
Success is defined in terms of professional achievement of the individual	Employment is an outcome that indicates successful rehabilitation
Each person is unique and independent	Self-sufficiency is an ideal outcome

fits into the prescribed model. This segment typically consists of individuals who believe in the same values, can be readily employed, and are English speaking. Furthermore, because of large caseloads, it is usually impossible to develop relationships with an individual and family members. This is directly opposite to the ideals of provision of culturally responsive services to people from some diverse backgrounds.

Another focus group was conducted with families of persons with disabilities from the Dominican Republic. Many of these families felt that it would be shameful and exploitative for them to allow their family members with disabilities to work because it is the responsibility of the family to care for its members with disabilities. Clearly, this runs counter to the philosophy of the vocational rehabilitation system and the independent living movement. Working with families that hold such values does not mean accepting such values, nor does it mean scorning them. A culturally competent service provider will use strategies that involve peer families and community organizations in showing newly arrived families the possibilities that exist in the United States for persons with disabilities to improve the quality of their lives.

Activities of Daily Living

Activities of daily living (ADL) can be defined as those tasks necessary to maintain physical well-being, personal appearance, hygiene, safety, and general functioning in one's home and community. These tasks, along with instrumental activities of daily living (IADLs), span many domains of living and include bathing, dressing, eating, household chores, financial management, and cooking. There are three important questions to address about daily living routines implemented by individuals with disabilities who are also members of foreign-born groups:

1. Are there differences in daily living activities in the person's country of origin in comparison to how they are performed in the United States? For example, persons in rural India usually eat with their hands, sitting on the ground, whereas in the United States eating is usually done at a table, using silverware.

2. How are daily living activities performed by persons with disabilities in that culture?

3. How might individuals from another culture respond to assistance in performing these activities?

The importance, type, variety, and frequency of daily routines may differ considerably from one group to another and, moreover, between generations

Table 2.6   Examples of Daily Living Practices in Selected Cultures

Ethnic Group	ADL-Related Practices
Cambodian	Men keep the nail of the right little finger longer than other nails
	Young unmarried women wear an article around the waist that should not be removed, to prevent "love magic"
Russian	The gender of the personal assistance provider is not an issue
	Personal care can be provided by a nurse or an aide
Vietnamese	Hair should not be wet at night; going to bed with wet hair causes headaches
	Only a family member of the same sex should help with personal care

within the same ethnic group. Table 2.6 offers a sampling of several groups and some selected differing daily living practices.

The value of specific daily living tasks can differ, contingent upon a group's perception of one's role in life. For example, an individual with a cognitive disability cannot budget or read important documents but can serve as a family member and employee. If the latter roles are perceived as more important, financial management activities conducted by this individual may be considered insignificant.

It is important to keep in mind that not all members of an ethnic group will demonstrate identical daily living activities. Any information describing cultural aspects of personal care is intended to serve as a cue to learn the unique characteristics of an individual and family.

Some individuals with disabilities may need the assistance of another person or a product to complete these tasks. Moreover, individuals with disabilities sometimes have added unique activities that the nondisabled population will not experience, such as accessing other forms of transportation and care of adaptive equipment.

The nature of assistance with daily living skills for persons with disabilities can be affected by many individual characteristics including geography, religion, socioeconomic factors, and the type of disability. For example, many Muslim women do not expose any skin, except for the hands and part of the face, to any man, except her husband (*Family Education and Resource Program*, 1998). Issues such as this are particularly important for personal care assistance provided by other individuals.

Worldview, or how one perceives the world and related personal roles, can also affect the nature of how daily living skills are performed. As described in a previous section, people who adhere to the traditional U.S. mainstream culture of individualism might uphold assertiveness and self-advocacy as admirable characteristics. Behavioral indicators might be manifested when an individual with a disability disagrees with family members regarding types of daily living supports. These individuals may prefer the help of paid employees as personal assistance service providers because this relationship promotes independence and self-advocacy, as opposed to relying on family members for personal assistance. Findings indicate that family providers are generally not the ones consumers find the most satisfactory for many reasons, including encouraging continued dependency (Nosek, Fuhrer, Rintala, & Hart, 1993).

Not everyone holds this opinion; for example, groups that abide by collectivistic worldviews. Southeast Asians, Ethiopians, and Haitians may feel strongly that only family members are appropriate personal care assistants. Because family members often assist an individual with a disability to complete daily routines, the family becomes the assistive technology. The suggestion that a device replace traditional family functions may not be regarded positively (Sotnik & Hasnain, 1998).

Diversity

There are many different types of diversity within a society, among them culture, gender, age, and economic. Although the focus of this chapter is cultural diversity, all the different types of diversity within a society are integral to understanding cultural diversity, and some of them will be discussed in the next chapter in relation to the role of disability service providers as culture brokers.

Specific values, beliefs, and behaviors are not universal across groups, but all human groups have a set of values and beliefs that guide their behaviors. When we are learning about specific ethnic or culture groups, it is important to keep in mind that there is as much diversity within groups as there is between groups. For example, when we talk about Native Americans, we are talking about more than 400 different tribal groups. Historically, most of these tribes had little contact with each other, spoke different languages, and did not have the same values and beliefs, and therefore could not be considered in the same culture group. It is inappropriate to consider Native Americans as one culture and to assume that all Native Americans have the same values and beliefs. This is a form of stereotyping. Native Americans may have some of the same values, but there is diversity among tribes as well as between members of the same tribe.

Stereotyping

Very often, when we first begin to learn about different culture groups, the tendency is to take the facts we learn and apply them to everyone who is a member of the group. We do this without evaluating the extent to which the individual members adhere to the dominant values and beliefs of the group. This is a form of stereotyping. Stereotyping refers to the assumption that all members of a group share the same characteristics, values, and beliefs. For example, a service provider may have read that in Mexican families, the man is the decision maker and that women in the family will not make service decisions by themselves. Based on this information, the service provider who applies the stereotype will not spend time discussing service decisions with a Mexican woman without her husband or father present. In some Mexican families, the man may be the primary decision maker, but in other families of Mexican origin, women assume autonomy in making decisions that affect them personally. By assuming the woman will not make decisions about the services she needs, the provider may be raising a barrier to effective intercultural communication and may be undermining a positive service outcome for this consumer. People within a culture group adhere to the basic values and beliefs of the group to varying degrees. The degree of adherence depends on many variables, among them gender, age, and exposure to other culture groups.

In another example of stereotyping using the situation just described, a service provider may read about Mexican families and assume that every Hispanic group adheres to the same values as those of Mexican descent. *Hispanic* is an umbrella term that encompasses people from Mexico, Puerto Rico, and some parts of Central and South America as well as Spain. These varied culture groups have a common language but have been separated culturally for many centuries. In addition, even though their common language is Spanish, the nuances of the language have evolved differently over the centuries.

One way to avoid stereotyping is to look at new knowledge about an ethnic group as a generalization, which is a *beginning* point that indicates common trends for beliefs and behaviors that are shared by a group. Stereotyping is viewed as an *end* point; that is, no attempt is made to learn whether the individual in question fits with what is known about the group.

Stereotyping assumes that every member of the group possesses certain characteristics, adheres to the same beliefs, and behaves in the same manner in any given situation. Generalization, as a beginning point, acknowledges that additional information is needed to determine whether the information known about the group applies to a particular individual within the group and to the particular situation in question. For example, one might read that most Mexican people are members of the Roman Catholic religion or that most people from the Middle East are Muslim. For the rehabilitation service provider to assume that every Middle Eastern consumer adheres to Islam and therefore prays five times a day is stereotyping. It could lead the provider to anticipate behaviors that do not exist and to make inappropriate scheduling decisions.

Possessing knowledge about Islam may increase the service provider's ability to give culturally competent care to Middle Eastern consumers. Stereotyping can be avoided by asking questions about their preferences, such as the opportunity to pray at certain times of the day. Galanti (1991) provides a useful discussion of stereotyping versus generalizing as well as discussions of many other basic concepts related to cultural diversity.

Acculturation

The degree to which one assumes the values and beliefs of a new culture is referred to as the degree of acculturation. Acculturation is influenced by language, length of time spent interacting with people in the new culture, and the intensity of contact with the new culture. Immigrants may be influenced by the U.S. culture, and their values, beliefs, and behaviors may change, based on frequency and intensity of contact. For some, this change will occur rapidly, and for others, the change will occur slowly or not at all. Acculturation essentially becomes a melding of a person's primary culture with that of the new culture. We can never assume that someone who has immigrated to the United States from another culture will assume the values and beliefs of the dominant U.S. society. Acculturation is also influenced by education, economic status, gender, and personal choice.

The following example serves as an illustration of how acculturation evolves in the various members of a newly immigrated family. The young children who come to the United States from another culture and who attend public school tend to acculturate faster and more completely than their parents. Daily exposure to U.S. values through the classroom environment, the pressure to learn English, and peer pressure and the desire for peer friendships all contribute to acculturation in the child. In contrast, the children's mother may be in the home most of the time, especially if there are preschool children in the family and she is not working outside the home. Her closest friends may be women who have immigrated from the same geographic location. This woman may not be under any pressure to learn the ways of the U.S. culture or to become fluent in English. Her social world may revolve around her ethnic community, where her primary language, rather than English, is spoken. The child's father and other family members acculturate depending, in part, on their work outside the home and the need to speak English in their work environments. Their degree of acculturation also depends on their need to attend to activities of daily living, such as shopping, accessing transportation, and interacting with various immigration and social service agencies.

Culture Competence and Sensitivity

Culture sensitivity is the awareness by one person of the differences in values, beliefs, and behaviors of another, and the understanding that these values, beliefs, and behaviors are the basis for the way people interact with each other. Cultural sensitivity precedes cultural competence, but it is not considered enough for service providers to be culturally sensitive to the diversity in others. Culturally competent service is responsive to issues related to culture, race, gender, and sexual orientation. Culturally competent service is service provided within the cultural context of the consumer (American Academy of Nursing Expert Panel Report, 1993). Randall-David (1989) defines cultural competence as a set of behaviors, attitudes, and policies that enable a system, agency, or individual to function effectively with culturally diverse consumers and communities. In the context of providing disability services, cultural competency requires recognizing and understanding how economic conditions, race, culture, ethnicity, the social context, and environment define health, disability, and the provision of services (Rorie, Paine, & Barger, 1996).

Rorie and colleagues (1996) provide a useful framework describing a continuum from incompetence to competence. On the incompetent end of the continuum is cultural destructiveness (attitudes, policies, and practices are exhibited that can be destructive to a culture). Movement along the continuum proceeds to cultural incapacity (a biased, authoritarian system that lacks capacity to facilitate growth in culturally diverse groups), then on to culture blindness (the "we're all human" approach in which it is thought that culture, ethnicity, and race make no difference in how services are provided). Next on the continuum is cultural pre-competence (cultural sensitivity wherein there is a decision made and attempts are made to deliver services in a manner respectful of cultural diversity). Following along the continuum is cultural competence (an acceptance of and respect for cultural norms, patterns, beliefs, and differences, along with self-assessment regarding cultural competence), and finally, there is cultural proficiency (motivation toward adding to the knowledge base of culturally competent service provision and developing a culturally therapeutic approach). It should be noted that each time a service provider encounters a consumer from an ethnic group with which the provider is not familiar, the provider may have to move through at least part of the competence continuum. Developing competency takes time with each new cultural encounter.

In 1993, an American Academy of Nursing panel of experts on culturally competent health care was convened to outline the major components of providing culturally competent care to diverse groups of patients. Although the panel concluded that there are no well-tested and tried models that can facilitate the provision of culturally competent care, the panel did identify a number of useful and effective models that have been used to enhance both cultural sensitivity and the delivery of culturally competent services. Jezewski's culture-brokering model, described in the next chapter, was identified as one practice model that offered guidance for the delivery of culturally competent care. Although it was originally developed in the context of health care, it has applications in many fields, including rehabilitation services. If culture is such an important influence on human behavior, how can the disability service provider work *through*, rather than *against*, the culture of foreign-born consumers? In the next chapter, we will examine the role of the provider as a culture broker.

References

Adkins, P. G., & Young, R. G. (1976). Cultural perceptions in the treatment of handicapped school children of Mexican-American parentage. *Journal of Research and Development in Education, 9*(4), 83-90.

American Academy of Nursing Expert Panel Report. (1993). Culturally competent health care. *Nursing Outlook, 40*(6), 277-283.

Chan, S. (1986). Parents of exceptional Asian children. In M. K. Kitano & P. C. Chinn (Eds.), *Exceptional Asian children and youth* (pp. 36- 53). Reston, VA: Council for Exceptional Children.

Equal Employment Opportunity Commission and the U.S. Department of Justice. (1991). *Americans with disability handbook.* Washington, DC: Government Printing Office. Available at ftp://trace.wisc.edu/PUB/TEXT/ADA_INFO/HANDBOOK/FREG1.TXT

Family Education and Resource Program, Cultural Traditions—Saudi Arabia. (1998). Boston: Children's Hospital.

Galanti, G. A. (1991). *Caring for patients from different cultures: Case studies from American hospitals.* Philadelphia: University of Pennsylvania Press.

Harry, B. (1992). *Cultural diversity, families, and the special education system.* New York: Teachers College Press.

Ingstad, B., & Whyte, S. R. (1995). Disability and culture: An overview. In B. Ingstad & S. Whyte (Eds.), *Disability and culture* (pp. 3-32). Berkeley: University of California Press.

Jandt, F. (1995). *Intercultural communication.* Thousand Oaks, CA: Sage.

Jezewski, M. A. (1990). Culture brokering in migrant farmworker health care. *Western Journal of Nursing Research, 12*(4), 497-513.

Leung, E. K. (1989). Cultural and accultural commonalities and diversities among Asian Americans: Identification and programming considerations. In A. A. Ortiz & B. A. Ramirez (Eds.), *Schools and the culturally diverse exceptional student.* Reston, VA: The Council for Exceptional Children.

Lipson, G. L., Dibble, S. L., & Minarik, P. A. (1996). *Culture and nursing care: A pocket guide.* San Francisco: UCSF Nursing Press.

Locust, C. (1988). Wounding the spirit: Discrimination and traditional American Indian belief systems. *Harvard Review, 58*(3), 315-330.

Miles, M. (1995). Disability in an Eastern religious context: Historical perspectives. *Disability & Society, 10,* 49-69.

National Council on Disability. (1993). *Meeting the unique needs of minorities with disabilities: Report to the president and the Congress.* Washington, DC: Author.

National Council on Disability. (1999). *Lift every voice: Modernizing disability policies and programs to serve a diverse nation.* Washington, DC: Author.

National Institute on Disability and Rehabilitation Research, Office of Special Education and Rehabilitative Services. (1993). Disability statistics. *Rehab brief: Bringing research into effective focus, 14*(8). Retrieved December 7, 2003, from http://codi.buffalo.edu/graph_based/.demographics/.disstats

National Institute on Disability and Rehabilitation Research. (1999, December 7). Long-range plan for fiscal years 1999–2004. *Federal Register, 64*(234), 68576-68614.

Nosek, M. A., Fuhrer, M. J., Rintala, D. H., & Hart, K. A. (1993). The use of personal assistance services by persons with spinal cord injury: Policy issues surrounding reliance on family and paid providers. *Journal of Disability Policy Studies, 4*(1), 89-103.

Randall-David, E. (1989). *Strategies for working with culturally diverse communities and clients.* Bethesda, MD: Association for the Care of Children's Health.

Rorie, J., Paine, L., & Barger, M. (1996). Primary care for women: Cultural competence in primary care services. *Journal of Nurse-Midwifery, 41*(2), 92-100.

Samovar, L. A., Porter, R. E., & Jain, N. C. (1981). *Understanding intercultural communication.* Belmont, CA: Wadsworth.

Schmidley, D. (2003). The foreign-born population in the states: March 2002. *Current Population Reports,* P20-539. Washington, DC: U.S. Census Bureau.

Smart, J. F., & Smart, D. W. (1997). The racial/ethnic demography of disability. *Journal of Rehabilitation, 63*(4), 9-15.

Sotnik, P., & Hasnain, R. (1998). Outreach & service delivery to the Southeast Asian populations in the United States. In T. S. Smith (Ed.), *Rural rehabilitation: A modern perspective* (pp. 228-259). Arnaudville, LA: Bow River Publishing.

U.S. Census Bureau. (2003). *Disability status: 2000—Census 2000 brief.* Retrieved November 13, 2003, from www.census.gov/hhes/www/disable/disabstat2k.html

U.S. Department of State. (2000). *Fact sheet. U.S. refugee admissions and resettlement program.* Retrieved November 13, 2003, from www.state.gov/www/global/prm/2000_admis_reset.pdf

3

Disability Service Providers as Culture Brokers

Mary Ann Jezewski

Paula Sotnik

Introduction

Providing culturally competent disability services may require that service providers play a role beyond that for which they were technically trained. The concept of culture brokering may be new to disability service providers, but various components of the role may already be part of the service provider's practice. This chapter will present a model for culture brokering as well as discussing the relevance of the model for disability service providers. Examples of ways that culture brokering may be used in specific situations will also be included.

We define culture brokering as the act of bridging, linking, or mediating between groups or persons of differing cultural backgrounds for the purpose of reducing conflict or producing change (Jezewski, 1990). In other words, the culture broker acts as a go-between, one who advocates or intervenes on behalf of another individual or group.

The term *culture brokering* was first coined in anthropology when anthropologists observed that certain individuals in the communities they were studying acted as middlemen or brokers between colonial governments and peasant societies that were ruled by the colonial powers. Very often, these middlemen brokered to resolve conflicts between the local people and the government, or brokered to acquire favors for the peasant population. In the 1960s, health care researchers began to explore the idea of brokering within health care delivery systems. In this situation, the broker was, very often, a member of the consumer's community who also was knowledgeable about the health care system. At the same time, other health care researchers looked at the ways that health service professionals acted as brokers between their clients and the health service system, as well as between clients and other service providers. Today, there is a body of literature on the concept of culture brokering as well as the model discussed in this chapter, which can inform service providers on how to broker for consumers. A selected bibliography of the culture-brokering literature is provided at the end of this chapter.

Jezewski's Culture-Brokering Model

The culture-brokering model presented in this chapter is based on theory constructed through a series of studies that used a methodology specifically for theory generation (Jezewski, 1995). The model was first developed for health services but has been adapted here to make it relevant for disability services.

An effective culture broker needs knowledge, skills, sensitivity, and awareness of cross-cultural variables. Perfecting the role of culture broker takes time and practice, as is true of any role within a profession.

The culture-brokering model (Figure 3.1) has relevance for disability service providers in a variety of settings, even in areas where service providers may not recognize the presence of cultural differences between the rehabilitation service system as a cultural system and some of the groups that it serves. In the previous chapter, the term *culture* was discussed. These explanations, along with the discussions of worldview, acculturation, and diversity, form the basis of understanding the culture-brokering role. It is also important to remember that disability service systems are cultural systems themselves, and, as cultural systems, they have values and beliefs that strongly influence the behaviors and beliefs of the providers within them. Consumers who enter disability services come with their own cultural values, beliefs, and behaviors. The differences in the beliefs and values of the lay culture of the consumer from those of the cultural system of service providers need to be understood in order for effective and relevant service to take place. If cultural differences lead to conflict between the consumers and the service system, someone must resolve the conflict for effective service provision to take place. The service provider can act as a culture broker to resolve conflict or produce a change that will prevent further conflict from occurring.

Culture brokering is essentially a conflict resolution and problem-solving model. The culture broker is a problem solver. Certainly this role is not a new one for disability service providers. However, looking at the problem-solving role from a cultural diversity perspective may be new. Culture brokering (see Figure 3.1) has a set of intervening conditions that affect, either negatively or

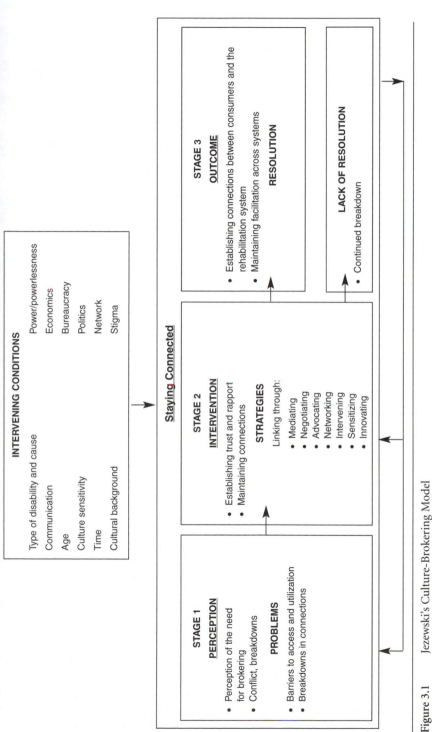

Figure 3.1   Jezewski's Culture-Brokering Model

SOURCE: Adapted from "Cultural Variation in the Experience of Health and Illness," McElroy & Jezewski, in G. Albrecht, R. Fitzpatrick, & S. C. Scrimshaw (Eds.), *Handbook of Social Studies in Health and Medicine.* © copyright 2000 by Sage Publications, Inc. Adapted with permission.

positively, the three stages of brokering. In some situations, an intervening condition facilitates brokering; at other times, the same condition hampers the brokering process. For example, bureaucracy can supply funding for services while at the same time placing barriers and red tape in the way of easy access to funds and services. Disability service providers must consider intervening conditions as they move through the three stages of culture brokering.

Stage 1 of the culture-brokering model is the recognition that there is a problem or potential problem in the consumer's encounter with the system. The service provider as culture broker looks at the problem from a cultural perspective. As the service provider becomes more proficient at culture brokering, potential problems will be anticipated and prevented or minimized. Conflict in the disability environment can occur because of problems in access and/or use of services. Different views about the intervention plan, breakdown in communication between providers and consumers, and differences in beliefs about what are appropriate services are other examples of problems that can be resolved by using the culture-brokering model as a guide. These problems are often based on differences between the culture of the consumer and the service system as a cultural system, and they can result in conflict and breakdown in the encounter. In Stage 1, the service provider determines that there is a problem and assesses the problem by attempting to understand the causes.

Reviewing and identifying which of the intervening conditions may be the basis for the problem also helps the culture broker to identify the problem and potential solutions. Knowledge of the meaning, scope, and diversity of culture, as well as sensitivity to the importance of culture in shaping the human view of disability, provides skills necessary to identify how cultural variables influence provision of disability services.

After the problem has been clarified, the broker moves on to Stage 2 of the culture-brokering model, the intervention phase. In this stage, strategies are put into practice to resolve the identified problem or problems. These strategies are used to prevent or minimize conflict situations, facilitate links between consumers and disability services, and assist consumers in staying connected to the system. The strategies used in brokering are varied and overlapping. Two strategies have been observed most frequently in the studies used to develop the brokering model: *mediating* and *negotiating*. Although strategies are difficult to separate, certain aspects in these two strategies are different. *Mediating* seems to be a more appropriate label for the strategy culture brokers use when conflict occurs and a go-between, or intermediary, is needed to resolve or minimize, and, in some instances, prevent conflicts between consumers and the service delivery system. Mediation is used to prevent conflict from occurring between service providers and consumers or family members. Mediation can be used whenever there is an element of conflict in the delivery of services.

Negotiating is a more appropriate label for the brokering process needed to reach an agreement. Negotiating involves conferring with the consumer in order to come to terms with the consumer's perception of the need for specific services. An example of this would be a service provider who needs to negotiate a particular service for a consumer that is not provided to the consumer currently, and one that, from the consumer's perspective, is necessary to optimize the intervention. This might include providing transportation to religious services or negotiating additional hours for an interpreter when a consumer, who does not speak English, must interact with a variety of English-speaking service providers. Negotiating through the broker can empower the consumer. To negotiate, the provider has to understand the consumer's perspective as well as possess knowledge of the system, thereby functioning as a true middle-person with knowledge about the actors on both sides of the negotiations.

Advocating is another strategy that is closely aligned with both negotiating and mediating. The advocate's role is one of defining and pleading the cause of, promoting the rights of, or changing the system on behalf of an individual or group. Advocacy involves activities that are aimed at the redistribution of power and resources to the individual or group that has demonstrated a need. The strategy of advocating is also closely integrated with the intervening conditions of power and economics, and the broker who is advocating must consider these intervening conditions in the brokering model. In disability services, advocacy can be further delineated as the act of informing and supporting consumers so that they can make decisions that serve their needs. Advocating can also encompass the responsibility to take appropriate action regarding instances of incompetence or unethical or illegal practices by a member of the service provider team. This would include a readiness to prevent any action on the part of others that is stigmatizing to consumers or prejudicial to their best interest.

Networking is another culture-brokering strategy by which the service provider as culture broker establishes links with other professionals who can provide services to consumers. These networks serve as a source of power for the service provider in facilitating provision of disability services to culturally diverse consumers, especially because culturally diverse consumers may have problems obtaining access to and using services.

The brokering strategies cannot be effective without understanding how and why the intervening conditions affect the consumer's situation. As the service provider is defining the strategies to resolve the identified problem, it is necessary to consider the intervening conditions.

Stage 3 of culture brokering focuses on outcome. The broker evaluates the degree to which the problem has been resolved. If resolution did not take place or the problem was not resolved satisfactorily, the culture broker reverts back to Stage 1 or Stage 2 to either reassess the problem (Stage 1) or use additional strategies to intervene (Stage 2). This reassessment, again, involves re-evaluating the role of the intervening conditions.

The *intervening conditions* are integral to the stages of culture brokering. Table 3.1 provides a very detailed explanation of each of the intervening conditions, as well as assessment questions for the culture broker to consider for each condition. In some situations where brokering is used, the intervening conditions influence each other. For example, two very important intervening conditions in the culture-brokering model are cultural background, which includes ethnicity, and culture sensitivity or competency. Consumers may be stigmatized based on their cultural background. This stigma or bias can affect consumers' access to and use of services. Particular disabilities may also have a stigmatizing effect. In turn, the economic and political conditions present in disability service delivery may limit development of an adequate number of service facilities. Situations in which stigmatizing and political/economic inequities prevail can complicate the service provider/culture broker's ability to negotiate access for the culturally diverse consumer. The intervening conditions can become a complex maze through which culture brokers need to weave their way in order to obtain optimal services for the consumer.

Several issues affect culture brokering. If brokers are people who function as go-betweens, with whom do they align themselves? Does the broker represent one of the two parties, or is the broker acting on behalf of both parties? Historically, in less complex brokering situations (peasant societies), the broker was a member of the community. The broker was able to function in both the community and the colonial government environment. A broker for disability services needs to have knowledge of both culture systems (the foreign culture of the consumer as well as the culture of the U.S. rehabilitation system) and be able to function in both systems. Because disability service systems are often complex, in many cases it may be difficult for persons who are not part of the system to function as culture brokers; they may not always have the knowledge necessary to "work" the service system. In today's complex rehabilitation systems, the broker most often will be a member of the service delivery system, because the delivery system may be far too complex for a layperson to negotiate and mediate in most conflict/problem situations. It is not impossible for laypersons to be culture brokers in the service system, but it is extremely difficult. Additionally, the service provider as broker must be knowledgeable and culturally competent to provide services to consumers of particular cultural backgrounds.

(*Text continues on page 49*)

Table 3.1   Operationalizing the Intervening Conditions in the Culture-Brokering Model

Intervening Condition	Explanation	Assessment Questions	Discussion
Understanding of Disability Type of disability and its cause.	Consumers' understanding of the cause and nature of the disability sometimes creates breakdowns in facilitating service. Diagnoses may be explained in ways consumers and families do not understand.	What impact does the consumer's disability have on access to or maintenance of services? Do consumers, providers, and family understand the disability in the same way? Is the understanding of the disability creating a barrier to open communication?	Family members may believe that some types of disabilities warrant the provision of rehabilitation services, whereas other disabilities should just be "accepted." Acquired disabilities may be viewed differently from lifelong disabilities, especially cognitive disabilities.
Communication Interpersonal communication (verbal and nonverbal) that takes place between consumers, families, and service providers.	When service providers act as brokers of information, consumers and families are better informed and better able to understand what is communicated. The broker of information uses language in a way that is sensitive to the consumer's or family's level of comprehension. Extra time and care need to be taken when consumers or families do not speak English. Communication breakdowns are sometimes just as severe when consumers and families do not speak the language of rehabilitation.	Is there open communication among all participants? What factors may be hindering open communication? What must the service provider do to encourage communication if there is a deficit? Do consumers and family members speak the same language as the providers? Do consumers and family members understand the language of rehabilitation? What is the language of rehabilitation?	Service providers need to act as information brokers between consumers and the system. This includes interpreting the language of rehabilitation to the consumer as well as interpreting and clarifying explanations communicated to consumers. The role of the culture broker becomes one of advocate and innovator when consumers and families do not speak the same language as the providers.

(Continued)

Table 3.1 (Continued)

Intervening Condition	Explanation	Assessment Questions	Discussion
Age Ageism–Age affects quality-of-life issues and rehabilitation options made available to the consumer.	When there are limited resources in disability service settings, preference sometimes is given to particular populations. Value judgments may be made regarding the consumer's age and disability services.	How does the consumer's age affect the service he or she receives? What are the values and beliefs of service providers toward the consumer, related to the consumer's age? Does ageism affect the way service is facilitated? Is the consumer labeled negatively (stigmatized) because of age?	Age is a subtle intervening condition in the brokering process. Ageism can be a potential form of stigmatization that can negatively affect service provision. It can also be a positive influence on the brokering process. If providers positively value the age of the consumer, it may be easier for the consumer to obtain optimal service.
Culture sensitivity/competence Awareness by one person of the differences in values, beliefs, and behaviors of another and the awareness that these are an integral part of the person's worldview.	The values and beliefs about disability may be very different for providers and consumers. Culture sensitivity does not have to do solely with ethnicity; it has to do with the similarities and differences in the values, beliefs, and behaviors of the cultural systems of the consumers and the service providers.	Do the providers know the consumer's views regarding disability? What are the consumer's explanatory models of disability? Are the service expectations of the consumer similar to or different from those of the providers? Is culture sensitivity present in providers who are interacting with the consumer?	The disability service system is a cultural and social system with a set of values, beliefs, and behaviors particular to that system. Culture sensitivity is a positive force in the brokering process. Culture insensitivity has a negative impact on the stages of brokering and leads to cultural incompetence. Culture sensitivity also increases awareness of stigmatizing behavior.
Time/timing 1. The time orientation (past, present, and/or future) of consumers and providers.	Brokering strategies are affected when the time orientation of the consumer differs from the provider's, especially when the	What are the time orientations of the consumer and the providers? Do they differ?	Awareness of differing concepts of time/timing informs the assessment of conflict and the strategies to resolve conflict, especially sensitizing

Intervening Condition	Explanation	Assessment Questions	Discussion
2. The time it takes to broker. 3. In some cases, there are right and wrong times to initiate certain interactions.	provider is future-oriented, emphasizing preventive, goal-oriented behaviors, and the consumer is present-oriented, emphasizing "survival is living life one day at a time." Brokering takes time and can't be rushed. The power of the broker evolves over time, especially the establishment of complex service provider networks.	Are differences in time orientations between provider and consumer creating breakdowns in the service interaction? Are they creating conflict between consumer and provider in their perception of appropriate service? Does the service provider see the value of taking time to broker for the consumer? How does a service provider make time to broker?	others to the presence of this intervening condition. Rehabilitation service providers may need to increase their own sensitivity to the concept of time orientation. There is a need to consider the timing of discussions with consumers in situations that require complex decisions.
Cultural background Similar to cultural sensitivity, but narrower in scope. This intervening condition implies that the cultures of the consumer and provider are embedded in their ethnicity and, in turn, ethnicity influences values, beliefs, and behaviors.	Differences in cultural background influence interactions. Cultural backgrounds affect communication patterns, time orientation, and beliefs about disability. Differences in cultural background impact negatively on the brokering process if providers are not sensitive to the influence of culture.	What are the cultural backgrounds of the provider and consumer? Are they different, and if so, in what ways? Do provider and consumer cultures impact positively or negatively on the service interactions? Is the potential for conflict increased as a result of cultural differences? How do the consumer and provider cultural backgrounds affect the other intervening conditions?	Cultural background affects most of the other intervening conditions. Culture is the framework in which the meanings of the other intervening conditions are formed and interpreted by the consumer and provider. The broker needs knowledge of the meaning of culture.

(Continued)

Table 3.1 (Continued)

Intervening Condition	Explanation	Assessment Questions	Discussion
Stigma Refers to the negative beliefs and values one person has for another based solely on a label ascribed to the person. The values and beliefs about the label usually are determined by the dominant culture. The stigmatizing label provides a discrediting attribute, which is likely to bring about social exclusion.	Stigma has a negative impact on access and utilization. The labels *migrant farmworker* and *homeless* may stigmatize because of perceived differences and stereotyping on the part of providers. One type of stigma is linked to age. Elderly consumers sometimes are circumvented in favor of their family members' decisions, even though the elderly consumer is competent to make decisions.	Is the consumer labeled in a stigmatizing way that results in a negative view of the consumer or family member? What is the source of the stigma? What information or educational processes are necessary to reduce the stigma associated with a particular derogatory label?	When stigma associated with the label *disabled* overlaps with stigma resulting from racial or ethnic affiliation, the stigmatizing effect may be increased. The effects of stigma are compounded when consumers' disabilities have a stigmatizing effect, such as mental retardation or impaired speech. Disability itself is sometimes stigmatized, regardless of the type of disability. Disabilities associated with accidents or war may sometimes be less stigmatizing than lifelong disabilities.
Power/powerlessness Power is defined as the ability or capacity to act or function effectively in interactive situations, to control one's own actions and/or exercise control over the actions of others.	Power versus powerlessness was ever-present in the studies that formed the basis for the culture brokering theory. The consumer usually is less powerful than the providers. The potential for abuse of power is present, especially in the provision of services to those persons who are relatively powerless socially, economically, and politically in our society, such as mentally ill persons.	Is there asymmetry of power in the service system? Are providers using their power to influence consumer decisions? Are service professionals exercising power to control consumers' access to or use of services? Are providers withholding service that they have the power to offer to consumers? Why is the service not offered? How can the consumer be empowered?	Powerlessness is often present when lack of health insurance is a factor in access to or use of rehabilitation services. In some conflict situations, providers withhold information from competent consumers under the guise that it is in the best interests of the consumer, despite the fact that consumers and/or family members want the information. Additionally, policy and protocols are influenced by those with the most power.

Intervening Condition	Explanation	Assessment Questions	Discussion
Bureaucracy An administrative system in which there is the need to follow complex procedures based in policy and/or legislation. Bureaucracy can impede the provision of rehabilitation services. Bureaucracy entrenches policy in a system.	Bureaucracy is the "paper chase" and "red tape" that can impede the brokering process. Bureaucracy in the form of complex protocols impedes brokering in interactions and mandates the need for an intermediary. Disability service settings often have the red tape of social service programs. The regulations of Medicaid create barriers rather than facilitate coverage for groups who economically are eligible for this rehabilitation service coverage but who may not meet all the regulations for eligibility.	Does the administrative paperwork affect the consumer's autonomy? Are there forms that consumers must fill out or sign? Does the consumer understand what he or she is signing and why? Are the forms necessary? Are there committees that periodically review forms and policies that consumers must deal with directly? What aspects of providing rehabilitation service and resolving conflict are entrenched in the bureaucracy? How do bureaucratic mandates affect service?	Consumers have difficulty understanding the jargon present in the bureaucratic paperwork and protocols. Differences in cultural values may make it difficult for some consumers to understand the forms they must sign or the necessity of signing such forms. Consumers may not have knowledge of the politics of regulations imposed by local, state, or federal governmental agencies on disability service agencies. Disability service providers act as intermediaries between the bureaucracy and the consumer.
Politics Defined in the context of culture brokering as conducting and engaging in activities that are designed to influence and determine decisions that affect rehabilitation service delivery.	Politics is "what is possible," more dynamic and changing than the bureaucracy. Policy development through politics affects the bureaucracy. Disability service providers may not be involved in the politics of their institutions. Politics in the institutions control, to some extent, who will and will not receive service.	Is there a role for the service provider in changing policy to prevent conflict in particular situations in disability service interactions? Does the service provider have the ability to change protocols to reduce the possibility of conflict in disability service interactions?	It is difficult to prevent political decisions from becoming immutable bureaucracy. Service providers who are active in policy decisions have more power to prevent or resolve conflict in service encounters. Politics affect economic conditions. Politics and legislation affect

(Continued)

Table 3.1 (Continued)

Intervening Condition	Explanation	Assessment Questions	Discussion
		Do service providers sit on committees that are active in changing policy?	insurance coverage under the Medicaid program.
Networks Networks are established links between the culture broker (service provider) and others in rehabilitation services. Others may have the power and know-how to assist the broker. The broker needs to know who the others are to facilitate brokering.	Networks facilitate the power of the broker to effect conflict resolution. Networks are either formal (administrative, contractual) or informal (personal, social). Referrals can be an important part of brokering disability services. Referrals are facilitated by networks. Referrals may be made to outside agencies for follow-up. Referrals may also be made within agencies.	Service providers can ask themselves, "Whom do I know, and what do they know that can help me facilitate service for consumers?" Are there formal networks in place to facilitate consumer services? What are the informal networks in place? Are there potential access problems for the consumers within agencies?	Networks provide power for the disability service providers practicing in a variety of settings within the community.

The above discussion does not imply that the culture broker needs to be a rehabilitation professional or a nonconsumer. Organizations run by and for persons with disabilities for self-help and advocacy, such as Centers for Independent Living (CILs), play an important role in helping persons with disabilities become more independent. Because of activities such as peer counseling and individual advocacy, the staffs of CILs and other community-based service organizations are included in this chapter as important parts of the disability service system. These persons usually have an understanding of how the rehabilitation service system works. Moreover, their understanding of the consumer perspective may make them particularly effective as culture brokers.

The brokering role is central to CILs. Although they provide some direct services to consumers, the majority of their activity is referral and advocating for service on behalf of the consumer. CILs assess, discuss, explore, arrange, advocate, design, and work with the consumer to see that the needed services are obtained. For the staff of CILs, culture brokering should be regarded as a skill in helping persons to receive services not only within the CILs themselves but also, and more important, from service providers outside the CIL. In fact, CILs and Client Assistance Programs (CAPs) were developed precisely to provide a third party to broker the interaction between the consumer and the service system.

The service provider as culture broker raises another question: If the broker is an employee of the system, might there not be a tendency to represent the interests of the system more than those of the consumer? The answer is yes, in some respects, but there also are attributes inherent in the successful broker. If these attributes are not present, the service provider will have difficulty functioning in the role of culture broker. Attributes necessary to be an effective culture broker include a willingness to be a risk taker, the ability to tolerate ambiguous roles, and a degree of comfort functioning at the margins of various systems (the consumer's cultural system and the service delivery system). Additional attributes of an effective broker include good communication skills, the ability to network, effective problem-solving skills, flexibility, and a willingness to learn and perfect the culture-brokering role. Disability service providers possess many of these attributes already; if they do not, the skills can be learned and cultivated.

A case study may illustrate some aspects of the brokering role in rehabilitation services.

Alvernia: A Case Study

Alvernia R., a 20-year-old woman, moved from Puerto Rico with her mother, Mrs. R., 2 years ago. Alvernia was diagnosed with cerebral palsy as a young child. She has difficulty walking, moving her arms, and engaging in fine motor activities. Currently, she is assisted by her mother and is using poorly fitted crutches to move about and complete daily living activities. She attended school sporadically in Puerto Rico and received some clinical services. Alvernia enjoyed school and being with other children. Mrs. R. became frustrated with the disability service limitations in San Juan for Alvernia and left a professional, well-paying position to move to New York.

At the time of Alvernia's diagnosis, her parents were told to place her in a mental institution because she would always be a burden. Close relatives agreed with this determination and described Alvernia's disability as a punishment from God. Mrs. R. felt particularly responsible for her daughter's condition and constantly relived her activities during her pregnancy. Because of these beliefs concerning responsibility, Mrs. R. vowed that she would care for her daughter to the exclusion of her own or other family members' needs. She was convinced that she would find the best services elsewhere in the United States and therefore left Puerto Rico.

Alvernia's extended family still resides in Puerto Rico. Although they maintain contact through telephone calls, letters, and visits, Mrs. R. and Alvernia miss them greatly. Prior to their move, the family maintained almost daily personal contact. Mr. R. has no intention of moving and will not divorce Mrs. R. because of strong religious beliefs. Mr. R. is embarrassed by his daughter's condition. He feels guilty because of this emotion and because he is not able to help her.

Alvernia attended special education classes in her high school and is now eager to get a job. Mrs. R. is uncertain of her daughter's education and had difficulty understanding information pertaining to her daughter's disability. She tried to participate in school meetings but felt stupid and helpless because she did not understand the jargon and necessary action steps. Alvernia wants to be a hairdresser, but her mother strongly discourages this preference because of her mobility and fine motor difficulties. Mrs. R. is also afraid that others would tease her.

Alvernia and her mother met with a vocational rehabilitation counselor through school, but Mrs. R. felt that the counselor was discounting her role as a mother. The counselor encouraged Alvernia to follow her dream job despite what other people felt about her capabilities. Alvernia became hopeful of attaining her career choice following her meeting. Mrs. R., however, did not want her daughter to have contact with the counselor again and became suspicious of the vocational rehabilitation service system. This difference in opinion caused a conflict within the family. Alvernia and her mother continue to argue about Alvernia pursuing a job and receiving vocational rehabilitation services. Mrs. R. has become increasingly depressed because of her daughter's increasing assertiveness and because of the great distance from Mr. R. and the rest of her family. Alvernia now talks about becoming independent by getting her own apartment and dating. Mrs. R. still feels that her priorities must center on the protection and care of her daughter.

In using the culture-brokering model to analyze this case, a service provider would do well to focus on several of the following considerations:

- Puerto Rican culture
- Worldview (values, beliefs)
- Religion
- Family
- Role within the family
- Other family members' roles
- Time orientation
- Degree of acculturation
- Communication
- Beliefs about what it means to be healthy and independent
- Beliefs about what Alvernia's disability means to different members of the family
- Beliefs about the explanatory model of disability and about the role of rehabilitation
- Financial status
- Education level
- Stigmatization

Figure 3.2 shows a partial analysis of this case using the culture-brokering model. This example identifies some of the principal factors in this case and some possible strategies that one might consider as starting points. However, alternative interpretations and solutions are possible.

Tools for Culture Brokers

Cultural assessment of persons with disabilities is an important skill for those who wish to provide culturally competent services. A complete cultural assessment of the consumer is a complex task and involves obtaining information about all aspects of the consumer's culture. In most instances, however, a comprehensive assessment is not necessary even when the consumer's culture and the service provider's culture are vastly different. It is important for the provider to understand how the consumer perceives and lives with disability. Understanding the consumer's perspective will alert the provider to cultural components that need further exploration.

Consumers construct their own explanation of their disabilities, and service providers are not always aware of these explanations. The assumption

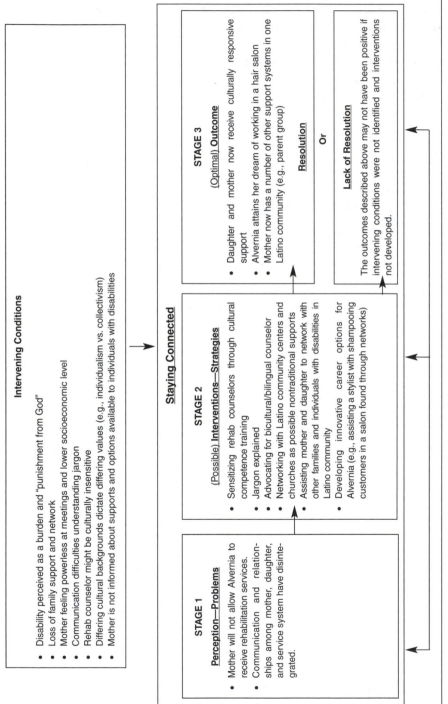

Intervening Conditions

- Disability perceived as a burden and "punishment from God"
- Loss of family support and network
- Mother feeling powerless at meetings and lower socioeconomic level
- Communication difficulties understanding jargon
- Rehab counselor might be culturally insensitive
- Differing cultural backgrounds dictate differing values (e.g., individualism vs. collectivism)
- Mother is not informed about supports and options available to individuals with disabilities

Staying Connected

STAGE 1

Perception—Problems

- Mother will not allow Alvernia to receive rehabilitation services.
- Communication and relationships among mother, daughter, and service system have disintegrated.

STAGE 2

(Possible) Interventions—Strategies

- Sensitizing rehab counselors through cultural competence training
- Jargon explained
- Advocating for bicultural/bilingual counselor
- Networking with Latino community centers and churches as possible nontraditional supports
- Assisting mother and daughter to network with other families and individuals with disabilities in Latino community
- Developing innovative career options for Alvernia (e.g., assisting a stylist with shampooing customers in a salon found through networks)

STAGE 3

(Optimal) Outcome

- Daughter and mother now receive culturally responsive support
- Alvernia attains her dream of working in a hair salon
- Mother now has a number of other support systems in one Latino community (e.g., parent group)

Resolution

Or

Lack of Resolution

The outcomes described above may not have been positive if intervening conditions were not identified and interventions not developed.

Figure 3.2   An Application of the Culture-Brokering Model—Alvernia Case Study

frequently made by the provider is that consumers understand the causes of their disabilities and the types of services they need in the same way that the providers understand these issues. This is frequently not true in a cross-cultural environment.

More than 20 years ago, Dr. Arthur Kleinman, a psychiatrist and medical anthropologist at Harvard Medical School, realized that the medical students and residents he was teaching did not understand how their patients perceived their illnesses. He also noticed that patients did not always agree with the treatment that was prescribed. Kleinman developed a useful tool for providers that helped them to elicit from patients their understanding of their condition (Kleinman, Eisenberg, & Good, 1978). Eliciting and understanding patients' explanatory models of their illnesses has proven to be a useful tool for health providers in a cross-cultural environment. Eliciting consumers' explanatory models, especially regarding their disabilities and the services they think they need, can be a useful tool for disability service providers as well.

The approach developed by Kleinman consists of a series of questions that require the respondents to express their understanding of their condition. The following list contains some questions that might be used by disability service providers to elicit consumers' explanatory models. The questions have been modified from Kleinman's questions to make them more relevant to disability contexts. Additionally, instead of the term *disability,* the provider may make the questions more specific to the individual by using terms such as *mobility impairment, vision impairment,* and *hearing impairment,* as appropriate.

Explanatory Model Assessment Questions

The questions below can help enable service providers to understand consumers' ideas about their disability, how it affects their lives, and the types of services they think will best meet their needs.

- Do you consider yourself well or ill?
- What do you think caused your condition?
- How does disability affect your everyday life?
- How severe do you consider your disability to be?
- What have you or others done about it?
- What kind of services do you think you should receive?
- What is the most important result you hope to receive from the services at _____?
- What are the chief problems caused by this disability?
- What does your family think about this disability?

- How does this disability affect your family? Your friends?
- What do you fear most about disability?

These questions attempt to elicit the consumer's understanding of etiology, symptoms, treatment, and the interaction of their disability with their social and cultural environment. Most important, eliciting the consumers' perceptions of their disabilities assists service providers in providing culturally competent care.

First, it is important to know whether the consumers view themselves as ill or well, because these terms are subjective and in fact may change from time to time. In all probability, we would assume that consumers consider themselves essentially well, but the provider should not assume to know the answer to the first question.

The remaining questions help the provider understand the consumers' perceptions of the cause of their disability; what they do to adapt to the disability; what they expect of the service provider, their friends, and their family; and, most important, what disability services they think should be available to them.

The experiences of Kleinman and others demonstrate that the explanatory models of providers very often differ with those of culturally diverse consumers. When these differences in understanding persist, poor provision of services can persist. Kleinman suggests that in order to provide culturally competent services, providers should negotiate shared explanatory models. First, the providers must assess their explanatory model of the consumer's disability and then compare their model with the consumer's. Any differences, particularly discrepancies or conflicting explanations, need to be discussed with the consumer and differences negotiated. Without this negotiation of differing explanatory models, provision of culturally competent services is in jeopardy and in all likelihood will not take place.

For example, a service provider asking the consumer the fifth question may find out that the consumer regularly uses alternative medical practices, including a variety of herbal remedies and religious healing ceremonies. This information should alert the provider to probe further into the consumer's response. For example, how do the religious ceremonies help the consumer? What specific herbal remedies is the consumer taking? There are resources available to providers to research different herbs to understand their chemical and medicinal properties as well as their potential interactions with over-the-counter and prescription medications. Most herbal remedies are not harmful, and some may have some medicinal properties. Nevertheless, it is the responsibility of the consumer's service providers to be proactive to resolve potential contraindications in consuming both herbal remedies and prescribed medications.

Caveats for the Rehabilitation Service Provider as Culture Broker

COMMUNICATION

Communication is of primary importance in providing rehabilitation services. Communicating cross-culturally presents unique challenges to service providers. The challenges of cross-cultural communication need to be understood, and strategies to overcome barriers need to be addressed by providers of rehabilitation services.

The primary challenge in effective cross-cultural communication is to be aware and sensitive to differences in both verbal and nonverbal ways of communicating. Verbal and nonverbal communication approaches vary cross-culturally. Awareness, sensitivity, and knowledge are three necessary prerequisites to developing effective strategies to communicate cross-culturally. This section of the chapter will explore both nonverbal and verbal communication patterns from a culturally diverse perspective.

VERBAL COMMUNICATION

Obviously, when the service provider speaks one language and the consumer speaks another, an interpreter will be needed in order to communicate. The role of translation and use of interpreters will be discussed later in this section. Culture influences how we use language to communicate, and there are culturally determined nuances in the way that people communicate.

First, we will explore the dominant American style of verbal communication. Americans place a heavy emphasis on the precision of the words used. Words should be exact and technical. Meaning is conveyed in the words apart from situations and events. Americans are taught early in their development to "say what you mean." American conversation is dependent on what is said more than what is not said. During conversations, Americans are expected to make their point with a minimal amount of elaboration. When description is lengthy, the American listener often becomes restless and impatient. Additionally, Americans generally do not value emotions in conversation. Often, they are embarrassed when communication becomes emotional. Americans emphasize factual, logical communication; emotions assume a secondary role to logic and facts. American conversation is categorized as low-context communication; that is, Americans do not rely on the situation to inform their understanding as much as they rely on the spoken word.

In contrast, many cultures depend on a style of communication that relies on context (situation dependent). Communication is less direct and depends on the common experiences of the communicators. For example, the status of the communicators is known and understood. What is said and how information is conveyed is highly dependent on the status of each of the communicators. Conclusions may not be stated explicitly; listeners are left to draw their own conclusions. In such a high-context situation, saving face (how you are viewed in the eyes of another and how you protect the feelings of another) is very important. Direct confrontation is considered rude because it does not take into consideration the feelings of others. Communication may be in a form meant to conceal feelings in order to avoid embarrassment for both speaker and listener (Stewart & Bennett, 1991). For example, there are as many as 16 ways to say "no" in Japanese, many of which will not embarrass the one to whom the reply is directed. American service providers may simply state to the consumer, "No, I can't" or "No, you can't receive services tomorrow." To a recently immigrated Japanese consumer, this logical, factual statement may be interpreted as rude, uncaring, and lacking concern for the feelings of the consumer. Repeated interactions such as this could lead to the Japanese consumer losing trust and faith in the intentions of the service provider.

Another variable in cross-cultural communication is also related to the dominant high- or low-context communication patterns: the importance placed on greeting and leave-taking rituals. In American culture, greetings are short, and the matter at hand is usually approached immediately after the greeting. Conversations are very often started, "I want to talk to you about . . ." (getting down to business). In many cultures (Middle Eastern, Asian), an elaborate greeting is expected. Such greetings include inquiries about one's family, health, and other personal matters. The greeting may also entail an offer of food or drink. In these circumstances, it is considered rude to refuse or to "get down to business" too soon. The prolonged greeting serves to set the context for the conversation and is far longer than a conventional American conversational greeting (Stewart & Bennett, 1991). Americans generally become very frustrated with this extended preliminary formality, and people from cultures where this is the norm find the American way to be brusque and to reflect a lack of concern for the welfare of others. Again, this points out the importance of service providers understanding the context in which information is optimally provided to culturally diverse consumers. Taking the time to properly greet consumers who value the contextual importance of a more elaborate greeting will improve communication between providers and consumers.

Another important aspect of intercultural communication is the degree of conversational formality that is considered appropriate to the individual speakers. Americans tend to value informality in conversation. This stems from the value of equality and is reflected by treating everyone the same, especially in conversation. Americans frequently engage in conversations with strangers they meet in their everyday life (waiters, clerks, cab drivers, etc.). This equality carries over in the frequent use of first names, even with relative strangers or those recognized as having higher and lower status. In the American value system, treating everyone the same is considered respectful. This is in contrast to other cultures, where respect is demonstrated by acknowledging status by a more formal approach and the use of specific titles. To do otherwise is a sign of disrespect and reflects a fault in one's character. For the service provider, it is always better to err on the side of formality when talking with immigrants, until a time when the provider understands the culture of the consumer. As the provider gets to know consumers and their culture, it may be appropriate to move toward a more informal conversational pattern.

This contrast between high- and low-context communication can result in breakdowns in communication between American service providers and recently immigrated consumers. It is impossible within the context of this chapter to go into a detailed discussion of the implications of communicating between persons in high- and low-context cultures, but there are many excellent resources that elaborate further on this rather complex aspect of cross-cultural communication. Some valuable resources are Stewart and Bennett's *American Cultural Patterns* (1991), Kavanagh and Kennedy's *Promoting Cultural Diversity* (1992), and Jandt's *Intercultural Communication* (1995).

NONVERBAL COMMUNICATION

The service provider as culture broker must also be aware of cross-cultural differences in nonverbal communication. This is an integral component of everyday communication and has added importance in cultures where high-context communication patterns prevail. Misinterpreting nonverbal cues or giving inappropriate nonverbal cues can be a major barrier to effective cross-cultural communication.

Cross-culturally, personal space can vary. In communication, personal space is the amount of distance individuals want between themselves and others at any given time. Socially, we feel uncomfortable when someone else invades this personal space by standing or sitting too close to us. In conversation, there is a range of space in which individuals feel most comfortable. The amount of space during communication depends on our relationship with the other person. The distance at which Americans feel most comfortable talking with colleagues, coworkers, or service providers is approximately 3 to 4 feet, and 18 inches is handshake distance (Hall, 1959). Usually, after shaking hands, Americans move apart to the comfortable conversation zone. This comfort zone is culturally determined. For instance, Arabs stand closer for conversation with colleagues than Americans do. When members of the two groups are conversing, very often each tries to maintain his or her comfort zone, with the American stepping away and the Arab stepping closer. Unconsciously, we tend to move away when someone invades our personal space. In a provider/ consumer situation, Middle Eastern consumers may interpret the distance at which the American provider stands when talking with the consumer as reflecting a cold or uncaring attitude. The consumer may not take the provider seriously because of the nonverbal messages conveyed simply by the distance at which the provider stands from the consumer. Once the provider is aware that distance between communicators is important, the provider can allow the consumer to set the distance to facilitate communication.

The gestures we use are also culturally prescribed and affect our communication cross-culturally. These include hand gestures, body movements, facial expressions, and eye contact. Communication includes the actions and movements of our bodies. Initial greetings between people differ among ethnic groups, from a firm handshake (United States) to an embrace (South America) to kissing both cheeks (France) to a bow (Japan).

Hand gestures can be misinterpreted. For example, crooking the index finger while the arm is extended toward another person means "come here" in the United States, but the gesture is very offensive and insulting in some Asian countries because it is used only to call animals. In other cultures, crossing one's legs while sitting facing another is impolite. The use of a thumbs-up sign varies in meaning from "that's great!" (United States) to "get stuffed" (Greece). The "OK" sign used in the United States, with thumb and forefinger circled, has a vulgar, insulting connotation in Brazil.

The amount of eye contact during conversation varies cross-culturally. Maintaining eye contact while speaking to another in American culture signals that the listener is interested in what the speaker is saying. Maintaining eye contact in other cultures may be a sign of disrespect. Lowering the eyes can be a sign of respect, especially when the speaker is of higher status or is perceived to have greater knowledge, as in the case of a service provider. Americans often perceive lack of eye contact as lack of interest in the conversation or as preoccupation. The service provider should not assume the same meaning of lack of eye contact from a culturally diverse consumer until the provider understands the consumer's cultural norms.

The use of silence also varies across cultures. In the United States, very little silence is tolerated during a conversation. Americans usually become uncomfortable when there is a lull in conversation. Eastern cultures of Asia, however, value silence. In these societies, silence can be a sign of thoughtful respect, affirmation, or cooperation. Service providers should not view silence as indicative that the consumer did not hear or did not understand what the provider said. Thus, it is important to understand the meaning of silence for the culturally diverse consumer.

WORDS, MEANINGS, AND TRANSLATIONS

Disability service providers often take for granted the meanings of certain words, but those words may have different connotations in other cultures. The following scenario is an example of the multiple and varied meanings of the term *disability*. Mr. Sam K., director of a Cambodian mutual assistance association, listened to an interviewer carefully as she asked questions about the population with disabilities that might be served by his center. He was sure that his community did not include people with disabilities. Some individuals who came to the center had lost arms or legs to land mines, and others had nightmares from terrible conditions experienced during Pol Pot's regime. However, these individuals were able to cook, clean their homes, go to temple, and work. None of these individuals were crazy or violent, and none acted like some people he knew of in Cambodia who would be considered "disabled." He remembered some individuals who were hidden by their families and not allowed out of a room in their house. The talk in his Cambodian village was that evil spirits made these individuals scream all day and night. These poor souls did not migrate to the United States, so he was certain there were no people with disabilities in the Cambodian cultural enclave.

As the interviewer described what having a disability means and asserted that individuals with disabilities can perform many activities, Mr. K. found that he could think of several young and middle-aged individuals who were different from most other people in the community. He considered one young girl who, at the age of 3, could hardly walk or talk. Her parents described her as a lazy child and hoped that she would overcome this obstinate conduct as she got older. Other family members and neighbors speculated that the parents were not capable of properly disciplining their child. Although health care clinicians recommended a developmental assessment for the child, the parents had not yet followed through. Mr. K. also recalled that the young girl did not interact with other children her age during the center's recreation activities.

The interpreter used the term *disability* to denote varied characteristics determined by the U.S. mainstream culture. Mr. K.'s original interpretation of this word was different and more narrowly defined. When he heard the word *disability*, Mr. K. visualized people who were threatening, violent, and had limited capacities. The meanings of the word *disability* and other related labels often differ between cultures, populations, generations, and service systems.

In a culture where daily affairs can be managed by someone with a healthy body, ordinary common sense, and elementary skills, the label *mentally retarded* would apply only to someone whose competence is severely impaired (Harry, 1992).

Many terms used by rehabilitation service providers on a daily basis may have no meaning in other languages and may be difficult or impossible to translate. Assistive technology terms exemplify how a lack of certain words in a vocabulary as well as related meanings can affect one's understanding of rehabilitation supports for individuals with disabilities. Outside the scope of traditional disability services, the terms *reacher* and *sound-activated light* might be difficult to depict. Furthermore, many terms and words naming adaptive products cannot be translated to any other language. The words *reacher* and *assistive* were contrived in the disability field within the last two decades, and the meanings assigned within that field cannot be found in generic dictionaries or a thesaurus.

Service providers should be aware that, for many reasons, persons who accompany the consumer as translators may vary in their background and ability to communicate the meanings of the service provider to the consumer. First, family members may themselves not have a full command of English. Second, if children or younger persons play the role of translator, this may introduce a demeaning element for the older consumer. Third, many persons who accompany consumers as translators may not have a very good understanding of disability terminology in either language, making it difficult for them to translate certain ideas.

Service providers should make an effort to speak slowly and use simple terminology, without speaking in a condescending way to either the consumer or the translator. The service provider should make an effort to speak to and maintain eye contact with the consumer, even when a translator is involved in the communications. Finally, the translator's task will be made easier if the speaker pauses after a few sentences to allow the translator the opportunity to translate at short intervals, rather than requiring that the translator remember a long, detailed explanation.

Time

Mainstream U.S. culture is often regulated by schedules, clocks, and watches. Medical professionals recommend feeding and sleeping schedules to ensure a well-adjusted baby. Upon entering school, we initially learn how the day is organized into periods of learning and playing. As adults, we wear watches and are guided by calendars. As a culture, we value punctuality and effective time management. We are concerned about being late and equate tardiness with irresponsibility.

Perception of time is culturally derived. In many other cultures, time is viewed and treated differently. Generally, life may be more relaxed and less hectic. Priority might be placed on personal interaction rather than being on time for the next appointment. For example, a director of a small agency serving Latinos, herself a Latina, would usually arrive late for committee meetings with directors of other community organizations. Some of the participants from mainstream agencies, frustrated and feeling insulted by the consistent delays, confronted the latecomer. Surprised by the frustration of her colleagues, this director described sessions with families conducted prior to her committee meetings. She could not imagine asking families to leave so that she could be on time for a committee meeting. One way of understanding how cultures use time was described by Edward Hall (1983). Hall conjectured that Northern Europeans and Americans plan the order of their use of time, doing one thing at a time, and labeled this monochronic time. Polychronic time, characteristic of Latin Americans and Middle Easterners, stresses the involvement of people and completion of transactions over adherence to schedules (Jandt, 1995). Table 3.2 provides a brief overview of the different time concepts.

Cultures also vary in their perceptions of the future, present, and past. Some cultures have a strong connection to their past that determines such beliefs as the role of the dead in everyday life and the extent to which the living are affected by the behaviors of their ancestors or heirs. For example, many Southeast Asian cultures believe strongly in the influence of ancestors, as described in *The Spirit Catches You and You Fall Down* (Fadiman, 1998). The Hmong believe that illness can be caused by a variety of sources, including being punished for one's ancestors' transgressions. This belief also can be generalized to explain the incidence of disability in families. Southeast Asian causal beliefs of disability range from those that focus on the behavior of parents, to those that center on sins committed by ancestors, to reincarnation (Sotnik & Hasnain, 1998). In contrast, the Western industrial societies place greater value on the future. Phrases such as "working toward" and "goal setting" are indicative of a future-oriented society. The term rehabilitation denotes a future-oriented activity. Rehabilitation takes place over time, and very often goals are set with the consumer with the idea that they will be met over time. For the consumer who is not future oriented, it may be difficult to see the benefit of working toward a goal that may be elusive by the very fact that it cannot immediately be met.

Table 3.2   Monochronic and Polychronic Cultures

Monochronic Culture	Polychronic Culture
Interpersonal Relations	
Interpersonal relations are subordinate to preset schedule	A preset schedule is subordinate to interpersonal relations
Activity Coordination	
Schedule coordinates activity	Interpersonal relations coordinate activity
Appointment times are rigid	Appointment times are flexible
Task Performance	
One task at a time	Many tasks performed simultaneously
Breaks and Personal Time	
Breaks and personal time are sacrosanct, regardless of personal ties	Breaks and personal time are subordinate to personal ties
Temporal Structure	
Time is inflexible and tangible	Time is flexible and fluid
Separation of Work Time From Personal Time	
Work time is clearly separable from personal time	Work time is not clearly separable from personal time
Organizational Perception	
Activities are isolated from the organization as a whole; tasks are measured by output per unit of time	Activities are integrated into the organization as a whole; tasks are measured as part of the overall organizational goal

SOURCE: Adapted from "What Are Monochronic and Polychronic Cultures," *Intermundo: Online Journal for Intercultural Communication.*

Conclusion

Although culture brokering may appear at first glance to involve a new set of skills for disability service providers, in reality it is an extension of skills that providers already practice. Assessment, problem solving, and communication are important skills for all rehabilitation service providers. Through culture brokering, providers may add new dimensions to these skills. Culture brokering is a learned role, one that requires awareness of the importance of considering a consumer's culture and the competence to provide culturally appropriate services to diverse consumers. Jezewski's culture-brokering model, presented in this chapter, offers a mechanism to understand and provide relevant cross-cultural services to a diverse population.

Appendix 3.1: Culture Brokering—A Selected Bibliography

Adams, R. (1970). Broker and career mobility systems in the structure of complex societies. *Southwestern Journal of Anthropology, 26,* 315–327.

Geertz, C. (1960). The Javanese Kijaji: The changing role of a cultural broker. *Comparative Studies in Sociology and History, 2,* 228–249.

Gentemann, K. M., & Whitehead, T. L. (1983). The cultural broker concept in bicultural education. *Journal of Negro Education, 52*(2), 118–129.

Hopkins, N., Ekpo, M., Helleman, J., Michtom, M., Osterwell, R., Sieber, R., et al. (1977). Brokers and symbols in American urban life. *Anthropological Quarterly, 50,* 65–75.

Jezewski, M. (1993). Culture brokering as a model for advocacy. *Nurse Health Care, 14,* 78–85.

Jezewski, M. (1994). Do-not-resuscitate status: Conflict and culture brokering in critical care units. *Heart & Lung, 23,* 458–465.

Jezewski, M. A. (1995). Evolution of a grounded theory: Conflict resolution through culture brokering. *Advances in Nursing Science, 17*(3), 14–30.

Lefley, H. (1975). Approaches to community mental health: The Miami model. *Psychiatry Annual, 5*(8), 315–319.

Loffler, R. (1971). The representative mediator and the new peasant. *American Anthropologist, 73,* 1074–1082.

McElroy, A., & Jezewski, M. A. (2000). Cultural variation in the experience of health and illness. In G. L. Albrecht, R. Fitzpatrick, & S. C. Scrimshaw (Eds.), *Handbook of social studies in health and medicine* (pp. 191–209). Thousand Oaks, CA: Sage.

Press, I. (1969). Ambiguity and innovation: Implications for the genesis of the culture broker. *American Anthropologist, 71,* 205–217.

Schwab, B., Drake, R., & Burghardt, E. (1988). Health care of the chronically mentally ill: The culture broker model. *Community Mental Health Journal, 24*(3), 174–184.

Singh, N. N., McKay, J. D., & Singh, A. N. (1999). The need for culture brokers in mental health services. *Journal of Child and Family Studies, 8*(1), 1–10.

Sussex, J., & Weidman, H. (1975). Toward responsiveness in mental health care. *Psychiatry Annual, 5,* 306–311.

Tripp-Reimer, T., & Brink, P. (1985). Culture brokerage. In G. Bulecheck & J. McCloskey (Eds.), *Nursing interventions* (pp. 352–364). New York: W. B. Saunders.

Weidman, H. (1975). Concepts as strategies for change. *Psychiatry Annual, 5*(8), 312–314.

Winters, L., & Dimino, J. (1984). Power brokering in training. *Training, 21*(5), 49–55.
Wolf, E. (1956). Aspects of group relations in a complex society: Mexico. *American Anthropologist, 58,* 1065–1078.

References

Fadiman, A. (1998). *The spirit catches you and you fall down.* New York: Noonday Press.
Hall, E. T. (1959). *The silent language.* Garden City, NY: Anchor Press/Doubleday.
Hall, E. T. (1983). *The dance of life: The other dimension of time.* Garden City, NY: Anchor Press/Doubleday.
Harry, B. (1992). *Cultural diversity, families, and the special education system.* New York: Teachers College Press.
Jandt, F. (1995). *Intercultural communication.* Thousand Oaks, CA: Sage.
Jezewski, M. A. (1990). Culture brokering in migrant farmworker health care. *Western Journal of Nursing Research, 12*(4), 497–513.
Jezewski, M. A. (1995). Evolution of a grounded theory: Conflict resolution through culture brokering. *Advances in Nursing Science, 17*(3), 14–30.
Kavanagh, K., & Kennedy, P. (1992). *Promoting cultural diversity.* Thousand Oaks, CA: Sage.
Kleinman, A., Eisenberg, L., & Good, B. (1978). Culture, illness and care: Clinical lessons from anthropological and cross-cultural research. *Annals of Internal Medicine, 88,* 251–258.
McElroy, A., & Jezewski, M. A. (2000). Cultural variation in the experience of health and illness. In G. L. Albrecht, R. Fitzpatrick, & S. C. Scrimshaw (Eds.), *Handbook of social studies in health and medicine* (pp. 191–209). Thousand Oaks, CA: Sage.
Sotnik, P., & Hasnain, R. (1998). Outreach & service delivery to the Southeast Asian populations in the United States. In T. S. Smith (Ed.), *Rural rehabilitation: A modern perspective* (pp. 228–259). Arnaudville, LA: Bow River Publishing.
Stewart, E., & Bennett, M. (1991). *American cultural patterns.* Yarmouth, ME: Intercultural Press.
What are monochronic and polychronic cultures? (n.d.). *Intermundo: Online Journal for Intercultural Communication.* Available at http://www.stephweb.com/forum/

4

Best Practices

Developing Cross-Cultural Competence From a Chinese Perspective

Gloria Zhang Liu

Introduction

The 2000 U.S. Census showed people of Chinese descent to be the largest single group of Asians in the country, comprising more than 20% of the 11.9 million Asians (Barnes & Bennett, 2002). The Asian American Health Forum (1990) revealed that more than 63% of Chinese Americans are foreign-born, 23% do not speak English well, 72.5% speak a language other than English at home, and 53% live in the western United States.

The Chinese in the United States are a heterogeneous group. They include people from mainland China, Taiwan, Hong Kong, and other Southeast Asian countries, and they are characterized by significant linguistic, social, economic, and political differences (S. Chan, 1998). For simplicity, the word "China" is used in this chapter to refer to mainland China, Hong Kong, and Taiwan. There are cultural differences among Chinese immigrants from different parts of the world, but the focus of this chapter will be on the common elements.

The philosophies, perceptions about disability, traditions, religions, communication patterns and styles, cultural norms, and practices of people of Chinese origin are described in this chapter, with case illustrations to help health and rehabilitation professionals gain insight into the many variations within this culture. I believe that cross-cultural information of this kind may help professionals appreciate and understand Chinese culture and thereby strengthen service provision to individuals with special needs who are of Chinese background.

Cultural Overview

According to Fung (1998), "Chinese customs, religion, and health practices are rich and complex and have stood the test of time over many millennia" (p. 3). China has one of the four oldest civilizations in the world and a written history of 4,000 years. The Chinese are very proud of their culture and history. They value their own culture and religion, but they are open and pragmatic toward the religions and cultures of others.

Chinese people in general are peaceful, hardworking, and easily contented. They follow norms of social order. For example, they respect authority figures and elders, and they are patient with their peers. The Chinese value modesty, reserved behavior, and humility. They believe in harmony and tend to avoid confrontation. They will, however, push and sacrifice for their children.

History of Immigration to the United States

Chinese migration to the United States on a large scale has a history of more than 150 years. It is a complex, fascinating story of change, adaptation, and survival that reveals how the Chinese family system is affected by the immense power of political, legal, social, and economic forces (Lee, 1996).

THE FIRST WAVE: THE PIONEER FAMILY (1840–1919)

Although there were Chinese in the United States prior to 1800, they began to arrive in large numbers in the 1840s in response to the demand for cheap labor provoked by the discovery of gold in California and the construction of railroads (Sue & Sue, 1999).

The Chinese Exclusion Act of 1882 barred Chinese laborers and their relatives (including wives) from entering the United States. The act later was broadened to include *all* Chinese people and was not repealed until 1943, when China became an American ally during World War II.

Early Chinese immigrants lived in a virtually womanless world without family life (Lee, 1996). While the Chinese immigrant population declined, those remaining survived in the face of antimiscegenation laws, special taxes directed against them, institutional racism, persistent humiliation, racial violence, loss of property, loss of livelihood, and sometimes loss of life (S. Chan, 1998). All of this had a profound impact on the development of family life among the early Chinese in the United States (Lee, 1996).

THE SECOND WAVE: THE SMALL BUSINESS FAMILY (1920–1940)

The discriminatory Immigration Act of 1924 allowed American citizens of Chinese ancestry to work in the United States but without their wives and families. The law changed in 1930 to allow wives of Chinese merchants and Chinese women who were married to American citizens before 1924 to immigrate to the United States. As a result, sizable family units began to come together in "Chinatowns." Meanwhile, many first-wave laborers left the mines and railroads and used their savings to start small businesses (Lee, 1996).

THE THIRD WAVE: THE REUNITED FAMILY (1943–1964)

In 1943, after years or even decades of separation from their husbands, many wives were reunited with their husbands for the first time as a result of changes in American immigration law. In response to reforms in immigration policies, many Chinese men returned to their native land to find wives, who were usually 10–20 years younger than them, and brought them back to the United States. Consequently, from 1943 to the repeal of the quota law in 1965, most Chinese immigrants were female (Lee, 1996).

THE FOURTH WAVE: CHINATOWN, DUAL-WORKER FAMILIES, AND STUDENTS (1965–1977)

The 1965 Immigration Act replaced a 21-year-old exclusionary system of immigration. The 1965 act assigned a flat annual quota of 20,000 immigrant visas to every country outside the Western Hemisphere. Following the passage of this act, Chinese immigration reached its peak (Pan, 1990). Most of the Chinese immigrants who arrived under the Immigration Act of 1965 came as families. Many initially settled in or near Chinatowns in the major metropolitan areas. Approximately half were of the working class. Most husbands and wives sought employment in labor-intensive, low-capital service businesses such as garment sweatshops and restaurants. Economic survival was the primary goal for many Chinese families, especially the new immigrants (Lee, 1996).

Before 1978, when the United States established diplomatic relations with mainland China, Taiwanese constituted most of the 20,000 quota. Taiwanese students have been settling in the United States under the quota system since the 1960s. Unlike the earlier immigrants of humble rural origin, many of the Taiwan arrivals came from well-to-do, well-educated families, and many were students who, upon graduation from American universities, stayed on to work in the United States (Pan, 1990).

THE FIFTH WAVE: STUDENTS/SCHOLARS AND REFUGEES (1978–PRESENT)

Taiwan retained its right to a 20,000-per-year immigration quota when the United States normalized its relations with mainland China—that is, the People's Republic of China (P.R.C.)—in 1978. The P.R.C. was given its own quota of 20,000, with an additional quota of 600 immigrants from Hong Kong that was increased to 5,000 on October 1, 1987. That meant that a total of 40,600 Chinese—counting those from the P.R.C., Taiwan, and Hong Kong—could come to the United States each year (Pan, 1990).

The reestablishment of diplomatic relations between the Unites States and the P.R.C. in 1978 provided an opportunity for students and professionals from China to study and lecture in the United States, and many of them elected to stay (Lee, 1996). The U.S. government granted special permanent residency status to a large number of Chinese students and visiting scholars in the United States immediately following the 1989 Tiananmen protest demonstrations (Pan, 1990). Most of these students and scholars came from prestigious universities in the P.R.C.

Another group of immigrants to the United States were refugees of Chinese descent from Vietnam, Laos, and Cambodia. A significant number of them were survivors of incarceration, forced migration, rape, torture, and deprivation of food. There were also "overseas Chinese" who emigrated from countries such as Japan, Korea, the Philippines, Singapore, Malaysia, Thailand, Mexico, Canada, and countries in South America and Europe (Lee, 1996). In summary, as Lee (1996) pointed out, "the influx of immigrants and refugees from many different parts of Asia and from many different socioeconomic and political backgrounds has contributed to the complexity of existing Chinese American communities" (p. 252).

Chinese Concepts of Disability

The traditional Chinese terms for disability are *canfei,* meaning "handicap" and "useless," and *canji,* meaning "handicap" and "illness." This demonstrates how the Chinese used to view disability. The term *canji ren,* meaning "handicapped" and "sick people," is also common. The term *gong neng zhang ai zhe,* meaning "individuals with disabilities," is rarely used.

In many areas of China, disability is viewed as a punishment for the disabled person's sins in a past life or the sins of the person's parents. When encountering health problems, many religious people, especially those from rural areas where medical resources are not readily available or sufficient, will visit temples or Taoist priest houses to pray, worship, or perform rituals in order to identify the cause of their condition and seek a solution.

Mental health is believed to be achieved through self-discipline, exercise of willpower, and the avoidance of morbid thoughts. Emotional problems are understood to be associated with weak character (Lee, 1996). In some cases, mental illness is blamed on evil spirits or punishment from god(s). Another belief is that an unbalanced diet, eating food that should be avoided, or emotional disturbance during pregnancy will cause illness or disability in the newborn. For instance, grief or having temper tantrums during pregnancy is thought to be a possible cause of a mother losing her baby or giving birth to a baby with disabilities. C. Lam (1992) discussed an example of a mother who blamed her child's epilepsy on the lamb she ate during pregnancy. The Chinese term for epilepsy, *yang dian feng*, translates as "shaking of the lamb." The mother believed that the lamb she ate passed the "shaking of the lamb" to her child. In general, disability is viewed as something shameful, a skeleton in the closet. As an example, one of my cousins was diagnosed with schizophrenia in his early twenties. No one in the family wished to talk about it, certainly not to persons outside the family. It remained a well-kept family secret for many years.

C. Lam (1992) described shame and guilt as a complicated mix in the family of persons with disabilities. Shame from the outside world is felt by the family, especially the head of the family, as well as by the disabled persons themselves. The stigma attached to disability may result in the family's fear of exposure to criticism and disgrace. Guilt might be felt by persons with a disability toward their family or by the family toward the individual with disability, as well as toward ancestors. These feelings often create conflicts and barriers to acceptance among family members (C. Lam, 1992). Although shame and guilt are often associated with disabilities in Chinese culture, as in American culture, Chung (1996) pointed out that the Eastern system focuses on the *cause*—that is, why it happened—whereas in the West, the focus is usually on the *solution* or treatment. It is essential, therefore, to educate the Chinese consumer and family about the nature and cause of the disability, as well as about treatment methods and available services.

Misunderstanding and lack of knowledge about a specific disability can cause a tremendous amount of fear, hostility, alienation, and blame. I was stunned by an article in the most popular Chinese newspaper, *World Journal* (Wu, 2000). It told a sad story of a 9-year-old Chinese boy, Ning Li, who acquired AIDS from a blood transfusion, received for a broken arm in 1996. Immediately after his diagnosis, Ning Li was terminated from his school, and to date no school has accepted him due to the nature of his illness. He has since lost all his friends, as have his parents. A neighbor even moved after learning the boy had AIDS. The neighbor's house is still empty because no one will purchase it. Ning's father took him to see a doctor, who told Ning, "don't touch my desk" when he learned the boy had AIDs. This happened in a small town in mainland China.

Wang, Chan, Thomas, Lin, and Larson (1997) summarized Chan and colleagues' 1984 and 1988 findings that Chinese participants were more positive toward people with physical disabilities than toward people with developmental disabilities and mental disorders. Chinese students were less positive in their attitudes toward people with physical or mental disabilities than their American counterparts.

ACQUIRED AND LIFELONG DISABILITIES

Chinese people are generally more accepting and sympathetic toward an *acquired* injury that causes physical limitations than toward a congenital physical or mental disorder. The same section of the previously mentioned *World Journal* contained an article about a 29-year-old woman, Lan Mao, who has received loving care by numerous health care professionals and strangers despite her severe disabilities (Dong, 2000). Unlike Ning Li, Lan was born in Beijing, the capital city of mainland China, where she lives today. Lan was almost burned to death in a fire 27 years ago. She is reported to be the only survivor of such severe burns in Chinese medical history.

Lan's face remains severely maimed even after numerous reconstructive surgeries. She lost her hands, her hair, and many facial features and will never be able to stand. Lan's parents left and never returned after seeing her on her hospital bed after the fire. She has remained in the hospital for 27 years, cared for by team after team of physicians, nursing personnel, and volunteers. The hospital received many donations that paid for all the expenses of her stay, including her medical bills. To facilitate Lan's independent living in the community, her hospital assisted her in selecting a "new home." Recently, she transferred to an excellent independent living and vocational training residential facility (Dong, 2000).

Because of the political, economic, and social differences among mainland China, Hong Kong, and Taiwan, provision of rehabilitation and social services to people with disabilities varies considerably. For instance, mainland China, a communist country that went through 10 years of cultural revolution and many other socialist movements, has adopted many aspects of the Western medical/rehabilitation system, and it has aggressively developed its own system over the past two decades. Hong Kong, a British colony for 99 years and a Special Administrative Region of China today, has a very advanced rehabilitation system. C. Lam (1992) noted that one of its major rehabilitation services, vocational rehabilitation, is quite similar to that of the United States. Taiwan, a strategic partner of the United States during the Cold War era, also is strongly influenced by the U.S. health care and rehabilitation systems.

The Role of Family, Community, and Religion

FAMILY

The roles of members of a Chinese family are highly interdependent (Ong, 1993). Traditionally, the family has been the most fundamental and important unit of society among the Chinese, and this is still true. The family is also an important economic unit. In today's China, it is still very common for three generations to live under one roof. C. Lam (1992) noted that Confucian philosophy advocates the virtue of sacrificing individual needs for the good of the group.

Parents are the highest authority in the family. To maintain family harmony, child rearing focuses on obedience, proper conduct, control of emotions and personal desires, moral training, impulse control, achievement, and the acceptance of social obligations. Chinese are brought up to remain an integral part of their families throughout their lives, rather than being trained to function independently (Bond, 1986).

The Chinese are willing to sacrifice for family members. They tend to seek help from immediate and extended family first before turning to neighbors, communities, and professionals. Seeking help, such as social welfare and benefits from the government, can be very intimidating. Because respect for the elders and filial piety are so important, rehabilitation professionals should attempt to establish a working relationship with parents or significant extended family members. Their involvement will be vital to the success of the rehabilitation process (Ong, 1993).

Some contemporary Chinese American families are "Americanized" but still hold some traditional values. It is important for American professionals to have knowledge of the Chinese traditional values and family structure, but it is also important for us to recognize that economic and political changes in mainland China, Taiwan, and Hong Kong have had dramatic impacts on the Chinese family system and values and that Chinese American families may not adhere to traditional values. As a result of the communist takeover of mainland China in 1949, Confucian thought and religion were banned. A one-child-per-family policy replaced the traditional extended family system (Lee, 1996). The 10-year Cultural Revolution caused many families to suffer forced separation. Filial piety and respect for the elderly were seriously questioned by Red Guard youths. In recent years, China's open-door policy and its economic boom have brought another wave of Western influence and urbanization (Lee, 1996) that has placed additional stress on traditional families.

Outside the mainland, Hong Kong and Taiwan underwent rapid growth in light industries and exports after World War II. The forces of industrialization, Westernization, urbanization, and economic affluence brought a change in their social and family structures. Although older and middle-generation Chinese still maintain some traditional beliefs and practices, the younger generation has tended to reject conservatism and traditionalism (Lee, 1996).

Lee (1996) emphasized that as a result of the social, political, and economic changes described above, there is no one "typical" Chinese family. Most families share many of the same beliefs and traditions, but different families and even members of the same family also have differences and variations in values.

Case Study: Carol

Zhang (1994), a counselor from China, used the following case study to argue that American counseling is deeply rooted in individualism, often at the expenses of family and community. He questioned the suitability of American counseling strategies for other cultures.

Carol, 29 years of age, blames herself for her family's tension and dissension. Her father is out of work and depressed most of the time. Her mother feels overburdened and ineffective. In the past, Carol has assumed responsibility for her family's problems and has done a great deal for her parents. She is convinced, however, that if she were more hardworking and competent, most of her family problems would diminish greatly. The fact that she is increasingly unable to effectively change bothers her. Therefore, she is asking for counseling help.

Zhang's (1994) American classmates all maintained that Carol was too submissive and should not continue to put family interests above her own. They encouraged Carol to think of her own needs first, leave her family, live alone, and make sure not to let her parents override her wishes. They also suggested assertiveness training for Carol.

Zhang (1994) could not understand why putting the family's interests before one's own is not considered correct or "normal" in the American culture. According to Chinese culture, a morally responsible son or daughter fulfills the duty of taking care of parents, even if it means sacrifice. To Zhang, it would be extremely selfish for Carol to leave when her family is in such need of her. In China, that kind of assertiveness is considered aggressive and immoral. Zhang thought the parents were the ones who needed change, not the daughter. He thought the parents needed to be more sensitive to their daughter's needs and more aware of the difficulties they had caused her. Zhang suggested inviting

Carol's parents to come in for a family session. If Carol feared that her parents would not tolerate having an "outsider" involved in this family matter, Zhang suggested inviting Carol's relatives or friends to come in and discuss intervention strategies they could use to help the parents come to terms with the difficulties they had caused their daughter. Zhang reasoned that in Chinese culture, it is all right for an individual to stand up for one's own rights; however, one needs to do it in an indirect, subtle way, especially when dealing with one's elders, lest it cause others to "lose face."

Case Study: Jim

Jim is a 25-year-old, single male of Chinese descent. Jim was born in mainland China and immigrated to the United States with his parents in 1997. Jim's primary language is Cantonese. He also speaks Mandarin and is able to communicate about basic needs in English. Jim's only sister still resides in Guang Dong (Canton), China. When he first came to the United States, Jim had several jobs, such as waiting on tables in Chinese restaurants and delivering newspapers for a Chinese newspaper company in New York City.

In July 1998, 1 year after he came to the United States, Jim's delivery truck was struck by another truck, and he sustained traumatic brain injury (TBI) as well as physical disabilities. He remained in a coma for more than 6 weeks. After emerging from his coma and receiving intensive inpatient rehabilitation, Jim was transferred to a skilled nursing facility with a TBI unit for extended care and further rehabilitation.

Jim's father was so disturbed by the accident that he had a nervous break-down and returned to mainland China for psychiatric treatment. Jim's mother has to work 7 days a week (5 days a week in a Chinese restaurant and 2 days as a home attendant for a Chinese home care agency) to earn a living. Jim is determined to go back to work and has stated that if returning home to live with his mother means adding to her burden, he would rather remain in the nursing home for the rest of his life. He is also eager to help his sister immigrate to the United States and was referred to a local Chinese agency that handles immigration matters. With the support of the Home and Community-based Waiver program, Jim was later discharged into a two-bedroom apartment, sharing with his parents (Jim's father returned from China). Jim and his mother requested all Chinese-speaking providers. Jim could not find a service coordinator (SC) who spoke Chinese, so he chose a health care agency with Chinese-speaking staff who would at times accompany the SC for home visits and be available for translations. Jim's counseling provider was able to hire a Cantonese-speaking counselor from the local Chinese American council. Because of difficulty finding consistent Chinese-speaking home care workers under the waiver program, home attendant service with Chinese-speaking aides was applied for on Jim's behalf, under another funding stream.

Although Jim's mother does not speak any English, she has become both Jim's and his father's primary caregiver and has been involved with every team meeting. Jim is still facing many challenges individually and with his family. His providers, however, now have a better understanding of his cultural differences and are proactively assisting him with these issues rather than complaining about the difficulty of working with him resulting from his demands, such as only wanting Chinese-speaking staff.

These cases illustrate several lessons that should be kept in mind when providing services to consumers born in China:

1. Find persons who speak the consumer's and family members' native language to work with them. If it is impossible to find providers who speak their native language, work through translators.

2. Understand the consumer's family structure and work around it. It is as important to work with the family, especially the caretaker and main advocate, as with the consumer himself or herself. Involve the family, especially the older generation, in meetings concerning care.

3. Explore services within the family's ethnic community. The city and county departments of health and the mayor's office of large cities usually have a department of minority affairs, where it may be possible to obtain resource information about a specific ethnic group.

4. Refer the consumer and family to community organizations where staff speak their language and are able to address such special issues as immigration with which the rehabilitation provider may not be familiar.

5. Provide the consumer and family with as many written materials in their native language as are available or have a translator translate basic information about program offerings into the consumer's and family's native tongue.

6. Indicate on marketing brochures or provider lists the different languages that are spoken by the staff.

COMMUNITY

Confucian philosophy advocates that individuals put group needs above personal needs. Chinese, with their Confucian background, have a strong sense of community.

The sense of being part of something greater than oneself gives the Chinese a feeling of belonging and security. They know that they do not stand alone (Sung, 1985). Lee (1996) believes that the community association model provides the psychological services of an extended family to many Chinese immigrants. To survive and make a better living in a foreign land, Chinese immigrants form many unique communities where they all speak the same language, shop at Chinese supermarkets or stores, see Chinese doctors, and have an understanding of each other's religion, culture, and beliefs. Each of these communities has advocacy groups, medical associations, churches/temples, and nonprofit organizations that address immigration, legal, medical, educational, disability, vocational, and many other needs.

Because of their unfamiliarity with and lack of understanding of Western medicine and the medical, social, and rehabilitation system, many community members prefer to seek medical help first from a Chinese doctor in their community. Some feel nervous, even skeptical when referred to an American medical professional outside that community.

Case Study: Joe

Joe is a 55-year-old man who sustained a traumatic brain injury (TBI) from a gunshot wound when he was mugged on the way home from work more than a decade ago. He is of Chinese descent and immigrated to the United States while in his high school years. He lived with his parents and sister in an apartment he now shares with his sister; both his parents are deceased. His mother died 1 year after he sustained his TBI. Joe worked in the food service industry prior to his injury and is very eager to resume work. He speaks Cantonese and Chao Shang dialect with his sister at home but also speaks English fairly well.

Since his injury, Sue—who is younger and is his only sister—has been his primary caretaker and advocate. She is very involved in Joe's care but often feels a lack of support from social workers and therapists. She commented that the social worker at the hospital told her to apply for benefits and services on her own, saying, "You speak English very well. You can do all this." Sue feels that she really doesn't understand the medical, rehabilitation, or social systems and is at a loss when dealing with all the jargon. She is often depressed and overwhelmed because she has been struggling to do her best but feels she gets little cooperation and appreciation from Joe. Joe, on the other hand, is very frustrated about his dependence on his younger sister. As the older brother, he thinks he should support the family and be the one to give orders. He cannot accept the fact that because of his memory loss, he has to depend on Sue to remind him to do things and give him advice. As a result, Joe often yells at Sue, "I don't need you telling me what to do!" He uses his sister as an outlet for his anger because he has nowhere else to release his temper. Joe and his sister fight all the time but are inseparable.

Joe's main focus is getting a job. Because he is so eager to be gainfully employed, he tends to put considerations of all his cognitive, medical, and physical limitations aside. This hinders his vocational rehabilitation. His service providers and vocational counselors find it very difficult to work with him because they can neither set realistic goals with him nor motivate him to achieve one step at a time. They complain that Joe wants to find a paid job right away but does not want to go through any training. Joe feels, however, that no one ever clearly explained in language and terms he can understand why the training is so essential.

Joe lost all his former friends after his injury but has been visiting Chinatown on a daily basis and has formed some new "tea friends," friends with whom he drinks tea and chats. He does not trust or like most of his service providers. One of the few providers with whom he relates well is his primary care physician (PCP), a Chinese doctor in Chinatown. This doctor has limited knowledge about the identification, treatment, and resources for TBI. Joe's service coordinator thought that Joe would be better served by a doctor who specializes in working with individuals with TBI, so he changed Joe's PCP to an American doctor who specializes in TBI. After seeing his new PCP once, Joe asked to be transferred back to his Chinese doctor because he felt much more comfortable with her.

This case illustrates several important points:

1. Do not assume that immigrants who came to this country decades ago and speak English well know the American medical, social, and rehabilitation concepts or systems well.

2. Be aware of family structure and conflicts. Find out what shapes the structure of the family and what causes any conflict.

3. Acknowledge culture as a predominant force in shaping behaviors. According to the Chinese tradition, the oldest son of the family is considered the head of the household, particularly if the father is deceased. He is expected to take charge of everything. It is considered shameful for an older brother to depend on his younger sister for a living and for advice.

4. Be sensitive to the consumers' needs and be respectful of their choices. As a professional, it is very tempting to refer the consumer to the best medical professionals and services. It is important, however, to find out from the consumers which medical professionals they want. The consumers may want to remain with a doctor with whom they feel comfortable and who speaks the same language, even if that doctor is not the most expert. Respect the consumers' rights and choices. Find a way to involve the doctor the consumers choose instead of forcing them to change.

5. Be aware of the consumer's community and try to find services within that community.

6. Acknowledge that cultural differences can have an impact on service delivery. In this case, being the oldest son and the only surviving man in the family, Joe has a strong desire to work and be the family breadwinner that could hinder his vocational and rehabilitation process. Counseling could help address his issue as well as his role in the family and his expectations related to vocational services.

RELIGION

China is a multireligious country. The majority Han nationality, the largest ethnic group in mainland China, practices Buddhism, Christianity, and Taoism. All Chinese are greatly influenced by Confucianism as well. Chinese philosophies promote harmony. Taoism and Buddhism, the most popular religions in China, have some differences between them but no conflicts (J. Lam, 2000). Based on Dao De Jin, Taoism promotes the belief that persons will gain power and strength if they behave in harmony with the nature of the universe and will suffer later in life if they act against the nature of the universe (J. Lam, 2000). This may explain why some believers in Taoism delay in seeking treatment.

Mental illness is viewed as being caused by deeds from past lives or acts against the nature of the universe. In traditional Chinese medicine, humankind is viewed as a microcosm within a universal macrocosm. The energy in each human being interrelates with the energy of the universe. If there is imbalance of the yin and yang, the immune system of the body is disturbed and the body is susceptible to illness (Lee, 1996).

In J. Lam's (2000) analysis, Confucianism is the philosophy that guides Chinese in governing behavior. It emphasizes the importance of family and social order. Children must respect and be obligated to their parents and grandparents, the junior follow the senior, and servants serve the rulers.

Buddhism was introduced to China from India. J. Lam (2000) maintains that the reason for the wide acceptance of Buddhism in China is the concept of rebirth and its reinforcement of the principles of Taoism and Confucianism. Buddhism is a human-centered religion, not god-centered. It tells people that life is suffering. No one but yourself can save you from suffering. Craving is believed to be the cause of all sufferings. To achieve happiness, one must overcome craving, desire, or endless wanting, hatred, and complaints. "In congruence with the belief that birth, aging, illness and death are the inevitable of life, some patients, particularly those advanced in age, may accept illness and death as de facto and seek treatment only passively" (Fung, 1998, p. 36).

Many Chinese are Buddhists and attend occasional services, practice rituals, and visit a temple on a regular basis. It has been estimated that more than 68 million Chinese still consider themselves Buddhists, though it is not likely that they all practice the religion regularly ("Chinese Cultural Studies," 1995). Many Buddhists do pray to Bodhisattvas to seek help to relieve their or their family members' sickness or ill fortune (Fung, 1998).

Islam was brought to China mainly from central Asia, and by 1995 there were believed to be more than 4 million Chinese Muslims ("Chinese Cultural Studies," 1995). Islam insists that its god is the only god in the universe (J. Lam, 2000). This belief is somewhat contradictory to that of Buddhism, but the two religions coexist peacefully in China.

Christianity arrived in China with Jesuit missionaries in the early 17th century. It is believed that as many as 2 million Christians practice their faith in China ("Chinese Cultural Studies," 1995), and a great many Chinese converted to Christianity after immigrating to the United States. Chinese Americans formed churches within their communities, where they worship in English or Chinese, depending on preference. The Chinese churches provide a very important support network to their members and beyond, especially to new immigrants whose social network is limited.

It is common for Chinese to honor their ancestors, especially during major holidays such as the Chinese New Year. Incense burning and the eating of special foods usually occur on special occasions. Good luck symbols may be displayed in homes.

Interactions With Service Providers in the United States

LANGUAGE

Sung (1985) found that the language barrier was the problem most commonly cited by immigrant Chinese. Language is the conduit through which we interact with other people. It is the means by which we think, learn, and express ourselves. Although many first-generation immigrants have learned some English, either formally or through their exposure to it via the media, most are fluent only in their native tongues (Hernandez & Isaacs, 1998). To complicate the situation, there are many different dialects in the Chinese language.

When I began working as a case manager many years ago, I was asked to interpret for a Chinese family. Knowing Mandarin and two other Chinese dialects, I went into the meeting with confidence. As soon as the conversation started, however, I realized that I did not understand a word the Chinese family was saying. I even asked whether they were actually Chinese. Later, I learned that the family spoke only Hakka, a Taiwanese dialect. This experience taught me a good lesson: Any health care professional seeking Chinese interpreters should first find out what dialects the consumer and the family speak. Many Chinese immigrants are multilingual, fluent in the official language and a local dialect, and speak some English as well. Many, however, do not speak English at all.

Case Study: Sun

I worked as a case manager for a 25-year-old woman, Sun, a Chinese American who was legally blind, nonverbal, and diagnosed with moderate mental retardation. Sun was able to understand Cantonese, which was the only language that her parents spoke, and a few words in English. She responded to questions by nodding, shaking her head, or making certain sounds. When I started working with her, she had been attending, for a few years, a traditional day treatment program for people with mental retardation. She seemed to be comfortable there, but on the occasion of a home visit to see her and her parents in their Chinatown apartment, it became apparent that Sun's parents really preferred that she attend a special school for the blind. They said that even though they had this wish for a long time, they were not able to make their needs known because of language barriers.

Sun's past case managers spoke only English. They would periodically check as to whether Sun's parents were satisfied with the day treatment program, and the parents would always say "Yes," unable to express their wish for a more appropriate setting for their daughter. I worked with Sun's parents and located an excellent program for adults and children with visual impairment. Sun was transferred to this program and appeared to be happier because she was more comfortable with the environment and was able to engage in activities designed for the blind. Sun has been attending the special program ever since.

This case study illustrates the impact that language barriers have on delivery of quality services and the difference it makes when the provider speaks the consumer/family's native tongue.

Hernandez and Isaacs (1998) pointed out that members of an immigrant family settling into a new community will learn English at different rates, so there might be many levels of English fluency within a family. It is always helpful for health professionals to take the time to learn as much as possible about the family's unique cultural and linguistic backgrounds. Although taking the time up front may be difficult for the provider and may even cause conflict with some agencies' policies, the knowledge and understanding that results will help the provider build a trusting and helping relationship with the individual or family and make more effective service provision possible.

COMMUNICATION STYLES

Besides confronting language barriers, Chinese and Americans differ in their styles of communication. Chinese in general communicate less directly and less explicitly, and their communication often relies on body movements, facial expressions, eye messages, and other nonverbal signals (Engholm, 1994). Interpreting nonverbal expressions can be quite difficult, however. Chinese may have completely different meanings for nonverbal expressions than do Americans. For instance, to most Americans, smiling generally means a positive reaction and agreement. The Chinese, however, may smile when they feel embarrassed or shy. Americans are taught to look at others when speaking to them, and they view eye contact as an indication of mutual understanding, trust, and attention giving. For the Chinese, looking a superior or an elderly person directly in the eye indicates disobedience and challenge.

Sue and Sue (1999) discussed the concept of high-low context communication proposed by Hall (1976). High-context (HC) communication emphasizes the physical or social context of the situation and relies heavily on nonverbal cues and identification or understanding shared by the communicators.

"In traditional Asian society, many interactions are understandable only in light of high-context cues and situations" (Sue & Sue, 1999, p. 82). For example, if you have dinner at a traditional Chinese home, the host will, on numerous occasions, offer you drinks and food to show hospitality and sincerity. The host will not accept no for an answer and will continue to offer the fine food or drinks until the end of the dinner. It is expected that the guest will turn down the offers to show his politeness.

Another example relates to the Chinese way of greeting. One of my friends, a third-generation Italian American, used to complain to me about a Chinese neighbor "Mei," who would always ask her "Did you eat?" and "Where are you going" every time she saw her. The friend would ask me, "Why is Mei so nosy? Why does she have to know everywhere I go? Why does she ask me 10 times a day whether I ate or not? I am Italian, alright, but that doesn't mean I eat 10 times a day!" For many Chinese, asking "Did you eat?" or "Where are you heading?" is a way of greeting or starting a conversation, as when Americans say "How are you today?"

The United States is a low-context (LC) culture. LC cultures place emphasis on the verbal part of the communication (Hall, 1976, Sue & Sue, 1999). LC cultures are associated with opportunism, being more individual-oriented than group-oriented, and having a greater focus on rules of law and procedures (Smith, 1981, Sue & Sue, 1999). Communicators from these HC and LC cultures often do not understand each other, and service providers should be aware of the differences in approaches to communication and attempt to accommodate them.

When dealing with criticism, LC white Americans are more likely to be direct and up front, getting right to the point. Conversely, their Chinese counterparts (with HC orientation) may view such behavior as rude and blunt. Because the Chinese tend to go to extremes to avoid offending or embarrassing others, they may seem ambiguous or "wishy-washy."

Chinese people are often shy, especially in an unfamiliar environment (Chin, 1996). Gentle and friendly tones of greetings are helpful. It is appropriate to address older consumers and family members by "Mr." or "Mrs." because addressing older people by their first names can be seen as a sign of disrespect. Be aware that married women from mainland China generally carry their maiden names. If a consumer's parents or other older relatives are participating in a conversation or meeting with a rehabilitation counselor, it is important to give the older family members attention while discussing the care of the younger family member.

Sue and Sue (1999) compared communication style differences among Asian Americans, African Americans, and white Americans. Their findings are shown in Table 4.1. The description of the Asian American way of communication can apply to that of the Chinese. It is important to consider the general Chinese communication styles because they may affect service providers' perceptions of and ability to work with Chinese consumers. It is equally important, however, to remember that these style differences are generalizations of traditional communication behaviors and will not apply to every individual of a specific background. There is simply no "one size fits all."

Table 4.1   Communication Style Differences

Asian Americans	Whites	African Americans
1. Speak softly	1. Speak loudly/quickly to control listener	1. Speak with affect
2. Eye contact avoided when listening or speaking to older or high-status persons	2. Eye contact when listening or speaking	2. Direct eye contact (prolonged) when speaking, but less when listening
3. Seldom interject; offer verbal or non-verbal cues to encourage communication	3. Provide head nods and other nonverbal markers	3. Interrupt (turn-taking) when appropriate to take a turn in conversation
4. Mild delay in response time	4. Quick response	4. Quicker response
5. Low-key, indirect communication	5. Objective, task-oriented communication	5. Affective, emotional, interpersonal communication

SOURCE: Adapted from Sue and Sue, "Culturally Appropriate Intervention Strategies," in *Counseling the Culturally Different: Theory and Practice* (1999, p. 89).

Interactions With Service Providers

The contrasting concepts of the Western individualistic (that is, independent) orientation versus the Chinese collectivistic (that is, interdependent) orientation have a strong impact on service provision to Chinese with disabilities in the United States. The client-centered approach used by many rehabilitation counselors in the United States may create discomfort and confusion for some Chinese consumers because this approach lacks the structure that they may be used to and expect. Moreover, Chinese Americans tend to view counselors as authorities and expect them to solve their problems for them, as opposed to offering empathy and nurturance through the counseling process. Because rehabilitation professionals may be viewed as authority figures and Chinese culture emphasizes controlling one's emotions, it may be very difficult for Chinese consumers to initiate conversations (F. Chan, Lam, Wong, Leung, & Fang, 1988). Chan et al. (p. 23) concluded that "these different expectations of counseling and low levels of self-disclosure and emotional expressions are often in direct conflict with the expectations of individual western therapists."

The language barrier is another problem when counseling Chinese Americans, in the light of the verbal interaction and rapport-building function of the counseling relationship (F. Chan et al., 1988). Interpreters can help with this issue, but greater success may be possible if the service provider bears in mind the recommendations listed below.

Recommendations for Service Providers

WORKING WITH THE COMMUNITY

When accessing the community, be aware of the following:

- There are subcultures within the general Chinese culture; that is, there are differences between people who originated in Hong Kong and those who originated in mainland China or Taiwan. In addition, cultural values and beliefs can be quite different between first-, second-, third-, and fourth-generation Chinese Americans. Questions such as "Which part of China did you come from?" or "How long have you been in the United States?" are important to ask because China includes so many varieties of linguistic, cultural, political, economic, health, and rehabilitation systems.
- There are differences in the availability of minority community organizations in urban and rural areas (Grant-Griffin, 1994). There are dozens of Chinese organizations, associations, and groups in New York City, for instance, but rarely will you find any in most rural areas, even those close to large cities.
- Hire Mandarin/Cantonese-speaking staff directly from the communities in need.
- Use Chinese media, such as Chinese newspapers, radio stations, and TV channels, when conducting outreach.
- Conduct outreach in "Chinatown's" schools, senior centers, churches/temples, and community health center. Distribute double-sided materials in English and Chinese.
- Collaborate with existing community organizations and service providers.

WORKING WITH FAMILIES

- Involve family members in the rehabilitation intake and treatment process. Keep family members well informed of the process.
- Be aware of family differences in cultural beliefs, traditions, religions, and values. Provide services to families in ways that do not conflict with their beliefs, customs, and cultural values (Grant-Griffin, 1994).
- Work with interpreters. These professionals should have both bilingual and bicultural skills, as well as knowledge of rehabilitation vocabulary and concepts, so that they can provide accurate translation. It is highly recommended that service providers meet with interpreters before meetings with the consumer or family to keep the interpreters abreast of the purpose and content of the meeting, familiarize them with relevant terminology, and obtain

information about acceptable communication that may be appropriate for the particular consumer or family.

- Expand family care programs to include relatives as providers (Grant-Griffin, 1994).

WORKING WITH INDIVIDUALS

- Recognize individual differences. Be careful not to make stereotypical assumptions about a consumer who is of Chinese heritage.
- Be sensitive to the language and dialect the consumer speaks, which can be different from the advocate's.
- Be aware of interpersonal skills and nonverbal communication cues (Grant-Griffin, 1994). For instance, when invited into Chinese homes and offered something to eat or drink, remember that it is considered impolite to say no.
- Promote the consumer's participation in choice of services. Keep in mind that younger consumers may tend to follow the lead of older family members.

Conclusion

Differences between Chinese and American cultures cannot always be easily identified. First, "Chinese" refers to a very heterogeneous group. There are many subcultures within its main culture. Second, many factors, such as different levels of acculturation and differences in socioeconomic status and political background, come into play. Although it is beyond the scope of this chapter to attempt to analyze every cultural difference, some common concepts and themes were brought to the attention of disability service providers, including individualism versus collectivism, high versus low context in communication, and general attitudes toward disability. The basic philosophies, traditions, religions, cultural norms, and family/community structures of Chinese origin were discussed, with case examples to illustrate the implications of such cultural differences. I hope that this chapter will serve as a resource to remove any previous misconceptions and overcome barriers that may hinder the rehabilitation process. It is also intended as a resource to broaden the perspective of service providers, to help them better understand and meet the complex needs of consumers of Chinese origin and enable them to provide services more sensitively and appropriately.

References

Asian American Health Forum. (1990). *Asian and Pacific Islander American population statistics* (Monograph Series 1). San Francisco: Author.

Barnes, J., & Bennett, C. (2002). *The Asian Population: 2000* (Census 2000 Brief C2KRB/01–16). Washington, DC: U.S. Bureau of the Census.

Bond, M. H. (Ed.). (1986). *The psychology of the Chinese people.* Hong Kong: Oxford University Press.

Chan, F., Lam, C. S., Wong, D., Leung, P., & Fung, X.-S. (1988). Counseling Chinese Americans with disabilities. *Journal of Applied Rehabilitation Counseling, 19*(4), 21–25.

Chan, S. (1998). Families with Asian roots. In E. W. Lynch & M. J. Hanson (Eds.), *Developing cross-cultural competence* (pp. 251–355). Baltimore, MD: Paul H. Brookes.

Chin, P. (1996). Chinese Americans. In J. Lipson, S. Dibble, & P. Minarik (Eds.), *Culture and nursing care: A pocket guide* (pp. 74–81). San Francisco: UCSF Nursing Press.

Chinese cultural studies: Philosophy and religion in China. (1995). *Compton's Encyclopedia.* Retrieved from http://academic.brooklyn.cuny.edu/core9/phalsall/texts/chinrelg.html

Chung, E. L. (1996). Asian Americans. In M. C. Juliá (Ed.), *Multicultural awareness in the health care professions* (pp. 77–110). Needham Heights, MA: Allyn & Bacon.

Dong, T. (2000, July 2). Hospitalized for 27 Years, Lan Mao Is Finally Discharged. *World Journal,* p. 2.

Engholm, C. (1994). *Doing business in Asia's booming "China Triangle."* Englewood Cliffs, NJ: Prentice-Hall.

Fung, K.-K. (1998). *Understanding Chinese cultures: A handbook for health care and rehabilitation professionals.* Toronto: Yee Hong Centre for Geriatric Care.

Grant-Griffin, L. (1994). *Best practices: Outreach strategies in multicultural communities.* Albany: New York State Office of Mental Retardation and Developmental Disabilities.

Hall, E. T. (1976). *Beyond culture.* Garden City, NY: Anchor Press.

Hernandez, M., & Isaacs, M. (1998). *Promoting cultural competence in children's mental health services.* Baltimore: Paul H. Brookes.

Lam, C. (1992). *Vocational rehabilitation development in Hong Kong: A cross-cultural perspective.* Stillwater, OK: National Clearing House of Rehabilitation Training Materials.

Lam, J. (2000). *Chinese philosophies and religions.* Retrieved from www.index-china.com/index-english/people-religions-s.html

Lee, E. (1996). Chinese families. In M. McGoldrick, J. Giordano, & J. K. Pearce (Eds.), *Ethnicity and family therapy* (2nd ed., pp. 248–267). New York: Guilford.

Ong, W.-M. A. (1993). *Asian American cultural dimensions in rehabilitation counseling.* San Diego: San Diego State University.

Pan, L. (1990). *Sons of the yellow emperor: A history of the Chinese diaspora.* Boston: Little, Brown and Company.

Smith, E. J. (1981). Cultural and historical perspectives in counseling Blacks. In D. W. Sue (Ed.), *Counseling the culturally different: Theory and practice* (pp. 141–185). New York: John Wiley.

Sue, D. W., & Sue, D. (1999). Culturally appropriate intervention strategies. *Counseling the culturally different: Theory and practice* (3rd ed., pp. 74–96). New York: John Wiley & Sons.

Sung, B. L. (1985). Bicultural conflicts in Chinese immigrant children. *Journal of Comparative Family Studies, 16*(2), 255–269.

Wang, M.-H., Chan, F., Thomas, K. R., Lin, S.-H., & Larson, P. (1997). Coping style and personal responsibility as factors in the perception of individuals with physical disabilities by Chinese international students. *Rehabilitation Psychology, 42*(4), 302–316.

Wu, X. (2000, July 2). Transmitted AIDS from blood transfusion. . . . Schools rejected, neighbors ignored. A nine-year-old boy, Ning Li's miserable world. *World Journal,* p. 2.

Zhang, W. (1994). American counseling in the mind of a Chinese counselor. *Journal of Multicultural Counseling and Development, 22*(2), 79–86.

5

An Introduction to Jamaican Culture for Rehabilitation Service Providers

Doreen Miller

Introduction

The literature in the field of rehabilitation is replete with information emphasizing the value of cultural awareness and competence for effective rehabilitation service delivery to minorities with disabilities (Schaller, Parker, & Garcia, 1998; Walker, Belgrave, Banner, & Nicholls, 1986; Walker, Belgrave, Nicholls, & Turner, 1991). A significant portion of this literature addresses the needs of African Americans (Belgrave & Walker, 1991; Fiest-Price and Ford-Harris, 1994; Harley & Alston, 1996; McGoldrick, Pearce, & Giordana, 1982). When African American rehabilitation issues have been discussed, the nature of the discussion has encompassed the rehabilitation concerns of all Africans who have been a part of the diaspora. Frequently, all immigrants who share the same race as African Americans are subsumed under one heading. Little, if any, distinction is made among immigrants from countries such as Jamaica.

Legislative mandates, such as Section 21 of the 1992 amendments to the 1973 Rehabilitation Act, have established that adequate, equitable, and effective rehabilitation service for minorities is imperative. Given the pluralistic nature of American society, there are many immigrants with minority status who would qualify for services. The fact that Jamaicans who migrated during the mass migration periods of the 1970s and 1980s may now be vulnerable to age-related disabilities makes it likely that rehabilitation professionals will be required to provide services to them. This is particularly true in regions of the country where large pockets of Jamaicans reside. In New York State, there are more than 1.8 million residents of West Indian descent, including many Jamaicans (U.S. Census Bureau, 2003).

Although cultural awareness and cultural competence are paramount for effective service delivery, systematic integration of information about Jamaicans into rehabilitation training programs is lacking. If rehabilitation service providers are to meet the needs of Jamaicans with disabilities, it is necessary that they acquire knowledge about Jamaican culture, including views on disability and rehabilitation. The purpose of this chapter is to provide such information. The chapter will address the following topics: general background, history and reasons for emigration to the United States, Jamaicans' concept of disability, views on acquired and lifelong disabilities concept of independence, Jamaican culture, typical patterns of interactions between consumers and rehabilitation service providers, family structure, the role of community and gender differences in service provision, eating habits, recommendations to rehabilitation service providers, and ways in which service providers can become more familiar with the culture.

Case examples are provided to clarify cultural concepts that might be unfamiliar to the reader. These case examples are based on personal experience and hypothetical scenarios.

Cultural Overview

GEOGRAPHY AND POPULATION

The country of Jamaica is a West Indian island, approximately the size of Connecticut, located near the center of the Caribbean Sea, 579 miles from Miami. Jamaica has an area of 4,411 square miles and is 146 miles long. The breadth of the island varies from 22 miles at its narrowest point to 51 miles at the widest (Gleaner Co., 1995; Statistical Institute of Jamaica, 1998; Superintendent of Documents, 1999).

In 1999, the Statistical Institute of Jamaica reported that there were 2,590,400 people living on the island. The ethnic composition of Jamaica reflects the historical legacy of African enslavement. The cessation of the slave trade precipitated a need for new sources of labor to maintain the sugar estates. To meet the demand for labor, East Indian immigrants came to Jamaica in 1842. Today, the ethnic composition of Jamaica is as follows: African descent, 90.4%, East Indian, 1.3%, white, 0.2%, mixed, 7.3%, and other 0.6% (Superintendent of Documents, 1999).

EDUCATION

Formal education in Jamaica is delivered via a four-level system under the auspices of the Ministry of Education, Youth and Culture. The four levels are preprimary (early childhood), primary, secondary, and tertiary (postsecondary) education. Education is compulsory from primary through secondary school.

Although basic education is compulsory for all children, literacy remains a national challenge (Statistical Institute of Jamaica, 1998). Overall, the literacy rate for the country is 86.5%. This figure may be misleading, however, because a literacy survey conducted in 1997 indicated that there might be a large group of people who can be categorized as functionally illiterate (Planning Institute of Jamaica, 2000). The literacy rate is higher among women (81%) than men (69%). It is also high among the younger population (86.5%) and declines among people 65 years and older (Statistical Institute of Jamaica, 1998).

Despite the literacy levels indicated by the 1997 survey, many Jamaicans residing in the United States may be functionally illiterate. Rehabilitation service providers must realize that rehabilitation outcomes might be affected by a lack of literacy competence.

In a country where education is highly valued, illiteracy carries a great deal of shame and stigma. It is sometimes carried as a family secret for many years. Tremendous effort is placed on keeping the secret because illiteracy indicates a lack of intellectual mastery and is a blight on the individual and family. One of the ultimate insults is to implicitly or explicitly suggest that someone is illiterate.

It is important for service providers to be aware that some consumers who are illiterate might be resistant to rehabilitation because they feel vulnerable to exposure. For example, some consumers may terminate the rehabilitation process prematurely or fail to keep evaluation and assessment appointments because of the desire to avoid embarrassment.

RELIGION

Religion is an integral component of Jamaican life. It is woven into the fabric of the history, education, and social behavior of the people. The religious fervor of Jamaicans has its genesis in the abolition of slavery and the slave experience. During the period of enslavement, religious groups played an important role in protecting slaves from maltreatment and had a great deal to do with the eventual abolition of slavery. Groups such as the Baptists were fervent in their outcry against the inhumane system of slavery. Religion, therefore, was understood by many to be the only hope for a better life.

Religious traditions are maintained through the Jamaican educational system. Religious education is a core subject in the curriculum in all levels of education from preprimary through secondary. It is also a subject for examination in secondary school exit examinations. In the early years, the curriculum focused only on Christianity, but recently it has become more eclectic. Devotional periods are also important segments of a school day. Early religious indoctrination is considered to be important in the development of children. For example, parents who may not be members of a church usually ensure that their children attend Sunday school to receive proper religious education.

Jamaicans are ardent churchgoers, and they are affiliated with many religions and sects. There are more than one hundred Christian religions practiced in the country (Jamaica Information Service, 2000). The country is predominantly Protestant (61%), with a small percentage of Roman Catholics (4.1%). Although a large segment of the population subscribes to traditional religions, a number of people belong to other religious groups, such as the Ethiopian Orthodox Church and Hindu, Muslim, and Bahai faiths. The largest religious group is the Church of God (Jamaica Information Service, 2000).

Some people spend an unusually large amount of time doing church-related activities. For example, they may attend up to 4 hours of Sunday school and worship services on Sunday morning and return for an evening service. Many churchgoers regularly engage in daily activities such as prayer meetings, Bible study, and choir rehearsals. Tuesday morning prayer meetings and Wednesday night midweek service are part of the religious tradition.

For those who are not regular churchgoers, holidays such as Easter, Christmas, and New Year's Eve require almost mandatory attendance. The ritual of being in church at the dawn of the New Year bears special significance for regular or irregular churchgoers, or even for those who rarely attend or never. Many people stop whatever they are doing, wherever they are, and rush to the nearest church before midnight on New Year's Eve. People leave parties and bars to be in church before the stroke of midnight, then resume their pre-midnight activities after the church service. The New Year's ritual is sustained by the belief that whatever one is engaged in when the New Year arrives will set the tone for the year. Being in church at midnight on December 31 establishes a positive note for the coming year.

Membership in different religious groups is related to social class, status, prestige, and religious practice. Upper- and middle-class people tend to gravitate to religions that are somewhat stoical and nonemotional. Religions that permit emotional expressions such as hand clapping and vocalizations are viewed by them with derision. Some middle- and upper-class members covertly believe that the more emotional religions are for the uneducated and ignorant. Upper- and middle-class people are more often members of traditional religions such as Anglican or Methodist.

Lower-class people also have their view of upper- and middle-class religious affiliation. Lower-class people perceive certain churches as being for the rich and powerful. For example, members of the Anglican Church are sometimes described as "ristos" because it is perceived that participation is limited to the aristocrats. One explanation for this perception may be related to the historical relationship between the Anglican Church and the early Jamaicans. During British colonial rule, the Anglican Church or Church of England was considered to be the "planters church," the church of aristocracy—the state church.

Church attendance serves many functions in the lives of Jamaicans. Status can be raised by attending churches where prominent community members are found. By association, individuals are viewed to be members of an elite group. Active participation as a lay reader or member of a church board is also a status-enhancing practice.

Church attendance strengthens extended family and kinship bonds. The church is a source of information and an emotional and financial support in times of crisis. For example, if a church member becomes ill, it is not unusual for other members to participate in family caretaking. Church members sometimes provide nightly respite care to relieve family members. This type of relationship between the church and congregation can be found in urban areas, but it is more characteristic of rural communities.

Among the traditional religions practiced in Jamaica are a number of religions of African origin. In general, the African themes are blended with Christian ideology. African-centered religions generally are practiced by people who are poor or disenfranchised. The three main Afro-Christian religions are Kuminu, Revivalism, and Rastafarianism. Among the African-centered religious groups, Rastafarianism is growing. Members of the middle class are now embracing the religion after many years of opposition.

VALUE OF INDEPENDENCE

The collective psyche of a people is often shaped by its history. In the case of Jamaica, the history of the *maroon* experience and many other slave rebellions are inexorably bound to the fierce sense of independence and resilience among many Jamaicans. Enslaved Africans in Jamaica waged fierce resistance to slavery, and in the case of the *maroons* rebellion it resulted in self-government and *maroon* communities that still exist today.

The indomitable will of the *maroon* is the spiritual essence that permeates the soul of many Jamaicans, and it is the legacy passed on from generation to generation. The attributes of survival, resistance, persistence, and independence among many Jamaicans are visible in contemporary Jamaican society. These characteristics have been a double-edged sword for some Jamaicans residing in the United States. On one hand, these characteristics have helped many to succeed, but on the other hand they have been a disadvantage for some Jamaicans who are perceived as pushy, aggressive, and unable to take "no" for an answer.

The confidence, assertiveness, and persistence observed among Jamaicans is often misconstrued. Some people describe Jamaicans as stubborn or intolerant of authority and authority figures. The historical experience of Jamaicans predisposes them to a belief that they can and will do what they think they can. Generally, they do not accept "no" as the final answer because they truly believe there is another way to achieve their goal. Jamaicans are ambitious and goal oriented. Once a goal is set, the urge to achieve will not allow anyone to interfere or create obstacles. What is often seen as aggressive, pushy, stubborn, competitive, and defiant behavior is really a single-minded desire to accomplish a goal.

Jamaicans see themselves as independent thinkers. They take pride in making their own decisions and controlling their own destiny. Many object to others telling them what they "should," "ought," or "must" do. They reject authority when they believe that their intellectual capacity to act on their own behalf is being disregarded or when the authority figure is perceived to be condescending. Intellectual condescension is a pet peeve of many. Those who are unable to read are particularly sensitive to patronizing intellectual behavior and are not afraid to confront those who disregard their capacity to think. One might say, "mi can't read but mi a no fool, mi know wa mi a do." (I can't read, but I am not a fool; I know what I am doing.)

History of Immigration to the United States

Jamaicans have a strong migratory spirit. Motivated by ambition and a desire for better economic conditions, they migrate. Wherever they perceive opportunities for a better life, they will move. Jamaicans have traveled to many distant places in search of opportunity. The most frequent destination is the United States.

In the late 19th century, Jamaicans began to migrate to the United States. Presently, among Latin American and Caribbean U.S. immigrants, Jamaicans rank fourth (Planning Institute of Jamaica, 2000). Banana ports like Boston were the earliest destinations. Later migrants relocated to Baltimore, Philadelphia, and New York. Today, the largest concentration of Jamaicans (350,000) is in New York, New Jersey, and Connecticut. (Black, 1997).

Mass migration to the United States in the 1970s and 1980s can be tied to political violence and the threat of communism. During this period, Jamaicans left the country in droves because they feared that their lives were in danger as the Peoples National Party (PNP) and the Jamaican Labor Party (JLP) struggled for power. In the 1980s, approximately 800 people died in politically motivated violence (Virtue, 1999). People felt so threatened that they were willing to abandon everything in the name of safety. They left professions, belongings, family, and a middle-class standard of living for the uncertain living conditions in other countries.

For some, the sacrifices did not pay off. Many middle-class professionals and entrepreneurs found themselves grossly underemployed or unemployed. Some found work as cab drivers, bus drivers, restaurant workers, or domestic care providers for elderly or terminally ill persons. Many who wished to return to Jamaica were unable to do so because they had uprooted their lives and there were no personal resources to allow them to remain in the country, as illustrated in the following example.

> George and Hyacinth Rogers owned a thriving business in Kingston. The business had been in the family for more than 30 years. Fearful that they might be victims of violence, they sold their home and business for half of their value, asked friends to care for what could not be sold, and fled to the United States. Unemployment, drastic changes in lifestyle and status, and dwindling financial resources began to take a toll on their marriage. Within a year, the marriage was in disarray. Mrs. Rogers wanted to return to Jamaica, but her husband, realizing that there was nothing to return to, refused. Eighteen months later, Mrs. Rogers returned alone because her husband had requested a divorce after 20 years of marriage. When she returned to Jamaica, squatters had taken over the property that she had left behind. She had no money, had no place to live, and was dependent on the goodwill of family and friends. Having suffered many major losses in a short period began to take a toll on her mental health. Six months after returning to Jamaica, she was hospitalized for severe depression.

The 1990s were reminiscent of the 1970s and 1980s. Jamaicans again fled the country in large numbers because of violence related to drug trafficking, particularly in Kingston. These periods of mass movement have had devastating consequences on the human resource capital of the country. Jamaicans with technical and professional skills are sought by countries such as the United States. The opportunity for increased income is enticing, so Jamaica has a great deal of difficulty retaining trained personnel.

Among Jamaicans residing in the United States, a considerable number have entered the country as illegal aliens. Those who enter the United States illegally are often less skilled and are generally confined to low-paying and hazardous employment. These individuals may be predisposed to acquired disabilities and are likely to require rehabilitation services. In providing rehabilitation, personnel must be aware that consumers who are reticent and uncooperative may be concealing their immigration status in an effort to avoid deportation. For example:

> Gladstone arrived in the United States as a visitor. When his visitor's permit expired, he did not return to Jamaica. His goal was to enter college once he had earned enough money and gained permanent resident status. Under an assumed

name and a fabricated Social Security number, he held a series of short-term jobs. He was a truck driver for about 6 months when he was involved in an accident and sustained a Lumbar 5 (L5) spinal injury. He was referred for rehabilitation services but refused to keep appointments or return his counselor's telephone calls because he wanted to avoid answering questions that might expose his status and ineligibility for services. He earned income as a taxicab dispatcher until he received permanent residence through immigration amnesty. Later, he contacted his rehabilitation counselor and resumed services.

Emigrants have also been a source of revenue for Jamaica in general and its residents in particular. Some émigrés with relatives in Jamaica provide regular financial support, which may be their only source of income. The following three examples illustrate patterns of remittance from the United States to Jamaica.

Etta migrated to the United States to attend college in 1969. She was supported by her parents while in college. Although her parents had planned for their retirement, devaluation of the Jamaican dollar in the 1980s coupled with an inadequate employment retirement plan placed them in a precarious financial situation. Since completing her degree, every month she had sent money for their support in an effort to assist them in maintaining their standard of living and quality of life.

Cynthia was 12 when her father was killed in an accident. Her mother became the sole support of the family, which included Cynthia's two sisters and a brother. Her mother, a domestic worker, managed to educate all of her children, three of whom were trained as nurses in Jamaica. As a way of improving the quality of life for their mother, Cynthia (the oldest) migrated to New York to work in a hospital. Later she sponsored her sister, who sponsored the third sister. The sisters provided support for their mother, which included a new home and living expenses. As their mother aged, they were able to provide for her medical care and a domestic caretaker until her death.

Calvin is a 30-year-old school bus driver by day and a taxi driver by night. All of his immediate family members have emigrated to New York. His mother's youngest sister, Mavis, lives in a rural community in Jamaica. Mavis has no income because her husband, who was the support of the family, died many years ago. Calvin has been supporting his aunt for the last 5 years. From his earnings, he sends his aunt $150 per month. Other relatives periodically send Mavis small amounts of money.

These examples are characteristic of Jamaicans living abroad and are consistent with their reasons for migrating (i.e., a better life for self and family). Given their financial responsibilities for family residing in Jamaica, adjustment to disability might be difficult. Inability to work or a reduced income could create complex psychosocial problems. It is important for service providers to understand that consumers' insistence that they must retain predisability employment may be based more on the desire to continue family support than on refusal to accept the disability. Consumers may experience feelings of failure if they are unable to support a family dependent upon them. The problem may be exacerbated if consumers can no longer maintain employment and must return to the family. For example:

> Kristen was a surgical nurse who was the sole support for her mother and brother who was mentally ill. Fifteen years after she was employed at a hospital, she was diagnosed with multiple sclerosis. Her condition deteriorated rapidly, to the extent that she was incapable of performing her duties as a nurse. In support of Kristen, the hospital's administrator offered her a position in the medical records department, but she refused the offer. Fearful that she could no longer support her family, she became very angry and considered filing a discrimination lawsuit against the hospital. She was encouraged to seek counseling through the Employee Assistance Program at the hospital. Eventually, she accepted the position in the medical records department, where she worked until she was eligible for retirement with benefits. Unable to care for herself adequately, she returned to Jamaica, where her family could assist her.

Jamaican Concepts of Disability

BELIEFS ABOUT CAUSES OF DISABILITY

Cultural concepts that influence views of disability and illness originate in religious beliefs related to Christianity and Afro-Christian sects such as Pocomania and Kumina. There are major beliefs that may have an influence on the way Jamaicans view disability: For example, disability is a punishment for wrongdoing. Other causes may be evil spirits, ghosts, duppies, obeah, or guzu, as well as natural causes (Heinz & Payne-Jackson, 1997; Leavitt, 1992). These belief systems are entrenched in Jamaican society. They have played a major role in shaping the attitudes toward disability and delayed the development of a comprehensive national rehabilitation program. Even professionals and the educated middle class tend to hold a strong belief that disability is a result of sin.

Jamaicans are firm believers in the power of God as a mediator between good and evil in their daily lives. God is seen as a force operating from a position of duality, at the same time forgiving and punishing. The nature of God is perceived to include a great capacity for a long-term vindictive memory. Those who sin or commit wrongful acts will always be punished. If the perpetrator escapes punishment, his or her offspring are certain to reap the negative effects of past wrongs. Jamaicans frequently cite the biblical verse, "The sins of the father shall visit the third and fourth generations." Thus, the causes of accidents or congenital deformities may be attributed to punishment deserved. This punishment can be the responsibility of past generations as well as the victim. For example, a child born with a birth defect may be seen as the recipient of punishment for wrongs committed by a grandparent. A young man who meets an accident and becomes paralyzed may be understood to have received punishment because of disrespectful behavior to his grandparents. Lack of respect for elders is unacceptable behavior.

The belief that disability is a result of punishment for past wrongs or sins is associated with tremendous shame and guilt. In an effort to minimize public shame, families often conceal the fact that a member of the family has a disability. Hiding a disability is particularly likely when it is congenital. A child who has a birth defect may be hidden from public view for life. Neighbors or the community may be aware that a child with a disability lives near but never have direct contact or a close view of the child.

> Mr. Spence was a businessman in a rural community. His home was located about half a mile from the main road in the village. When his grandson, Trevor, was born, it was discovered that he had a bone disease. For years, people in the community knew of Trevor but had never seen him. When he was about 3, caretakers pushing a pram could be seen from the main road. Stories circulated about the nature of Trevor's disability, but because he was never seen in public, the extent of his disability was unknown.

Obeah or guzu is the belief that there are supernatural forces that can be harnessed for good or evil, for health or sickness. Obeah (witchcraft) workers are believed to have the ability to create conditions through which one's desires can be fulfilled. For example, they can cause illness, death, separation, divorce, love, and prosperity. Any illness that cannot be explained by medical intervention is considered to be a result of obeah. If the condition is believed to be induced by obeah, the victim is generally taken to a "balm yard" or mission that is the holy ground of the Pocomania religion. At the balm yard, the female leader, who is called "the mother" or "shepherdess," and the male leader (the "shepherd") may perform rituals, prepare herbs for ingestion, or prepare baths and oils for anointing the body. Clients are often given biblical scriptures to read. Selected psalms are generally the spiritual prescription and must be read for a designated period. For example, selections from among Psalms 27, 30, 31, 33, 35, 36, 37, 40, 51, 59, 65, 66, 69, 71, 77, 91, or 139 may be given to be read three times each day for 7 to 9 days.

Some labels given to obeah practitioners include "obeah man," "guzu man," or "four eye man." These references are not gender specific; the word "man" refers to both male and female practitioners. The practice of obeah is illegal, so those who engage in it generally operate covertly in remote parts of the country. Both practitioners and those who seek them are viewed to be among the less educated. Although obeah workers use herbs in their practice, they should not be confused with the bush doctor or spiritual herbalist. Spiritual herbalists believe that the capacity of the body to combat physical illness can be enhanced by the use of herbs coupled with religious ritual (Lowe, 1995).

In general, Jamaicans tend to self-medicate and exhaust every possible home remedy before seeking professional medical assistance. Elders within the family are generally the repositories of herbal wisdom, and they often insist on the practice of self-medication. It is even combined with traditional medicine. Herbs are also used for health maintenance. For example, children are often given senna, Epsom salts, or castor oil to cleanse the bowel of worms and purify the body. This practice generally takes place just before the beginning of a new school year. Bowel cleansing for health maintenance is not limited to children; adults also take different combinations of herbs periodically. Reliance on non-traditional medical practices can be related to spiritual practice, but there is also an economic component. People who lack the financial resources to seek medical treatment are forced to use home remedies to cure illnesses or maintain health.

Even those who scoff at the use of obeah to influence changes in one's life will go to great lengths to protect themselves from its effects. The response is contradictory because they say obeah does not exist, yet they take precautions against being affected. For example, obeah holds that personal items such as shoes and clothing should not be left outdoors overnight. The fear is that these possessions may be used to harm the owner. It is believed that potions placed in shoes will cause the body to swell and ultimately result in death. As a protection against attack, people are selective about eating food handled by persons believed to be involved in obeah. Ingesting food from such a person might cause bodily harm. Men are often cautioned about eating food from women with whom they are unfamiliar or women who are seeking marriage, because they could be obeahed into falling in love and marriage, or remaining in relationships against their will.

Disability and illness are believed to be the result of contact with evil spirits sent by obeah or spirits that are simply malevolent. For example, an explanation for someone who becomes mentally ill is that a duppy or ghost attached itself to the individual's spirit. In such an instance, mental illness could be the work of an enemy imposing a vendetta. People in the community might say "a nu so im use to be a duppy dem set pan im. A imgal fren do im so. Das why im a wak an tak to imself." ("That is not his normal behavior. A duppy was sent to make him ill. It is the work of his girlfriend. That is why he walks and talks to himself.")

Spirits or ghosts are believed to be fond of babies. If a ghost plays with a child, that child could become harmed, sometimes fatally. To protect babies and toddlers, caretakers often place a Bible opened to one of the Psalms (preferably Psalm 27, 35, 37, 40, 91, or 139) above the sleeping child's head. If a child is thin and appears unhealthy, it is believed that ghosts or duppies might be sharing the child's food intake so the child is unable to gain weight. In such cases, something red or black is tied on the body of the child to provide protection from spirits. Parents are uncomfortable with a fretful or crying child at night because they believe that the child is most vulnerable to spirits at that time. If a child cries loudly at night, duppies might take his or her voice and render the child mute.

Duppies also have the power to cause accidents. For example, if a man falls from a tree, it might be the act of a duppy that pushed him. In such a case, the tree is marked, and others will refrain from climbing it. The belief in spirits, ghosts, or duppies can be traced to Pocomania and Kumina practices related to animistic African spiritual traditions.

Natural causes for illness and disabilities are generally the explanations used by those who are considered sophisticated. The disability may be deemed to be a mistake by the medical profession, a malfunction of a technique used to ameliorate a medical problem, or germs. It can also be a result of the failure of the body's natural mechanism to heal itself. Those who subscribe to the belief in natural causes seek medical attention and believe in the medical profession's ability to alleviate suffering or cure the illness.

ATTITUDES TOWARD DISABILITY

Acceptance of certain types of disabilities are affected by the views held about these disabilities. Physical disabilities are more readily accepted than mental or cognitive ones. Of all disabilities, mental illness is most stigmatizing, and very little is expected from persons living with mental illness.

Personal perceptions can have an impact on whether a parent will accept a child with a disability. Parents who experience intense shame because of giving birth to a disabled child may reject that child. There have been cases in which mothers have abandoned offspring by refusing to take a child home from the hospital.

A young mother, 20 years old, gave birth to a baby with a facial abnormality. She told the doctors that the baby did not belong to her because she could not have given birth to a child with what appeared to her to be inhuman features. The hospital staff tried to coax her into accepting the baby, but to no avail. She refused to touch the child and insisted that the doctors correct the face of the child; otherwise, she did not want to have any contact. When the staff failed to honor her request, she disappeared from the hospital, leaving the baby behind.

In contrast to parents who abandon their children, there are those who provide very loving and nurturing environments for their children with disabilities. Overprotection of children with disabilities is another way in which parents may react. The tendency is to behave as if the children are incapacitated and totally dependent on others, even when they might be quite capable of engaging in a variety of activities. Family members keep disabled children dependent by imposing a "sick" label. Everyone in the family knows that these children should not be expected to do very much because they are "sickly." A typical assumption is that disabled persons should not be required to work, but instead should be cared for by the family.

Seclusion of children with disabilities can occur as well. Some parents keep their children indoors away from public view, and the disability is kept as a secret within the family for years. Residents in the community may be aware of the children but would be unable to describe the nature of the disability. Keeping the children hidden can be attributed less to cruelty than to lack of information and education about the management of chronic disabilities. Parents are unaware of what children with a disability can achieve, given the proper accommodations and resources.

CONCEPT OF INDEPENDENCE

In a disability setting, the spirit of independence and resilience can be of value in helping consumers to reach their goals. Disability service providers may capitalize on the "can do attitude" and defiant spirit to help consumers regain control of their lives. These behaviors surface in very subtle ways, and if the providers are not aware of them, they might impede the rehabilitation process. For example:

Lorraine's 17-year-old son, Bryan, sustained a head injury during a motorcycle accident. Bryan was an honor roll high school student with a goal of becoming a doctor. Although his dream was no longer possible, Lorraine believed he still had an academic future. She wanted him to attend college, but because of evaluations, his counselor, Jerome Porter, thought it was doubtful that Bryan would be successful in college. Lorraine had many discussions with the counselor. She insisted on making college a goal because she believed with support, her son would be successful. Unable to get satisfaction, she refused to continue the rehabilitation program. A few months later, she contacted the state director for rehabilitation services and requested a meeting with him and Mr. Porter. In discussing the problem with the state director, Mr. Porter reported that Lorraine was unrealistic, stubborn, pushy, and demanding. He really did not enjoy working with her because she was difficult. During the meeting with Lorraine, the state director found that Lorraine was clear about the needs of her son but very insistent that he attend college as a goal for rehabilitation. Shortly after the meeting, Lorraine and Bryan moved to another state. Bryan re-entered the rehabilitation system. His new counselor felt that there was a chance that he might be successful, so she recommended that he attend the state junior college. In his first semester, Bryan was able to maintain a "C" average.

It is necessary for service providers to recognize that the desire for personal independence and an active role in decision making are essential for many Jamaicans with disabilities. The high regard for independence and self-reliance might affect consumers' views regarding independent living or institutionalization of family members. There is a strong sense of self-reliance as it relates to the use of public assistance. A Jamaican consumer might resist the concept of independent living because he believes that a family member with a disability is the responsibility of the family and should be cared for and not be forced to work. There is also a belief that a family member should not be placed in a facility outside the home unless it is a hospital or similar setting. Placing a family member in a group home would be considered an abdication of family obligations. Because of the belief that a disabled relative should not have to work, job placement might also be met with opposition.

Acquired and Lifelong Disabilities

Some of the major similarities in views about lifelong and acquired disabilities pertain to causation, personal responsibility, and preventability. In general, people tend to seek meaning in their life experiences and attempt to establish reason or blame. For instance, persons with disabilities might attempt to understand their experience of disability by determining "why" or "what" caused the disability. Acceptance becomes more likely when a reason other than personal cause can be found. For example, if a genetic reason can be established, there is a greater feeling of relief and ultimate acceptance.

When personal blame is the cause for the disability, it is more difficult to accept. For example, a mother who neglected prenatal care would experience more guilt than one who had done everything she could to prevent her child from developing a birth defect. Similarly, a man who falls off a moving truck during an epileptic seizure might feel less guilt than a man who falls because he consumed too much rum.

Among Jamaicans, causative factors are important not only for the individual with the disability but for family and community as well. There is diminished compassion, or even anger, directed at those who receive injuries or disabilities because of personal negligence. Although care is provided by the family, the persons with disability are reminded that they were responsible for the disability. For example, in a conversation with the author, Ms. Cynthia Parchment stated:

My son Michael graduated from Teacher's College and bought a little car. I was so proud of him. I never finished high school. He did what I could not do. Soon after graduation, he became friends with a group of boys who liked to drink rum. He stopped spending time with me and every weekend he was attending beach parties in Montego Bay. Before long he was a heavy drinker. I tried to tell him to stop but he would not listen. One morning, about 3:30 a.m., I heard a knock on my door. It was the police, who had come to tell me that Michael was in the hospital. He was in a bad accident. Michael was paralyzed as a result of the accident. If he had not been drinking, the accident could have been avoided. Now, I have to take care of him. I have to provide food, medicine, wheelchair, money for doctor's visits—everything. Sometimes I look at him and get real angry. Sometimes I wish that I could leave him and go away. I don't know what I am going to do because it is so expensive to take care of him without any financial assistance. He is my son, though; I have to do it. But he has caused all of our problems and I have to tell him so. He does not like to be reminded, but it is true. If he had listened, we would not be having so much trouble.

With regard to adjustment, parents may find it easier to adjust to the fact that their child was born with a disability rather than having acquired one during childhood. Grief over the loss of a child's potential is paramount. For instance:

Audrey McDonald's 15-year-old son, Delroy, was hit by a car on his way home from school. Three years have passed, and she is still grieving. She carries his report card and a photograph of him in her handbag. She tries to tell anyone who will listen about her son's accident. She often offers the report card to show that he was a good student and show his picture to tell them, "This is the way he looked before the accident. He was going to be a doctor."

As can be noted from this case, it is not unusual for family members to fixate on predisability status as a means of coping with loss. The views held by Jamaicans about lifelong and acquired disabilities may not be unique to them. These responses may be common to other parts of the world, including the United States.

The Role of Family, Community, and Religion

The roots of the Jamaican family structure are embedded in the historical experience of slavery. Marriage and households with both parents were characteristic of the European planters, while slaves cohabitated and were often separated from mates and children. Jamaican family relationships reflect the legacy of both planters and slaves. Upper- and middle-class Jamaicans tend to assimilate European standards and aspire to create families that embody these values. Formal marriages occur more often among upper- and middle-class families or among those who can afford the cost of a wedding. Among the upper and middle classes, cohabitation is frowned upon because it does not give legitimacy to offspring, lowers family status, and is viewed as immoral. When children are born to unmarried parents in these groups, illegitimacy is often a source of derision for the children.

Tremendous pressure is sometimes placed on cohabiting family members to marry their partners. This is particularly true for those who have children. Both maternal and paternal sides of the family often encourage the parties to marry or terminate cohabitation and find other mates who are considered "suitable" for marriage. Living together is a source of shame and moral guilt for family members.

Appropriate choice of a marriage partner is integral to the value system of those who marry. An upper- or middle-class person who marries someone who might be considered lower class would experience disapproval from parents and family. Such a person would be considered lacking in ambition and self-worth. Criteria such as skin color, class, occupation, level of education, and parental or family status in the community are important in considering mate selection.

Fundamentally, the selection criteria are also based on how well the man is able to provide for his family. It is a source of pride and dignity for a man to be able to support his family, and he will do what it takes to find work. If it means leaving the family for long periods, he will do so, as long as he is able to send money home for their care and support. A man who refuses to provide for his children is viewed with disdain. Conversations describing such a man's behavior often includes statements such as "He is a bad seed," "He has never given a copper penny to his children in Black River," or "He is no good." Parents warn their daughters against developing relationships with such a man because he is viewed as lacking in character. Marrying the wrong person is seen as a step down among ambitious and status-seeking members of the society. Marrying someone who is viewed as a lower-class person is tantamount to "royalty marrying commoners." Factors influencing mate selection, while known, are seldom discussed. It remains one of the social taboos derived from the colonial past of the country.

The residue of slavery on family structure and sexual behavior is still visible in contemporary Jamaica (Dechesnay, 1986). Although there have been increasing numbers of marriages, cohabitation continues to be the union of choice among poor and lower-class Jamaicans. This may be related to the historical precedents set by the prohibition by slaveholders of stable unions through marriage. According to Dechesnay (1986), those who practiced legally sanctioned marriages when it became possible were deemed social climbers.

Many people remain in cohabiting relationships for years. Although they are not legally married, people in the community tend to recognize partners as husband and wife and will address them as such. There is some level of respect given to cohabitants, especially when they have been together for a long time. Sometimes after rearing children into adulthood, parents will marry for a number of reasons, such as imminent death or pressure from children who are embarrassed by their parents' marital status. Pressure can also be brought to bear through religious affiliation. Ministers who perceive cohabitation to be "sinful" will encourage partners to marry.

Even when partners are legally married or cohabitating, additional intimate relationships are not unusual. Jamaican men are known for having more than one partner at a time. Frequently there are children (family) resulting from extra unions. While maintaining a stable union, the man can become a visiting parent.

Fathers who are the sole support of the family may travel to urban areas to seek employment. In such cases, they may visit on weekends or major holidays, such as Easter and Christmas, or when work schedules permit. If conditions do not permit, money will be sent home. Fathers may be away from home for long periods of time, leaving the child rearing and decision making to the mother. As a result, many women are heads of households. These women are often very independent because of the role that they have had to play. The legacy of independence is often passed on to their daughters, who model the behaviors of their mothers. The independent nature of Jamaican women is often mislabeled as bossy and stubborn.

Improved transportation has reduced the length of time these family members must be away from home. Those who can afford bus fare or cars can commute daily. The increase in the number of taxis and buses traveling to different parts of the country has helped to keep families together. Sometimes, however, even when the man is in the home, the woman may remain the head of the household and the decision maker because the man perceives his role to be only that of the breadwinner. It is generally the woman's job to manage the money and make sure the children are disciplined and educated. When children misbehave or err in some way, the woman is usually blamed by the husband and sometimes by the community.

Traditional Jamaican families tend to be quite extended. Grandparents frequently live in the home of one of their children, and is not uncommon for a child to remain in his or her parents' home long past the age of 18. Some never leave home and remain to head the household of aging parents.

Aunts and uncles are considered close family members and are often considered surrogate parents. Aunts and uncles are very significant in Jamaican families, and their role may include emotional and financial support. The successful development of the child is not the responsibility of the parents alone. Nieces and nephews are aware of the importance of their aunts and uncles, and they respond to them with the same degree of respect and care that they extend to parents.

Kinship bonds also extend to close friends and neighbors who contribute to the nurturing and rearing of children. On a variety of levels, children receive support in areas in which parents may be lacking. For example, when a child misbehaves, corrective feedback is given by others even in the presence of parents, who usually are not offended. Such friends and neighbors provide activities that enhance the development of the child. As a result, children can have many maternal or paternal figures in their lives. Where these kinship bonds develop among nonrelatives, children often refer to such individuals as aunts or uncles.

Although extended family structures have been the norm, contemporary Jamaican families are becoming more nuclear. One of the major contributors to the erosion of close kinship bonds is internal and external migration. Within the country, young people are moving away from villages to urban centers for better employment opportunities. The trend is that they marry and have children who have little contact with relatives in the rural areas. In an effort to retard the erosion of traditional extended families, grandparents often relocate to live with their children whenever it is feasible.

External migration is another major threat to the disintegration of the traditional family structure. Individuals migrate with the intention of reuniting with their children who are left behind with relatives, friends, or neighbors. The children are told by their parents that they must leave in order to create a better quality of life for the family. Sometimes the intentions of parents, although honorable, fail to materialize. Low-paying jobs, unemployment, illegal immigration status, establishment of second families, or other difficulties prevent them from reuniting with their children. A husband might tell his wife that he will reunite with her and the children but never do so, although he continues to send financial support. Children may receive support from parents for extended periods without ever seeing them. Some become adults before reuniting with their parents. There is a new phenomenon resulting from the abandonment of children by parents who support them but fail to reunite. The phenomenon of the "Barrel Children" is a growing concern for many communities. "Barrel Children" receive regular shipments of goods from their parents who reside in countries such as the United States and Canada. Children are left in the custody of grandparents, aunts, uncles, friends, or neighbors, who are told that care is temporary until the parents send for them. Sometimes children left at 5 and 6 years of age do not see their parents until they are 18 or may never see them. Margaret, a "Barrel Child," commented:

> I have not seen my mother since I was 5 and I am 18 now. She left me with my grandmother who died when I was 12 and then I went to live with my Aunt Hilma. I don't think my mother cares about me. When she had me she wasn't ready for a child. She has been in the United States for 20 years and she is still not able to send for me. The barrels keep coming and sometimes money, but it does not make up for her not being here. What is worse, I don't even get along with my aunt. I guess it is partly my fault because I am so angry with my mother. I used to get into fights at school over the fact that a friend said that my mother did not want me. That really hurt for a long time.
>
> I could have done better in school if I wasn't so worried about a future alone. In some ways I am lucky because my Aunt Jean, my mother's childhood friend, keeps encouraging me to stay focused on my schoolwork because I will be taking my Caribbean County Examinations (CXC) next month and that determines my future. Sometimes I used to feel cheated and sorry for myself, especially when my Aunt Hilma tried to discipline me. I know that my aunts have helped me a lot; without their help, I could have gone down the wrong road. During school hours, I went about my own business with my friends and could have gotten into trouble with drugs or the law. If I were to see my mother today, I would hardly know her. I wouldn't know what to say to her. I don't feel close to her, but I know that I love her because she is my mother.

Although changing rapidly, strong kinship bonds are characteristic of the Jamaican family. Even when family members are scattered, they try to maintain some contact with each other, and if a family member needs support, the family is mobilized to assist. The oldest child is often the standard-bearer, whose responsibility it is to help to keep the family intact.

Responsibility for the family is a role for both sexes, but it is even more demanding when the oldest sibling is male. The male role is frequently that of a surrogate father who makes sure that his sisters make appropriate choices related to education and mate selection. His responsibilities may be compounded as he takes on a family of his own. The role of the oldest female is often that of a caregiver and decision maker for aging parents. When a health decision is to be made for a family member, it is not unusual to have siblings, as well as extended family (aunts, uncles), participate in consultations with health professionals. The final decision, however, rests with the oldest sibling.

Following emigration, kinship bonds often continue to reflect an appreciation for the collective good of all the family, including cousins, aunts, and uncles. For example, it is not uncommon to find two or more immigrant families living together to help one another achieve goals. The belief in family is very strong, and many take pride in their loyalty and care for one another.

Even when there is a schism among family members, an outsider must be very careful not to raise the ire of quarreling relatives and receive the brunt of displaced anger. The saying "Blood is thicker than water" reflects the keen sense of family loyalty among Jamaicans.

Gender Differences

Women tend to take the leadership role in securing and utilizing services for themselves and their families. If a family member is ill, it is the woman who researches available resources and makes arrangements to get the person to the doctor or other medical professional, and women are more inclined to seek service for themselves than are men.

Men sometimes engage in denial of their own needs that may result in remedial rather than preventive services. As the chief breadwinners, they are reluctant to lose time and money from work to seek medical help, which may be indicative of their sense of duty and responsibility to the family. The denial of needs may also be related to the desire to appear "manly" and strong. Going to the doctor for what appears to be a minor illness is sometimes perceived to be a weakness.

When service is accessed, the woman accompanies the man to the doctor and is ultimately responsible for ensuring that the prescription is followed. For example, Audrey Guilling, a nurse at the Montego Bay Regional Hospital, said:

> Women tend to seek health care and will follow instructions; men tend to shy away. . . . Men come when they are dying or the problem has gotten out of control. It is difficult to get men to change lifestyle behaviors. . . . They continue to engage in the same behaviors that got them in trouble.

Men will refrain from accessing service to avoid financial embarrassment. If both the man and woman need service, the man will generally make sure that the woman's need is met. This is rooted in the belief that a man must be able to provide for his "woman" or his family.

Women with disabilities also appear to be more aggressive in accessing services than their male counterparts. For example, there are more women with disabilities than men pursuing educational opportunities and making significant improvements in their quality of life. Women have also occupied more leadership roles in advocacy organizations. For example, three women have served as the president of the Combined Disabilities Association (CDA), which is the major advocacy group for people with disabilities. Also, the committee convened to formulate a national policy on disability was spearheaded by a woman, Monica Bartley.

Religion

Because the role of religion is integral to the lives of many Jamaicans, it is vital to the rehabilitation process. It would not be unusual for a consumer to inject religious beliefs into the rehabilitation experience, so service providers must be prepared to address religious/spiritual concerns when they arise. Addressing the religious issues of the Jamaican consumer is paramount because service providers are expected to deliver holistic rehabilitation services that are culturally relevant.

Interaction Between Consumers and Rehabilitation Service Providers

Interaction between consumers and service providers may be influenced by the source of referral. Consumers who are referred by the medical profession will be apt to use the resources because physicians are among the authority figures of the society. Rapport building with physician-referred consumers will also be easier because of their desire to comply with the doctor's instruction.

The use of home remedies is a major health practice among Jamaicans. Modern medical treatment is generally sought only after home treatments have been exhausted. By the time medical intervention takes place, irreparable damage may have occurred. Even when medical care is sought, there is a practice of blending prescriptions with home remedies. It is very difficult for health professionals to convince consumers to rely solely on modern medicine. Cost is a factor. People may have to choose between going to the doctor and buying food. Second, there is a historical tradition of using home remedies that have successfully eliminated health problems. Elders, who are authority figures in the family, are more inclined to use home remedies before seeking medical attention.

Personal pride can also hamper the relationship between consumers and service providers. Some Jamaicans resist the use of public assistance because they are embarrassed by dependence on governmental or "poor relief" support. In an effort to maintain dignity and avoid being labeled "indigent," some will remain in dire need.

As mentioned previously, another source of potential conflict relates to the institutionalization of a family member with a disability. The belief is that home is the best place, and institutional care cannot be compared to what can be provided by family. Resistance to institutional care is often very strong because family members believe that they can manage without assistance. When placement occurs, it is under extreme conditions and with some pressure from physicians or other health care professionals. A factor that may influence placement is unfamiliarity with rehabilitation facilities because of the lack of them in most parts of Jamaica. The family must also contend with covert community stigmatization; institutionalization is frowned upon by those who share the belief that families must care for their own.

Recommendations to Service Providers

When working with Jamaicans with disabilities, it is imperative that service providers attend to cultural nuances that might be deemed trivial in the American culture but are very important in Jamaican culture. An understanding of these cultural idiosyncrasies can be vital in minimizing communication problems. Value-laden cultural beliefs can affect communication and result in poor client retention or failure of the client to comply with prescriptive health measures. The following are suggestions for working with Jamaicans.

Greetings or acknowledgment of an individual's presence is an important cultural value. Before any professional or social interaction, Jamaicans customarily preface their interactions by saying "Good morning (or "Good afternoon" or "Good evening"), how are you doing today?" Absence of the greeting implies a failure of interest in the well-being of the individual. For example, one might ask "a wha mi do yu dis mawning, you naw say notin ti day?" ("What have I done this morning, are you going to say hello today?")

The same value holds when an interaction is terminated. Some form of goodwill should be expressed. To depart without doing so is construed as disrespectful. For example, you might hear, "She lef an she never even say she gone," "She left without saying so," or "She left without saying good-bye."

For service providers, to take time to greet and engage in brief small talk can be very helpful for rapport building. Otherwise, clients might leave with the belief that the service provider does not care about their well-being ("dat de man dry sah, im neva even sat mawning, mi naw go back de"—"that man is not warm, he never said good morning, I am not going back there"). Greeting as a practice with Jamaican clients can serve to set the tone for the agency-client relationship and a potentially positive service outcome.

The titles of Miss, Mr., Mrs., or Doctor before one's name are important. If you visit a Jamaican office or observe people in social interaction, a title is always attached to a name. The last name (surname) is often used, but in less formal settings a title precedes a first name, as in "Miss Mary." If someone has a title, such as Doctor, it is frowned upon to address that person without the title.

Even if given permission to omit the title, some people still have difficulty not using it. This custom is based on respect for each other. When individuals have been friends for a long time, use of the first name is appropriate. It is considered a breach of familiarity to address someone you are meeting for the first time or with whom you are only vaguely acquainted without the formal title. For example, for a service provider to request a patient by calling aloud "Mary Jones" in a waiting room would be considered disrespectful by some Jamaicans.

Jamaicans pride themselves on being able to handle their own problems, and it is important to ensure that service delivery environments are supportive of this value. Individuals who feel that they might lose control in a service delivery system might not be inclined to use such services.

Jamaicans are very proud and will go to great lengths to maintain their dignity. Even in the face of tremendous distress, they might appear quite stoic. This should not be misinterpreted as unfeeling or uncaring.

Privacy is highly valued, so discreet and confidential treatment of information is important. Physical or personal privacy is also expected. For example, a patient in a hospital might be very fussy about being able to wear his or her own sleepwear instead of a hospital gown that has the potential for unexpected exposure. A request for one's own hospital wear therefore should not result in the staff labeling the patient as difficult and hard to work with.

Caring for a family member is often an obligatory role. If someone is in the hospital, it is not unusual for family members to insist on providing routine care similar to the role of nurses. For example, family members might want to bathe and feed a patient. They might even prefer to prepare meals at home and bring them to the hospital. When possible, accommodating the family's desire to provide care can be helpful.

Family members have strong kinship bonds that might appear unusual to some professionals. Providers should refrain from dismantling these bonds, particularly when a family member is ill or disabled. For example, an ill relative might be accompanied to the doctor by four or five family members. It would be unusual for the patient to visit the doctor, physical therapist, or rehabilitation office alone.

An aunt or uncle might accompany a child to the doctor or other service delivery agency. That aunt or uncle should be treated with the respect of a parent. To ask the aunt or uncle why they are the ones accompanying the child would be a surprising question because they consider their presence as good as that of the parents. For example, a rehabilitation professional questioned an aunt because she was making demands for special services for a niece. When he asked why the parents were not there, she replied. "I am here and she needs the service, so you will have to deal with me." The counselor reported that he thought that the aunt was difficult, stubborn, and hardheaded. The child did not return for services.

Appointments should be made as convenient as possible because Jamaicans have a strong work ethic and will miss an appointment before missing work. For example, a rehabilitation counselor set an appointment date for a family member to return with a child for evaluations. She informed the counselor that she could not keep the appointment that was given and requested other dates. The counselor reported that he was annoyed because the family member had the "nerve" to dictate appointment dates and she should have come when he told her. He felt that it was a sign of her stubborn behavior. The family member and child did not return for service.

Treat the elderly with respect. Voice tone, physical handling (e.g., manipulation of limbs), and instructing the elderly should be done with care and sensitivity. Jamaicans have a great deal of respect for the elderly. Their experience is considered to be a source of wisdom and should be appreciated. Displays of honor and respect are often shown by total strangers, who may refer to elderly women as mother (Madda), mamma, mammie, or mumsy and elderly men as "'pops," dads, daddy, or "papa." The reference is generally accepted with grace, and the elderly might respond by using the terms "mi son" or "mi daughter" (my son or my daughter). Disrespect of the elderly is frowned upon and will be brought to the attention of the offender. Strangers will stop to assist an elderly person if they deem it necessary.

Jamaicans have a strong antipathy toward the placement of elders or ill family members in nursing homes. The placement of family members in a nursing home represents the ultimate rejection and abandonment of one's own flesh and blood. It is considered a gross failure and disgrace for a family to consider the use of nursing home facilities. To care for one's family until death is admired and applauded, so counseling and support must be available for families who must utilize the service of a nursing home. Families should be reminded that life in America is not conducive to the maintenance of such family loyalty. Work demands, family members scattered across the country or remaining in Jamaica, and lack of financial resources needed to provide care at home make the choice of a nursing home a necessary decision. The suggestion of nursing home placement must be approached with tact and sensitivity. Family members might be receptive if they are coached into the decision.

Jamaicans place a high value on the intellect; therefore, information regarding cognitive dysfunctions should be presented with tact and sensitivity. For example, prognosis related to mental illness, learning disabilities, head injuries, and related neurological disorders might be sources of resistance for family members who might be in denial. Even if there is difficulty, family members often have high expectations for the patient and might refuse information that does not support their beliefs about the patient's capabilities. Again, tact and sensitivity are imperative.

Personal information is considered to be just that, so information gathering can be a tedious process. At the beginning, be sure that the client knows your reason for requesting personal information and how the information will be used. If clients feel that questions are invasive, they may avoid direct questions or may not return for service. Questions from doctors might be more readily answered because Jamaicans have a great respect for professionals such as doctors, nurses, teachers, and ministers.

Listen carefully to understand what is being said. Although English is the language spoken in Jamaica, most Jamaicans, especially the less educated, speak Jamaican Creole. It is a mixture of English and West African languages, particularly of Ashanti origin. Speech patterns are fast and rhythmic and are coupled with unfamiliar words, which may make communication difficult. American English accents may also pose communication problems for some Jamaicans. Simplify and clarify what has been said in order to prevent misunderstanding on behalf of both patient and service provider, but make sure that efforts to deliver clear communication are not conveyed in a condescending manner.

Acknowledge religious expressions of patients. Most Jamaicans are very religious, and they see God as their spiritual refuge and strength in times of crisis. The concept of God is fundamental to the Jamaican experience. Attention to references to God may be a bridge to rapport building and psychosocial adjustment to disability, because it validates what is important to them.

Network with Jamaican professionals in the field of rehabilitation who might serve as informal consultants or advocates on behalf of those Jamaicans receiving rehabilitation services. Communication with these professionals can be helpful in understanding unfamiliar behaviors or attitudes of Jamaican clients.

Suggestions for Becoming
More Familiar With Jamaican Culture

1. Be curious and willing to learn about other people and their way of life. You may wish to read Jamaican newspapers and novels and explore the Internet as a medium for listening to Jamaican radio stations to gain better insight into the Jamaican way of life.

2. Recognize that Jamaicans bring with them a cultural history and a strong national identity based on their historical experience.

3. Ask when in doubt. Most Jamaicans are proud of their country and are happy to talk about it.

4. Be both a teacher/counselor and a student. Learning about each other is a "two-way street."

5. Learn about the symbols and meanings in the culture and the national heroes. They provide insights into how the collective identity and consciousness of the country were developed.

6. Examine personal biases and stereotypes against Jamaican immigrants in the United States.

Conclusion

Rehabilitation services in Jamaica are very young in comparison to those in the United States. Many Jamaican consumers are unfamiliar with the concept of rehabilitation as a process that can improve the lives of people with disabilities. Given this lack of familiarity, rehabilitation service providers in the United States face a challenge when it comes to educating Jamaican consumers not only to access the rehabilitation system but also to complete the process. Jamaicans typically have many sources of strength that service providers can build upon to assist them in this process. These include confidence in the ability to achieve goals, a strong work ethic, and self-reliance. However, providers must also recognize that there are cultural factors that can hinder the rehabilitation process. Such factors include the belief that persons with disabilities should not work, live alone, or pursue an independent life. The provider must take into account such beliefs to ensure the success of the rehabilitation process.

If providers remain open to culture, they can provide holistic rehabilitation services to Jamaican consumers. Informing themselves about the differences and similarities between Jamaicans and the dominant culture will enable providers to leap over cultural barriers and provide the quality of service that reflects the fundamental principles of American rehabilitation.

References

Belgrave, F. Z., & Walker, S. (1991). Differences in rehabilitation service utilization patterns of African Americans and white Americans with disabilities. In S. Walker et al. (Eds.), *Future frontiers in the employment of minority persons with disabilities: Proceedings of the national conference* (pp. 25–29). Washington, DC: President's Committee on Employment of People with Disabilities.

Black, C. V. (1997). *History of Jamaica.* Kingston, Jamaica: Longman.

Dechesnay, M. (1986). Jamaican family structure: The paradox of normalcy. *Family Process, 25,* 293–300.

Fiest-Price, S., & Ford-Harris, D. (1994). Rehabilitation counseling: Issues specific to providing services to African American clients. *Journal of Rehabilitation, 60*(4), 13–19.

Gleaner Co. (1995). *Geography and history of Jamaica.* Kingston, Jamaica: Gleaner Co. Limited.

Harley, D. A., & Alston, R. J. (1996). Older African American workers: A look at vocational evaluation issues and rehabilitation education training. *Rehabilitation Education, 10*(2&3), 151–160.

Heinz, A., & Payne-Jackson, A. (1997, April). Acculturation of explanatory models: Jamaican blood terms and concepts. *MACLAS Latin American Essays, 11,* p. 19.

Jamaica Information Service. (2000). *What is our national heritage?* Kingston: Author.

Leavitt, R. (1992). *Disability and rehabilitation in rural Jamaica.* London: Associated University Press.

Lowe, H. I. C. (1995). Jamaican folk medicine. *Jamaica Journal, 9,* 2–3.

McGoldrick, M., Pearce, J. K., & Giordana, J. (Eds.). (1982). *Ethnicity and family therapy* (Guilford Family Therapy Series). New York: Guilford Press.

Planning Institute of Jamaica. (2000). *Economic and social survey Jamaica 1999.* Kingston: Planning Institute of Jamaica.

Schaller, J., Parker, R., & Garcia, S. B. (1998). Moving toward culturally competent rehabilitation counseling services: Issues and practices. *Journal of Applied Rehabilitation Counseling, 29*(2), 40–48.

Statistical Institute of Jamaica. (1998). *Statistical yearbook of Jamaica.* Kingston: Printing Unit.

Superintendent of Documents. (1999). *The world factbook.* Pittsburgh, PA: National Technical Information Service.

U.S. Census Bureau. (2003). *Census 2002 summary file 3 (SF 3)—sample data* (Table QT-P13). Retrieved April 14, 2004, from http://factfinder.census. gov/servlet/ QTTable?_bm=y&-geo_id=01000US&-qr_name=DEC_2000_ SF3_U_QTP13&-ds_name=DEC_2000_SF3_U&-_lang=en&-_sse=on

Virtue, E. (1999). Only the brave stay here. *The Gleaner,* pp. 8A-11A.

Walker, S., Belgrave, F. Z., Banner, A. M., & Nicholls, R. W. (Eds.). (1986). *Equal to the challenge: Perspectives, problems, and strategies in the rehabilitation of the nonwhite disabled.* Washington, DC: Bureau of Educational Research, School of Education, Howard University.

Walker, S., Belgrave, F. Z., Nicholls, R. W., & Turner, K. A. (1991). *Future frontiers in the employment of minority persons with disabilities.* Washington, DC: Howard University, Research and Training Center.

6

Disability and Korean Culture

Weol Soon Kim-Rupnow

Introduction

The purpose of this chapter is to provide information to rehabilitation service providers in the United States that will assist them in working effectively with persons who hold traditional Korean values. The topics of Korean history, immigration, culture, language, religion, and views on disabilities are included to provide the reader with a brief overview and background. For those who seek more detailed information, the references cited in each section can be used as a starting point.

Data about Koreans with disabilities in America are limited. The anecdotal examples cited in this chapter illustrate some typical Korean beliefs, behaviors, and attitudes but should not be applied categorically to all Koreans. Individuals will act differently depending on their degree of assimilation of American mainstream culture. The level of assimilation and acculturation of each individual will determine how much of this information will be relevant in each case. The author hopes that this chapter will enhance the reader's awareness and knowledge of traditional Korean culture related to disability issues. An additional aim is to increase the reader's knowledge and respect for Korean culture, which can result in enhanced interpersonal relationships with persons from this culture in general.

The Romanized writing system for Korean sounds used in this chapter is the McCune-Reischauer Romanization system, which is currently used by most academic libraries, including the Library of Congress in the United States.

Cultural Overview

Korea is a peninsular country located in the Far East, adjacent to China on the west and Russia to the north. It occupies approximately 86,000 square miles and is roughly the size of Minnesota or New York State. To the east, Korea faces the islands of Japan. The peninsula is strategically important because it has the advantage of easy access to continents and oceans. It has the disadvantage, however, of being a target of aggressive neighbors. Although Korea has never initiated wars to conquer other people's territory, it has often been a battleground for powerful neighbors over the past thousand years.

The discovery of Paleolithic sites suggests that people probably have inhabited the Korean peninsula for about 40,000 years. The first political state, called Kochoson, emerged in the northern portion of the peninsula more than 5,000 years ago. According to Korean mythology, all Koreans shared the bloodline of Tangun, the founder of the country and a descendant of the gods. The existence of a Korean state has been recognized through documented records since the three kingdoms period (57 B.C.–A.D. 668): The kingdoms were those of Koguryo, Paekche, and Silla. Silla unified the peninsula in 668, which led to the Tongil (unified) Silla period (668–935). The succeeding Koryo Dynasty (918–1392) is known by Westerners for its gorgeous pottery of blue and green celadon with intricate designs. The name Korea originated from "Koryo." Although the Mongol empire conquered Koryo in the 13th century, the dynasty continued its state structure under the Mongols (Korean Overseas Information Service, 2002).

The Choson Dynasty was established in 1392 and lasted until 1910, when Japan imposed colonial rule (1910–1945). Korea was liberated from Japanese rule in 1945 at the end of World War II. Korea then became entangled in an ideological battle, and the country was divided into two parts. The north established the People's Republic of Korea, backed by two powerful communist allies, China and Russia, while in the south the Republic of Korea was supported by the United States. In 1950, the communist government of North Korea launched an attack on South Korea, triggering the Korean War (1950–1953). United Nations forces from 16 countries, including the United States, intervened to defend South Korea until an armistice was signed in 1953.

It took almost a decade after the end of the Korean War for South Korea to establish stability and generate a consistent program of development. During the past three decades, South Korea has achieved remarkable economic growth, with per capita income now 13 times that of North Korea (Central Intelligence Agency, 2000). In the 1990s, South Korea established a civilian government, and it has maintained its commitment to democratize its political processes.

Koreans' sense of many thousands of years of shared history and culture has played an important role in uniting the Korean people whenever the country faced national difficulties, such as foreign invasion or colonial occupation. Seoul, the capital city of Korea, has become a tourist attraction because people can easily trace its millennia of history in old palaces and city gates and find state-of-the-art technology in its subways and many skyscrapers housing worldwide trade and commerce.

The Korean people are the descendants of a number of tribes that migrated into the peninsula from central Asia, Manchuria, Siberia, and other areas of the continent. Koreans and other Asian people share similar physical and cultural characteristics. Over several thousand years, foreign troops from China, Japan, and other countries have swept through the Korean peninsula at various times, yet Koreans never considered themselves part of those countries and maintained their own distinctive language, culture, dress, and cuisine.

The essence of Korean culture is harmony with order, contrasted with American mainstream culture that stresses individualism. Influenced by Confucianism, Koreans value harmony within family, community, and the society as a whole. They have strong ties to family and value education, hard work, and ambition to excel. The commonly cited virtues in traditional Korea include filial piety, respect for elders, benevolence, loyalty, trust, cooperation, reciprocity, and humility (Hur & Hur, 1999). Many Koreans have recently challenged, modified, and adapted these traditional values to accommodate portions of a complicated Western value system.

History of Korean Immigration to the United States

The first wave of Korean immigration to the United States began in 1903 and continued through 1920. Approximately 8,000 Koreans, mostly plantation laborers and their families or women "picture brides," immigrated to Hawaii during this period. The causes of this immigration were many. Some left Korea to escape from famine or from the Japanese colonial state. Others sought new opportunities for better lives, attracted by the promises of American Christian missionaries (Reardon, 1996).

The second wave, from 1950 through 1965, brought approximately 17,000 Koreans to the United States. Most of these immigrants were wives and children of American military men who had served during the Korean War (1950–1953) and orphans adopted by American families.

The number of Korean immigrants accelerated with the passage of the 1965 Immigration Act that eliminated quotas that had been imposed on Asians. The act opened the gates for a third major wave of Korean immigration. The annual number of Korean immigrants increased rapidly, from a few thousand in the 1960s to more than 30,000 between 1976 and 1990.

Unlike the immigrants who came before the 1960s, many of these Koreans had a university education and a middle-class background. They entered the United States seeking better education and opportunities for their children. By 1994, when Korea had achieved great economic prosperity as well as political freedom within a civilian government, emigration had decreased to about 16,000 per year. The approximately half million Koreans in the United States in 1994 constituted the third-largest Asian population in the United States, following Filipinos and Chinese (Hansen & Bachu, 1995).

CHALLENGES OF ADJUSTMENT

The language barrier was often among the biggest challenges experienced by the first generation of Korean immigrants (Kim & Yu, 1996; Kwak & Lee, 1991; Min, 1998). Until the late 1990s, classes in English taught as a foreign language in Korea had focused on reading comprehension based on rote memorization of vocabulary and grammatical rules. Opportunities to practice listening and speaking with native English speakers were very rare. Thus, when Koreans arrived in the United States, they found themselves experiencing communication difficulties similar to those of persons with hearing and speech impairments. The frustration of these immigrants is exemplified in cases of Koreans with advanced training who could find employment in the United States only in lower-level positions.

These Koreans did not have time to attend school to learn English because they needed to work full-time to make ends meet. The language barrier also caused miscommunications with American employers and service providers as well as difficulty participating in the American mainstream. Younger generations of Koreans who studied in the American educational system, however, quickly adapted to the American culture and language and became highly successful, both professionally and financially.

Cultural differences present additional hurdles that make it difficult for Korean immigrants to adjust to American mainstream culture. One of these is the American emphasis on individualism. Because Koreans emphasize harmony with order, they tend to be influenced by the opinions of other members of their family or community when making decisions. If they make a decision based on their own preferences without considering others, they are likely to be labeled "selfish." It is interesting to note here that language usage reflects subtle differences between individualism and collectivism. For example, the accurate Korean translation of the pronoun "my" as used in "my family" and "my country" is "uri," which means "our."

Koreans set a high priority on their children's education and are willing to make tremendous sacrifices to help them get the best education possible. Once these children are educated within the culture of the American educational system, however, they may not accept the values of collectivism and filial piety that require personal needs and goals to be downplayed for the good of parents or siblings. Resulting family tension caused by different degrees of assimilation among family members can become problematic. In addition to individualism, many parents are concerned about their children's easy access to illegal drugs, sexual freedom, and related problems in American society (Kwak & Lee, 1991; Pang, 2000).

In addition, racial discrimination against Asian Americans, including Koreans, has been well documented. The most infamous examples include discriminatory immigration laws intended to prevent Asians from coming to America or becoming citizens (Chin, Cho, Kang, & Wu, 2001). The current portrayal of Asians as "a model minority" that has succeeded through education and hard work, and whose income almost matches that of Caucasian Americans, is somewhat misleading. For example, immigration law has given priority to Asians who are highly educated, skilled, or wealthy enough to start their own business in the United States. Thus, the majority of recent Asian immigrants are already above average in terms of education and income. Although civil rights and immigration laws have been amended over the years to decrease overt racism against people of Asian origin, subtle racism continues to burden Asians. Asian stereotypes based on physical characteristics and heavily accented English are often perpetuated by popular media and political leaders, and there are still many cases of employment discrimination and victimization through racial violence (Abelmann & Lie, 1995; Chin et al., 2001; Kwak & Lee, 1991; Pang, 2000).

Korean Concepts of Disability

Their culture profoundly influences what Koreans believe about the causes and treatments of disability. Some Koreans believe disability can be caused by supernatural agents, such as punishment from God or the curse of the devil for their sins, or those of their parents, or even their ancestors. Others think that the mother did something wrong during pregnancy, such as creating an imbalance of metaphysical forces (Umyang in Korean), failing to follow prescribed dietary and nutritional practices, or violating certain taboos (Reardon, 1996). For example, even a bad thought or an accidental killing of an animal or insect by a pregnant mother can harm the natural development of the fetus according to the Buddhistic belief in karma, which holds that no living things should be killed.

Modern Koreans with education in biology and medicine believe that genetic defects or diseases often cause disability. It is common to observe

Koreans with a complex mixture of the belief systems described above, depending mainly on their education, religion, and family backgrounds.

Beliefs have a direct implication for prescribed methods of treatment. People who associate supernatural agents with disabilities tend to feel helpless or depressed, or they blame themselves or ancestors when they discover a disability in themselves or their family. They tend to seek little help and leave everything to fate. Those with a scientific education believe that disabling conditions may be overcome with appropriate medical intervention, and they actively seek medicine, therapy, or surgery from health professionals. Unlike Westerners, however, many Koreans use herbal medicines, acupuncture, and other natural remedies. Being spiritually oriented, many Koreans using Western medicine also offer prayers and conduct religious rituals to regain physical and mental health.

Korean professionals working in rehabilitation categorize disabilities as (a) impairments of the human body and internal organs; (b) disabilities in intelligence, behavior, or emotion; and (c) handicaps created by the society, which include limitations that stem from environmental factors such as negative perception and attitudes toward people with disabilities, poverty and malnutrition, and barriers in architectural structure. It is noteworthy that environmental factors are included as a cause of disability in addition to functional limitations. This integrative view is parallel to a holistic paradigm of disability as described in the Long Range Plan (1999–2003) of the U.S. National Institute on Disability and Rehabilitation Research (NIDRR):

> [D]isability is a product of the interaction between individual and environmental characteristics along a continuum from enablement to disablement. Individual or intrinsic factors include person, biology, and behavior, whereas environmental or extrinsic factors are related to socioeconomic status, education levels, access to health care, nutrition, living conditions, and personal safety. (NIDRR, 2001)

This integrative view explains the Korean professionals' perspectives on disability better than the medical model, which is structured to scientifically identify the causes of disability and treat the symptoms largely in isolation from other aspects of a person's life. Korean professionals believe that the best tools for removing societal barriers that confront people with disabilities are information and education, both of which can improve public awareness and cooperation.

Attitudes Toward Disability

Koreans are generally homogenous and conservative in terms of values and customs. People tend to stare at or gossip about those people whose dress code and behavior deviate from social norms. For this reason, people with disabilities are likely to be isolated. The general public tends to avoid people with disabilities because of uneasiness associated with not knowing what to do. When helping a person with disabilities, some people usually overprotect or overcompensate, which only serves to frustrate those they are trying to help.

In the special editorial section of *JoongAng Ilbo* [*Korea Central Daily of Hawaii*] ("Changaein munje," 2001 p. 22) written specifically for the 21st annual celebration of a "Changaein ui nal" (Day for People with Disabilities), the editor criticized the lack of a long-range planning and support by the government and nonprofit organizations:

> Korea's Employment Promotion Law for People with Disabilities requires employ-ers with more than 300 employees to reserve two percent of their positions for people with disabilities. A survey by the Korean Ministry of Labor, however, showed that employers do not fulfill that requirement. For example, only 0.91 percent of jobs in 1,900 privately owned companies with more than 300 employees, and 1.48 percent in state, city, and other government organizations are held by persons with disabilities.

Employers indicated that they would rather pay fines than hire people with dis-abilities.

Negative attitudes toward disabilities have not improved over a 15-year-interval. According to surveys conducted by a private research firm, 83.1% of the sample in 1984 and 82.4% in 2000 indicated that they would rather abort than raise a child with disability ("Changaein munje," 2001, p. 22). This single survey result demonstrates the unfavorable perceptions of disability and the hardships that persons with disabilities must endure in Korean society.

Efforts have been made to eradicate prejudices against people with dis-abilities and their accompanying stigma. For example, the Korean Broadcasting System (KBS) recently produced three special TV shows about people with dis-abilities within 3 months, an unprecedented number of shows on a single topic (Cho, 2001b). This set of programs, "Sunday Special," covered various topics during prime evening hours and received numerous awards and consistently high ratings. The three episodes focused on the hopes and dreams of people with disabilities and the attitudes of Koreans toward them.

The first episode (Cho & Cho, 2001) depicted the life of Kich'ang Kim, a famous artist who lost his hearing at the age of 6. He learned to read as a result of his mother's dedicated tutoring. He could not endure the ridicule and teasing at a regular school and dropped out. Rather than dwell on what he could not do, his mother discovered his talents in art and sent him to a master artist for private lessons. It did not take long before his artistic talents began to blossom and earn awards in national art competitions.

A woman artist with a prestigious college degree and wealthy family background fell in love with Kim and married him, despite her parents' opposition and threats to disown her because of his disability. Later in his life, Kim said that his deafness, combined with his wife's inspiration, had opened the door for him to pursue endless experiments with his art. In 70 years as an artist, he created more than 10,000 works encompassing a wide variety of genres, including traditional, contemporary, Oriental, and Western paintings. He overcame childhood ridicule and frustration to become an internationally renowned artist through exhibits in America and Europe. Most of his works were sold. Later in his life, he contributed much of his wealth to building an advanced facility to provide wellness services and job training for people with disabilities. Although he became a wheelchair user after several strokes, he never stopped painting until he died at the age of 88. Kim became a role model for young people with disabilities. He said, "Use your talents to learn the skills that are employable, then make money, get married, and support your family" (Cho & Cho, 2001).

The second program episode portrayed the love and dedication of an American couple with sight impairments (Cho & Nam, 2001). In spite of their own disabilities, the couple was successful in adopting and raising four Korean children who also had sight impairments and had been abandoned by their biological parents. Ellen, one of the adopted children, was a high school senior getting ready to go to a college. She remembered clearly the day her mother took her shopping and left her in a mall and never came back. Ellen was not sure what would have happened to her if she had been left to fend for herself without the unconditional love provided by her adopted parents. Now she wants to be productive and pay back her parents. The story raised the question, "Why can't everyone accept the differences in individuals and love them as this American couple does?"

The third program concerned several Americans with disabilities who regained mobility, communication capability, and sensory ability by taking advantage of highly advanced technology (Cho, 2001a). It urged a change in Korean public policy by pointing out that the employment rate of people with disabilities in the United States has increased fourfold since the passage of the Americans with Disabilities Act.

The three shows offered snapshots of Korean attitudes toward disability and provoked a new understanding of people with disabilities and the innovative tools that can support them. The presentation of these individuals with disabilities through the medium of television was powerful and beautiful. It showed them overcoming internal and external obstacles, striving to reach their full potential, and contributing to their own welfare and that of their families and communities. It remains to be seen whether Korean attitudes toward children with disabilities will move in a more positive direction.

The Concept of Independence

Because Koreans believe interdependence among family members is more important than independence, they accept that all people need help from others many times in their lives. In particular, dependency of young children, old grandparents, or sick family members is usually expected. Family members feel obligated to take care of their basic needs and to keep up their morale. It is common in Korean society to see infant babies and young children sleep with their parents in the same room. Korean parents often tell their children, "Don't worry about anything now. Just study hard, go to a college and get a good job; until then I'll take care of everything." Independence is expected after the completion of schooling, which usually culminates in college degrees. Children are expected to secure a job, earn their own living, save for the future, get married, start a family, and support that family.

Parents of adult children with disabilities often experience conflict between the child's independence and interdependence. They want to encourage the self-sufficiency of their children but, at the same time, protect their children's well-being. As their children with disabilities grow into adults, parents want them to find meaningful work consistent with their goals and talents and to make enough money to support themselves. The issues of independence and interdependence are the developmental issues parents struggle with in raising children with disabilities in Korean culture. It is often difficult for children with disabilities to grow and learn to be independent in Korean families that emphasize interdependence, with parents who often overprotect them. However, some adults with disabilities who have found employment say that work has played a key role in developing their self-esteem and a sense of belonging in society. They do not want to rely on the social welfare system. The sense of pride they have as taxpayers proves even more valuable than the income they bring in.

Acquired and Lifelong Disabilities

Some Koreans believe that lifelong disability is a kind of payback for something they did wrong in the past. As a result, many Koreans with disabilities and their families often suffer from shame, helplessness, denial, withdrawal, and depression. Many view acquired disability as the result of some sort of bad luck or misfortune. People generally accept illness and disability due to aging as a fact of life, however.

If a disability is acquired through a work-related accident or military service, a glimpse of pride may be observed in the client and his or her family, along with overwhelming distress. For example, a firefighter who was injured in the line of duty said during a TV interview, "I saved other people's lives through my sacrifice." The following paragraph, translated from a Korean newspaper article by T. K. Park (2001), describes the essence of Korean views on acquired disabilities.

> "I never realized that anyone could become disabled at the blink of an eye until I had a car accident and had to rely on a wheelchair to get around," said sobbing Mrs. Jo who became paralyzed from the waist down after a truck crashed into her car eight months ago. Mrs. Jo continued, "It is desperately needed that we, the society, should all be aware and consider the problems faced by people with disabilities like our own, not somebody else's. I want to be an independent mom for our children as soon as I can, so I bought a wheelchair and I have been getting vocational rehabilitation training."

It is alarming that 9 out of 10 people with disabilities become disabled because of automobile and industrial accidents and diseases. According to the Korean Ministry of Health and Welfare, in the year 2000, 89.4% of the 133,500 people with disabilities had acquired disabilities, and less than 5% were disabled by genetic defects or early birth and delivery-related complications. The most common causes of acquired disabilities included high blood pressure, stroke, and accidents (T. K. Park, 2001).

The Role of Family, Community, and Religion

FAMILY STRUCTURE

Koreans regard family as the basic social unit and consider harmony at home the first step toward harmony in the community and in the nation as a whole. Many Koreans consider themselves extensions of their families and often regard the welfare of the family as more important than that of individual members. The family relationship has been strongly influenced by Confucianism, which emphasizes harmony and order within a system of prescribed roles for husband, wife, son, and daughter. The relationships emphasize subordination and interdependence: Parents love their children, while children respect their parents and are filially pious.

Parents are expected to support their children's education, often sacrificing their own comfort in the process. In return, adult children are obligated to support their aging parents. Usually, the eldest son is expected to live with his parents. Even if the children live separately, they are expected to visit their parents often, especially on occasions such as birthday celebrations, memorial services to ancestors, and national holidays such as New Year's celebrations and Korean Thanksgiving.

The roles of family members are based on gender and age. Exchanging roles and sharing power are not encouraged because of strong beliefs that order and harmony exist when there are distinctions between the roles and duties of men and women. This results in the husband taking the lead and the wife following. Children are ranked by age, with the younger required to respect the older. Many first-generation Koreans retain the traditional authoritarian family system in which the father acts as decision maker in family affairs. Direct openness of expression and assertiveness by children is often seen as rude or aggressive. Expressions of feelings or needs are discouraged, especially for boys. Silence and humility are valued more than storytelling and bragging.

There is a growing body of research about the gap between first- and second-generation Korean immigrants (Kwak & Lee, 1991; Min, 1998). A major cause of this gap is the language barrier. Full communication between these groups is often difficult because many of the first generation do not speak English well, while most members of the second and third generations do not speak Korean.

Another reason for the gap is the different degrees of assimilation to American culture. The first generation often holds traditional Korean values. For example, parents may want to decide their children's future in terms of a school major, a career choice, and even a marriage partner. These parents tend to insist that the parents know what is best for the children. The American-educated children may ignore or rebel against their parents' authoritarianism.

ROLE OF COMMUNITY

Koreans generally have a strong group identity, as reflected in Korean American telephone directories, which have long lists of numbers of nonprofit organizations. Koreans may identify with a region, religion, surname, school, or economic group. In general, coworkers, friends, alumni from the same class, or religious colleagues are likely to provide extensive support in time of celebration, such as a wedding or the birth of a child, as well as in time of hardship, such as hospitalization or the death of a family member.

Depending on their age, people are often addressed as "brother," "sister," "uncle," "aunt," "grandma," or "grandpa" by neighbors or even strangers on the street. Such terms reflect Koreans' strong sense of collective group identity. In the work environment, individual identity is closely tied to the position held within an organization. An indicator of importance of position is the way Koreans address each other. They would never use personal names and instead call each other by their job titles, for instance, "President Kim" or "Director Lee." These terms reflect the fact that the traditional Korean community functions within a hierarchical order of human relationships based on age or status. In the same manner, to Koreans "friends" refer to close relationships within the same age group, a narrow definition compared with the American concept of friends. Trust is an important virtue among friends. Kindness and generosity are also highly valued. Gift giving and food sharing are common cultural practices in the Korean community and are gestures of appreciation or friendship.

RELIGION

For many Koreans, spiritual aspects of life and religion are a source of strength and support. Statistics indicate that most Koreans have a religion— Christian, 49%; Buddhist, 47%; Confucianist, 3%; Shamanist, Ch'ondogyo (Religion of the Heavenly Way) and others, 1% (Central Intelligence Agency, 2000). Koreans enjoy freedom of choice in religion and lead a rather harmonious life despite their diverse religions. The various belief systems are mutually reinforcing and do not conflict with values that underlie the daily lives of Koreans. Many Koreans tend to be open to the teachings of other religions and respect others' choices, so they are puzzled when violent wars break out over religious conflicts in other parts of the world.

Interactions With Service Providers

Service providers, such as doctors, nurses, teachers, and therapists, whose jobs require higher education degrees and intensive training, are well respected in the Korean community. Consumers tend to listen to their advice and follow their directions as passive recipients. Korean service providers are not familiar with the concept of empowerment of or partnership with consumers and tend to administer services as authority figures. Service providers generally are the primary decision makers, and few choices are given to consumers. Overall wellness and illness issues are defined by government agencies and experts.

The choice of treatment options for individual consumers is also usually determined by service providers. A recent trend, however, encourages consumers to become better informed by gathering information from a variety of sources, including informal social networks, and to be proactive in seeking second opinions before making decisions about their rehabilitation.

Some consumers expect clear and understandable explanations regarding procedures and treatment. They also want to have time to review and think before proceeding, particularly when considering treatment related to surgery or Western medicines or practices that are unfamiliar to them. Many believe that tampering with their bodies surgically or with strong medicines is disrespectful to their parents.

Recommendations for Service Providers

The following are general suggestions for building positive and collaborative relationships with consumers who hold traditional Korean values, regardless of their age or type of disability. The recommendations are divided into three sections: building a positive relationship, involving consumers and family members, and expanding support and services considered to be critical elements in the rehabilitation process. "You" and "I" are used in this section to make the recommendations more personalized. The term "consumer" includes categories such as client, student, and patient.

BUILDING A POSITIVE RELATIONSHIP

Building a positive relationship with consumers is fundamental to successful service delivery. This section focuses on recommendations for attitudes, manners, and ways to improve communication as a multiculturally competent service provider.

Be open and respect individual differences. Mutual respect and trust take more effort cross-culturally. We need to understand our own culture and its biases, as well as those of the consumers. We need to be open enough to understand the consumer's perspective. I have been a consumer and a service provider. As a strategy to enhance awareness and flexibility, I often ask myself questions such as "Am I thinking like an American?" and "Can I see this situation differently from a consumer's perspective?" Reversing the roles in my mind sometimes helps me better understand the consumer's position. When I do this role-playing, I am often pleasantly surprised. For example, some consumer attitudes that I have found bothersome may be considered appropriate in their cultures, and this mental role-reversal has helped me improve my working relationships with consumers.

In-ja's experience while she was recuperating from the delivery of her first son illustrates how a conflicting situation can be altered by cross-cultural appreciation. In-ja's sister flew from Korea to assist her with her newborn child for a month. In-ja's mother-in-law, a 65-year-old European American who had little exposure to Asian culture, also flew across several states to see her first grandson. During her visit, the grandmother became upset after In-ja's sister quickly stopped her when she approached the crying infant. In-ja's sister checked the baby's diaper, gave him a bath, and dressed him, while rejecting help from the grandmother. She could not speak English, so her intentions were indicated by hand gestures and saying "no." The grandmother complained to her son, who told In-ja that her sister was too possessive with the baby to allow the grandmother near him. In-ja told her mother-in-law that her sister's behavior indicated respect for an older person according to Korean custom, and her intention was to do the work for the grandmother. The grandmother understood, and her growing tension toward In-ja's sister switched to friendly smiles. In-ja also talked to her sister about the misunderstanding and suggested that she should share the responsibility of taking care of the baby with the grandmother. They not only got along well together for the rest of their stay but also appreciated each other's help. The grandmother learned to say "Thank you" in Korean, "Kamsa hamnida." In-ja's sister learned to respond automatically, "You're welcome."

In-ja created a win-win situation for both her mother-in-law and her sister by helping them understand different cultural values. This story illustrates well how individuals, both service providers and consumers, might experience problems when minority persons with cultural values and beliefs quite different from those of the majority culture seek rehabilitation services.

Avoid stereotyping and labeling. Stereotyping and generalization keep us from being open-minded. Every Korean is unique in terms of personality and the degree to which he or she has assimilated American culture. The information you have learned about Korean culture in this chapter and from other sources may not apply to some consumers with whom you are working.

Provide Korean American clients with an empathetic ear and learn from them about their own unique needs, values, and attitudes. Be flexible and let go of your own assumptions, which could negatively impact expectations, services provided, resources employed, and outcomes. They can also produce hurt feelings in both the consumer and the provider. Be in control of how you present yourself to consumers and how you perceive them.

Use Korean greetings to break ice and to build rapport instantly. One of the most useful phrases is "Annyong haseyo?" The word "Annyong" means "peacefulness" and "well-being," and "haseyo?" makes a noun into a verb and shows respect. This phrase means generally, " How are you?" You can use this phrase any time of the day—morning, afternoon, or night. You may use this greeting with a stranger or with those with whom you are acquainted. You may use the word "Annyong" alone with a person younger than you.

Another useful expression is "Kamsa hamnida," which means "Thank you." You may check the Web site (www.langintro.com/kintro/) created by

Eisenberg (2003) to hear the pronunciation. If Korean consumers hear you use a Korean greeting, they will feel instantly connected and appreciate your attitude toward them.

Show respect, especially to those who are older than you. Age difference is one of the most important elements that define relationships among Koreans. For example, we must not talk back to someone older than us. In addition, the language that we use varies depending on the age of the person to whom we are speaking. Calling adults by their first names may make them feel offended or uncomfortable. First-generation Koreans are not accustomed to Americans' use of the first name as a gesture of friendliness.

When you hand something to an elderly person, you should hold the object with both hands. Koreans bow their heads slightly as a greeting, rather than saying, "Hi!" or waving. These are just a few examples of how to express respect to older people. If you try to implement these expressions of respect and have a genuine interest in the culture, Koreans will respect you as a well-mannered person and will likely listen to you more seriously than to service providers who use more casual styles of greeting.

Have open and ongoing communication. Positive relationships begin with communication. Free exchange of knowledge about services, needs, and expectations might not take place with first-generation Korean immigrants because of their limited English proficiency. Ask consumers if they need an interpreter. If necessary, use a family member or friend of the consumer as an interpreter. This may compromise the objectivity of the interpretation, of course, because family members may sometimes feel embarrassed or ashamed to disclose certain information. Some consumers might feel offended if providers ask for private information such as socioeconomic and marital status in order to obtain intake information.

Building trust is another issue with which you must deal if you bring in an interpreter who is a stranger to the consumer. Although the person may speak the same language, the consumer may have strong reservations about airing family problems to an outsider. You may have to wait until the consumer gets to know the interpreter better and builds trust. Open and ongoing communication with consumers should involve informing them of the pitfalls as well as the benefits of the service system. In this way, you establish trust and respect.

Provide written information. The majority of first-generation Koreans, who were not educated in the American school system, may speak little English but may understand more than they can speak. Often they can read fairly well if they finished the equivalent of secondary school education in Korea. It is a good idea to provide brochures about any important information regarding the services you are providing. You may give written memos, especially regarding medicines, treatment-related terminology, and appointment dates and times. If they do not understand, they can use an English-Korean dictionary or can ask a friend to assist them later. Sometimes, you may be able to find Korean brochures that contain the same information as English brochures.

Take advantage of nonverbal communication. Although hand-shaking is common, many Koreans feel uncomfortable with physical contact with strangers, such as hugging or kissing on the cheek as a social greeting. They would rather bow slightly or smile, reserving friendly touching or hugging for family members and friends. It is common to see hand holding or shoulder holding between friends of the same sex, although most are not homosexual. Among strangers, however, touching is considered disrespectful or harassing, unless it is part of a physical examination or treatment. Particularly insulting is pointing at or touching the head of another.

Koreans usually do not make direct eye contact, considering it impolite, until they are comfortable with each other. Silence or long pauses during conversation usually means the person needs more time to think about the issue before giving an answer. Do not pressure clients for a prompt response.

Avoid potential misinterpretation. Some Koreans are not in the habit of using an automatic "you're welcome" as an immediate response to "thank you" or saying "excuse me" after burping or sneezing. Some Koreans tend to be less verbal or spontaneous in group situations as a result of the cultural emphasis on humility, as opposed to independent thinking and assertiveness.

In a group setting, being spotlighted in a negative sense may bring about an overwhelming sense of shame, so it is better to discuss such concerns privately. Keeping the head down when being scolded or disciplined is generally a sign of regret or acceptance of the consequences, while looking straight into the speaker's face is interpreted as a sign of defiance. American service providers usually expect consumers to exhibit openness and assertiveness, but Koreans may restrain their feelings and endure hardships because they have learned in Confucian ideology that harmony and order are maintained through perseverance and calm acceptance of authoritarian decisions.

INVOLVING CONSUMERS AND FAMILY MEMBERS

Active consumer involvement is an important element in successful rehabilitation. Considering Koreans' high regard for family, a service provision model that recognizes how consumers view themselves in relation to their family will likely succeed. This section will provide tips on involving Korean consumers and their family members as partners to enhance service provision.

Invite parents into the process from the beginning. The following case illustrates the benefits of parental involvement.

> Jin-nam is a young man with a sensory disability. Although it has now been corrected, he was teased in school about his hearing impairment. This, in addition to his status as a minority immigrant, made it untenable for him to remain in school. He passed the GED test for an alternative high school diploma through self-study and demonstrated responsibility as a cookie baker in his family business. Jin-nam worked to learn practical information about several careers in which he is interested and has taken tours of community college programs in his areas of interest. Jin-nam's parents were invited to the tours, and they were introduced to one of the vocational rehabilitation (VR) staff members who could speak Korean. Although his primary interest was agriculture, he chose technology as his career, according to his mother's wishes. His mother, who communicated regularly with the VR counselor through the Korean-speaking staff, encouraged Jin-nam to be a technologist because it is considered a white-collar job with more prestige than farming. He is now attending the office technology program at a community college. He is happy with his second choice because his parents' dream means a great deal to him.

If the VR counselor had not involved Jin-nam's parents from the beginning, she and Jin-nam might have spent much time exploring many other programs. Bringing in a staff member who spoke the same language as Jin-nam's parents also facilitated the communication process. Service providers should be aware of the possible pressures on some Korean young adults. Their parents might have high expectations that may not correlate with their children's abilities or desires. As illustrated here, many Korean young adults, by custom, are dependent on their parents for guidance and may need career counseling both individually and with their parents.

Diagnostic assessment for children and young adults should also involve parents. Some aspects of children's behaviors are considered normal in Korean culture but not in America. One example is attention deficit disorder (ADD). In Korean society, children, especially boys, are expected to be active. Some parents often encourage their boys to be active and tough rather than timid. They often laugh when their boys get a report card saying "not paying attention" or "easily distractible," considering this part of the growing-up process. One mother, whose son was diagnosed with ADD, complained to me that the teachers were picking on her son.

Professionals involved in assessment should not overlook culture in identifying certain disability types. In addition, compounding factors such as learning

English as a second language can hinder accurate diagnosis of a disability. For example, Jin-nam's hearing impairment was identified much later than it might have been because school personnel, as well as his parents, considered Jin-nam's hearing problem temporary and due to the difficulty associated with learning a new language.

Yong-hi's story offers another example of complex issues related to an accurate assessment of a minority child's disabilities. Yong-hi was a 5-year-old girl who came to the United States 6 months previously. When she started kindergarten, no one at her school heard her speak a word for about a month. The teacher contacted her mother to ask if Yong-hi had hearing or speech impairments. The mother could not believe that Yong-hi had been mute during the past month, so she decided to come and observe her daughter at school without letting her know. Knowing how talkative Yong-hi was at home, the mother was shocked to find out that her daughter would not say a word in her regular classroom, in the ESL (English as a second language) classroom, or on the playground. In addition, she exhibited no facial expressions and looked numb throughout the day.

Her concerned teacher approached me, a Korean-English bilingual tutor at that time, and explained the situation. I worked with Yong-hi in a small group of new immigrant students who were learning English as a second language. Yong-hi would neither speak nor smile for about a week. One day, I decided to deal with the problem indirectly by playing a game with the group, explaining rules and procedures in both Korean and English. When the game took an exciting turn and created a funny situation, she suddenly burst into laughter. The other students in the group followed her. She began to speak to me in Korean. I smiled with a big sigh of relief. In less than a year, she became a fluent English speaker and mainstreamed into a regular classroom.

Yong-hi's temporary state of muteness also illustrates newcomers' stress during their adjustment period. It is important to note here that immigrant students used to be called SLEP (Students with Limited English Proficiency) in the 1980s; now, the label has been changed to ESLL (English as Second Language Learners).

The two labels demote or promote a positive self-concept in these learners. The first term focuses on the individuals' limited English proficiency, implying a disability or limitation compared with the majority culture, while the second implies that the students have already acquired their first language and are now learning an additional language. Because they possess extreme senses of pride and shame, many Korean parents would not want their child to be placed in a special class because of discriminatory labels that would single out their child from the larger group. If they can afford it, they would rather find a private therapist or a tutor. Even parents of children with disabilities want teachers to be strict in discipline and to have high expectations for academic performance. Thus, they prefer much homework within a rigorous curriculum. Long-range goals for education and career are developed at an early age.

Respect healing rituals. A person's culture can serve as a barrier or a facilitator during the rehabilitation process. Some service providers might view Koreans' spiritual emphasis as a barrier to the supposedly expeditious rehabilitation process, but much depends on how individuals balance their inner world with extrinsic factors in their lives. Those who use meditation or prayer to boost their inner strength, in combination with scientifically developed medicines or therapeutic methods, are likely to have a better chance of recovery than those who insist on using only one of the two methods.

Make good use of natural supports. The American rehabilitation system values individual responsibility and individualized services, whereas Korean culture tends to emphasize the interdependence of family, friends, and community. Involving not only family members but also a circle of friends, especially members of their religious organizations, can benefit consumers by offering additional support. In group residential settings such as hospitals, nursing homes, and group homes, some Korean consumers may crave Korean food. If feasible, let relatives and friends bring in ethnic foods that they believe promote wellness and produce therapeutic effects.

Empower consumers and their parents. Some service providers admit that the more involved and assertive the consumer, the better the services. They recommend that consumers and parents should get involved in obtaining the necessary documents for services and participate in meetings for developing Individualized Educational Plans (IEPs), Individualized Family Service Plans (IFSPs), or Individualized Written Rehabilitation Plans (IWRPs). Most Korean consumers, however, are likely to be passive recipients. Koreans are not familiar with American concepts such as empowerment, advocacy, personal choice, and independent living that are valued by the mainstream rehabilitation service system in the United States. In addition, most people do not understand what planning documents are required, the importance of consumers' involvement in an IEP or IWRP, and the alternative types of services.

Once rapport and trust is established with Korean consumers, it may be necessary to explain their rights and responsibilities in the special education or rehabilitation system and to encourage them to be active participants by teaching the values of self-determination and assertiveness. Kalyanpur and Rao describe empowerment as changing the role of a service provider, from that of an expert to that of an ally or friend who helps families articulate what they need (National Center for the Dissemination of Disability Research, 1999). It might not be easy at first to establish a partner relationship with Korean consumers as defined above because they are accustomed to a hierarchical relationship.

Structured approaches with clear directions and expectations might suit most first-generation Koreans best. Providing many options and freedom of choice might not be widely appreciated as it is in American mainstream culture. Even worse, the service provider who offers too many options is likely to be considered incompetent. Korean consumers may be able to collaborate better when given a clear explanation of the pros and cons of a few options the provider has already screened based on his or her expertise and experience in the system.

EXPANDING CAPACITY AND SUPPORT

A truly productive working relationship extends beyond the provision of services, to the formation of a partnership at an individual level. This section deals with expanding capacity and support to ensure positive rehabilitation outcomes at a system level. A wide array of services and supports is needed by Koreans with disabilities and their families, but the three most critical are (a) interpretation (translation) services, (b) mental health services, and (c) policy and system level support.

Be creative in finding interpretation and translation services. As noted above, the language barrier is the most significant problem experienced by a majority of first-generation Korean immigrants. From the intake process and assessment to intervention strategies, the language barrier for Korean-speaking consumers with a disability will affect the outcome of the rehabilitation process. Along with culturally appropriate interventions and strategies, the incorporation of Korean language in all steps of the rehabilitation process is needed (J. Park & Turnbull, 2001).

There are several ways to reduce the cost for interpretation or translation services at the institutional or national rehabilitation level. There are some Korean information brochures available on the prevention and treatment of common diseases, as well as those about rehabilitation programs and services. Sharing information brochures at the national level, as well as an international exchange among rehabilitation research institutes, would help prevent duplication of cost and effort.

It is also useful to have access to staff members within the agency or related nonprofit organizations who speak Korean. Jin-nam's mother, in the story cited previously, felt very positive about the resourcefulness of his son's counselor and said in Korean, "Although she could not speak Korean, she introduced me to a Korean staff member. Whenever I am frustrated with communication, being able to explain the problems to her in my native language reduces my stress level." She was most impressed by the counselor's initiative and promptness in locating the appropriate human resources.

Provide mental health support. Many Korean consumers and parents view disabilities as the result of their incorrect behavior and are not only embarrassed but also suffer an extreme sense of shame. As a result, they are less likely to report a disability and to get the support and services they need. It is important to reassure them that no one should be blamed and that positive attitudes can facilitate recovery.

Be an empathetic listener as a way of providing emotional support that is not specific to the consumers' disability. Help them identify what they are feeling, and help them find healthy ways to vent their depression and frustration. Assist them in avoiding self-defeating behaviors such as isolating themselves, overeating, and drinking. Have them stop using their disability as an excuse for these behaviors. Encourage them to focus on the things they can control and do well, rather than dwelling on deficits. If there are too many issues for you to handle, seek external help. Remember that you are a human being first, then a service provider, and you may feel exhausted and simply need a break.

Some Korean family members often sacrifice their own needs to care for their loved ones who are ill or who have disabilities. This can result in severe emotional distress manifested by vague abdominal pain and depression (Min, 1998; Pang, 2000). Try to arrange respite services and external mental health support for them. Many Koreans underutilize mental health services because they may fear that mental illness is a sign of a spiritual crisis or fear losing face by exposing inner weaknesses. In addition to cultural stigma associated with mental health, other primary reasons for the pervasive undertreatment of mental illness include poverty, lack of health insurance coverage, and language barriers. Help consumers expand their formal and informal networks to find extra support from other Korean consumers with similar disabilities.

Policy- and system-level support. Service providers may need in-service training to develop culturally competent skills and to prevent discrimination against particular ethnic or disability groups seeking rehabilitation service and support systems. Compared with the overall disability community, Koreans are less likely to be identified as having disabilities and are also less likely to be served through public assistance and welfare services. This is due in part to guilt or shame associated with disability and the belief that disability is a private family matter.

Underidentification and underutilization of services by minorities with disabilities need to be addressed at the policy level. As a strategy to improve the underlying social and institutionalized inequities, minority persons including Koreans and other Asians, especially those with disabilities, need to be supported in becoming role models and leaders in the field of rehabilitation services. Having minority role models in the system can benefit both service providers and consumers by assisting them to bridge the cultural gap between mainstream and minority cultures (Stodden, Stodden, Kim-Rupnow, Thai, & Galloway, 2003).

Building strong links between various rehabilitation agencies and other service organizations by sharing Korean language materials and translators among agencies is another way to broaden opportunities and improve services.

Ways in Which Service Providers Can Become More Familiar With Korean Culture

Below is a list of ways to become more familiar with Korean culture.

- Socialize and make friends with persons from Korea.
- Read books, journals, and newspapers about Korea. References used for this chapter, including *Korean Journal* and *Journal of Korean Studies*, are available online at www.uhpress.hawaii.edu/journals/ks/ and are a good beginning. Korean newspapers written in English include *The Korea Herald*, *The Korea Times*, and *The Korea Economic News Daily*.
- Watch Korean movies, videos, and TV series. Cities with large numbers of Korean immigrants have Korean TV stations and stores that rent Korean videos and taped TV shows. Some of these shows may have English subtitles.
- Visit the Web sites used for this chapter. Some sites have related links to broaden one's perspective and understanding of the Korean culture.
- For the academically oriented, explore the resources offered by universities with Korean studies or Korean language programs. Examples include the following:

    Korea Institute of Harvard University (online information; www.fas.harvard.edu/~korea/index_home.html)

    Center for Korean Studies, University of California, Berkeley (online information; http://ieas.berkeley.edu/cks/)

    Center for Korean Studies, University of California, Los Angeles (Online information; www.isop.ucla.edu/korea/)

    Center for Korean Studies, University of Hawaii (online information; www2.hawaii.edu/korea/)

The Korean Studies Program at the University of Washington (online information; http://jsis.artsci.washington.edu/programs/easc/Korea Studies Program.html)

- For those who enjoy travel and feel adventurous, plan to visit Korea as a vacation destination. One may learn much in a short period of time, especially how difficult it is to live in a foreign land as a minority with limited proficiency in the language.

References

Abelmann, N., & Lie, J. (1995). *Blue dreams: Korean Americans and the Los Angeles riots.* Cambridge, MA: Harvard University Press.

Central Intelligence Agency. (2000). Korea, South. In *The world factbook 2000.* Available at www.odci.gov/cia/publications/factbook/geos/ks.html#People

Changaein munje nam ui il man anida [Problems of people with disabilities are not somebody else's business]. (2001, April 20). *JoongAng Ilbo* [*The Korea Central Daily of Hawaii*], p. 22.

Chin, G., Cho, S., Kang, J., & Wu, F. (2001). *Beyond self-interest: Asian Pacific Americans toward a community of justice: A policy analysis of affirmative action.* Available at www.sscnet.ucla.edu/aasc/policy/

Cho, D. H. (Executive Producer). (2001a, April 29). Hait'eku ka kajoon huimang: Miguk Changaein chongch'aek. [Hope brought by hi-tech: American Disability Act]. *Iryo special* [*Sunday special*]. Seoul: Korean Broadcasting System.

Cho, D. H. (Executive Producer). (2001b). *Iryo special* [*Sunday special*]. Seoul: Korean Broadcasting System. Review scripts and VOD (video on demand) services available (in Korean) at www.kbs.co.kr/special.

Cho, D. H., & Cho, I. S. (Producers). (2001, January 28). Kojang, ttonada: Wunbo Kim Ki-chìang ui sam kwa yesul [Master, farewell: Life and art of "Wunbo" Ki-chìang Kim]. In D. H. Cho (Executive Producer), *Iryo special* [*Sunday special*]. Seoul: Korean Broadcasting System.

Cho, D. H., & Nam, G. S. (Producers). (2001, Feburary 18). Poiji annun sarang: Ellen kajok iyagi. [Invisible love: Story of Ellen's family] In D. H. Cho (Executive Producer), *Iryo special* [*Sunday special*]. Seoul: Korean Broadcasting System.

Choy, B. Y. (1979). *Koreans in America.* Chicago: Nelson-Hall.

Eisenberg, J. D. (2003). *An introduction to Korean.* Available at www.langintro.com/kintro/

Hansen, K. A., & Bachu, A. (1995, August). *The foreign-born population: 1994* (*Current Population Reports,* P20-486). Washington, DC: U.S. Department of Commerce, Census Bureau. Available at www.census.gov/prod/1/pop/p20-486.pdf

Hur, S. V., & Hur, B. S. (1999). *Culture shock! Korea.* Portland, OR: Graphic Arts Center.

Kim, E. H., & Yu, E. Y. (1996). *East to America: Korean American life stories.* New York: New Press.

Korean Overseas Information Service. (2002). *Dynamic Korea 2002: CD-ROM.* Seoul: Author. Available at www.korea.net

Kwak, T.-H., & Lee, S. H. (Eds.). (1991). *The Korean-American community: Present and future.* Seoul, Korea: Kyungnam University.

Min, P. G. (1998). *Changes and conflicts: Korean immigrant families in New York.* Boston: Allyn & Bacon.

Mitchell, D. (1999, February). *Bridging the gap between expectations and realities: Special education in Asia and the Pacific.* Paper presented at the 15th Annual Pacific Rim Conference on Disabilities, Honolulu, HI.

National Center for the Dissemination of Disability Research Southwest Educational Development Laboratory. (1999). *Disability, diversity, and dissemination: A review of the literature on topics related to increasing the utilization of rehabilitation research outcomes among diverse consumer groups.* Available at www.ncddr.org/du/products/dddreview/index.html

National Institute on Disability and Rehabilitation Research. (2001). *National Institute on Disability and Rehabilitation Research (NIDRR) long range plan for fiscal years 1999–2003.* Available at www.ncddr.org/new/lrp.html

Pang, K.Y.C. (2000). *Virtuous transcendence: Holistic self-cultivation and self-healing in elderly Korean immigrants.* New York: Haworth.

Park, J., & Turnbull, A. P. (2001). Cross-cultural competency and special education: Perceptions and experiences of Korean parents of children with special needs. *Education and Training in Mental Retardation and Developmental Disabilities, 36*(2), 133-147.

Park, T. K. (2001, April 20). Changae nam ui il man un anida: Changaein yol e ahop saldaga tanghan pulhaeng [Disability is not somebody else's business: Nine out of ten people with disabilities have acquired the misfortune]. *JoongAng Ilbo [The Korea Central Daily of Hawaii]*, pp. 19, 23.

Reardon, T. (1996). Koreans. In J. G. Lipson, S. L. Dibble, & P. A. Minarik (Eds.), *Culture and nursing care: A pocket guide* (pp. 191-202). San Francisco: UCSF Nursing Press.

Stodden, R. A., Stodden, N. J., Kim-Rupnow, W. S., Thai, N. D., & Galloway, L. M. (2003). Providing effective support services for culturally and linguistically diverse persons with disabilities: Challenges and recommendations. *The Journal of Vocational Rehabilitation, 18,* 177-190.

7

An Introduction to Haitian Culture for Rehabilitation Service Providers

Erik Jacobson

Introduction

The goals of this chapter are twofold. The first goal is to provide service providers an overview of Haitian history and culture along with recommendations regarding working with Haitian clients. The need for such an overview is clear. News about Haiti is often limited to AIDS, voodoo, or political violence. This scarcity of information leaves service providers and others with less than a full picture of Haitian culture. This chapter does not attempt to capture every aspect of Haiti or of Haitian immigrant life in America. The Haitian community in the United States is diverse, and differences in social class and regional variations make it impossible to generalize about the population. However, there are patterns and customs that provide guidance in interacting with Haitian immigrants in the United States.

The second goal of this chapter is to encourage research on disability in the Haitian context. Unlike many of the other communities represented in this

Author's Note: This chapter was made possible through the work of Dr. Renald Raphael of the Haitian Family Support Program in Boston. The author relied on Dr. Raphael's insights on Haitian culture and his experiences dealing with disability issues. In addition, this chapter would not have been possible without the input of the families of the Haitian Family Support Program, whose experiences in trying to provide for family members with disabilities have taught me many lessons. They shared their thoughts, dreams, and disappointments with me over several years. This chapter was developed on their behalf, with the hope that their children can achieve their own dreams.

book, the Haitian community and disability issues within it have not been a focus of research. Most of the research on Haiti and Haitians has tended to deal with immigration patterns, language use, and health and sexuality issues. One reason for this is the lack of a rehabilitation or special education system in Haiti. Because the country does not have the resources to provide basic services, it is not surprising that there is little or no research on disabilities issues in Haiti. This chapter is a beginning and should help point to some important avenues of future research. It is my hope that service providers and researchers will take up this challenge.

Cultural Overview

GEOGRAPHY

Haiti occupies the western third of the Caribbean island of Hispaniola, which it shares with the Dominican Republic. Haiti is slightly smaller than the state of Maryland and lies just southeast of Cuba. Haiti is very mountainous. In fact, the word "Ayiti" was a Taino (the original inhabitants of Haiti) word for "land of mountains." The capital of Haiti is Port-au-Prince, which lies in the center of the country on the coast. Other important cities include Cap Haitien, which is in the northeast coast of the country, and Les Cayes, which is on the southwest coast.

Historically, 90% of Haiti was covered with forests. Now that figure is 4% or less. Most trees have been cut to make charcoal. This deforestation has led to erosion, rendering much of the land unharvestable. Runoff into rivers has also affected fishing. The economic and environmental downward spiral results in poor farmers harvesting more trees to earn money. Environmental conditions continue to deteriorate. What was once called the "Pearl of the Antilles" is now an ecosystem on the point of collapse.

COLONIAL HISTORY AND THE HAITIAN REVOLUTION

The original inhabitants of Haiti were the Tainos, who were part of the Arawak people. The island first came to the attention of Europeans when Christopher Columbus landed on it, thinking that he had arrived in India. Almost immediately, the colonizing powers of Europe set their sights on this island, rich with natural resources and stunningly beautiful lush forested mountains. During its early history of colonization, France, Spain, and England struggled to control parts of the island. Within decades of landing, Europeans wiped out the Tainos through outright slaughter and through the introduction of diseases to which the Tainos were not immune. This genocide meant that colonizers did not have the labor to collect the resources they wanted, so they imported slaves from the west coast of Africa. These slaves came from many different tribes and melded together to form the African population of Haiti.

There was a long period of struggle between European colonizers. By the early 1700s, France had established control over the western side of the island (Haiti), while Spain ruled the eastern side (the Dominican Republic). At this time, there were 40,000 colonists and almost 500,000 slaves within the French colony of Haiti (Farmer, 2003). There was also a sizable mulatto population. The mulattoes played an ambiguous economic and political role between the French and the African slaves. Slave owners, who for the most part owned large plantations, were known to be the most brutal of their class throughout the region. It was common practice for slave owners to torture and maim their slaves. Although there had been sporadic resistance to French rule, the final series of rebellions began in 1791. A former slave named Toussaint L'Ouverture took command of an army that consisted of rebellious slaves and mulattoes. The army killed thousands of colonists and chased the rest away; however, it was not an overnight success, taking years of violent struggle. Eventually, L'Ouverture was tricked into visiting Paris, where he was immediately jailed. He died in prison. Jean-Jacques Dessalines led the revolution to its conclusion, uniting the country and driving out the remaining vestiges of French colonial power. His rule was short. After his death in 1806, the country was ruled in the north by Henri Christophe and in the south by Alexandre Petion. Their control was short lived as well. Soon the country was reunited under Boyer (James, 1989; Ros, 1994).

This pattern of events has repeated itself throughout Haiti's history. During the 19th and 20th centuries, regime change was common. Often, rulers were violently forced out. The use of force was not limited to Haitians. From 1915 to 1934, the country was occupied by American troops. Diplomatic missions requested U.S. occupation in Haiti because they were concerned about the power vacuum created when a mob lynched President Vilburn Guillaume Sam. Although the willingness of the United States to intervene could be explained by its desire to protect the lives of Haiti's foreign residents, the fact is that the United States already had gunboats in Haitian waters. Occupying Haiti was one part of a larger U.S. effort to create an exclusive sphere of influence in the Americas. (Dash, 2001; Smith, 2001).

François Duvalier (known as Papa Doc) took control of the country in 1957. He ruled the country until 1971, when he stepped down in favor of his son Jean-Claude Duvalier (known as Baby Doc). The Duvalier regimes were marked by political violence conducted by Duvalier-associated militia known as the *Tonton Macoutes*. Violence and the economic conditions of the country caused thousands of Haitians to emigrate. After Baby Doc's exile in 1986, another series of governments followed. Some were sponsored by the military, whereas others were attempts at democracy. In 1990, a charismatic and politically progressive Catholic priest named Jean-Bertrand Aristide was elected president. Ousted by military coup, he returned to power in 1994 with U.S. president Bill Clinton's support and was re-elected in 2001. Tensions between Aristide's party and a confederation of opposition groups who are calling for another election created a political deadlock. This rift prevented the Haitian government from receiving promised international aid meant for development. In early 2004, opposition groups seized power and Aristide went into exile.

POPULATION

In 2000, the estimated population of Haiti was 8 million. Racial demographics are 95% black and 5% mulatto. Port-au-Prince has a population above 1,000,000. Across Haiti, 33% of the population lives in cities, while 67% lives in rural areas. With 700 people per square mile, Haiti is second only to Barbados for population density in the Caribbean. In the urban areas, women give birth to three to four children on average; in the countryside, they average seven. Infant mortality is 97 per 1000. There is one doctor per 4,000 inhabitants. Haitians have a life expectancy of 49 years (Arthur, 2002).

Hundreds of thousands of Haitians have created new Haitian communities in countries all over the world. After Port-au-Prince, New York City has the largest Haitian population of any city, followed by Miami and Boston, with Cap Haitien ranking fifth. These immigrant communities have been referred to as Haiti's "10th Department." This is a reference to Haiti's nine official governmental regions. Regardless of their distance from Haiti, the population of the 10th Department remains involved in Haitian politics and society. For this reason, the nation of Haiti is not geographically limited to the island of Hispaniola in terms of its influence.

ECONOMY

Haiti is often described as the poorest country in the Western Hemisphere. It has the lowest per capita income, and approximately 80% of the population lives in poverty. Many people do not have a steady job or income. Large areas of Port-au-Prince are occupied by people who left the countryside to look for work. Sections of the city, such as Cité Soleil, are infamous urban slums.

Almost 70% of Haitians depend on agricultural work, done mostly on small farms. The environmental devastation mentioned earlier leaves this workforce especially vulnerable to variability in weather and to the damage caused by crop erosion. Much of Haiti's economy depends on foreign aid and the resources of volunteer aid organizations. The track record of foreign investment and support is spotty. There is a history of large amounts of money being spent with little to show for the expense (Smith, 2001). Critics suggest that aid efforts have not focused on developing capacity for the long term. Projected development often stops soon after the aid agency and its adminis-trators leave the country.

Haiti's economy has been directly affected by policies of the United States, including a disastrous attempt to import American pigs. The pigs replaced Haitian pigs thought to have swine flu; however, the American pigs would not eat local food, and poor farmers were forced to buy expensive feed from American corporations. Many families went bankrupt trying to care for pigs that eventually died. This case is not an isolated example. It points to the fact that although Haiti may be the poorest country in the Western Hemisphere, its economy does not exist in isolation. Haiti is particularly vulnerable to policies generated in Washington.

One notable aspect of the Haitian economy is the role of group work. Communities engage in what is called a *konbit*, in which work and resources are shared. This is often called working *men-nan men*, or hand in hand. For example, on one day the whole community will help a single farmer harvest his crops. The next day, the same group may help a different farmer build a new farmhouse. Also notable is the key role played by traveling saleswomen called *Madan Sara*. These women go from town to town selling, trading, and exchanging goods. They are an informal distribution network. This aspect of the Haitian economy provides some independence for women.

LANGUAGES

Haiti has two official languages: Haitian Creole (also known as *Kreyòl*) and French. Kreyòl is spoken by 100% of the population, while 8–10% of Haitians can speak French. Like all French-based creoles, Kreyòl is a mixture of French and the African languages that Haitian slaves spoke. It is incorrectly described as a French dialect or, worse, as "broken French." In fact, it is a distinct language with its own vocabulary and grammar rules. This negative comparison to French is a legacy of colonialism. Even after Haiti became independent, French has been the language of government and of power for most of Haiti's history (Valdman, 1984). Although Kreyòl has increased in status, French continues to provide access to power and prestige. Not surprisingly, French is more likely to be spoken by urban elites than by farmers in the countryside. Because French appears to have more prestige than Kreyòl, many Haitians identify themselves as French speakers when they are not truly fluent in the language. This may create problems if parents in the United States introduce their Kreyòl-speaking children to bilingual teachers as French speakers. In some cases, children who underperform because of a linguistic mismatch are misdiagnosed as having a disability. Similarly, because of a lack of diagnostic resources in Kreyòl, some Haitian students in the United States are misdiagnosed as having mental disabilities because they are tested in languages they have not mastered (such as English or French).

EDUCATION

Access to education varies greatly. Although the Haitian constitution states that primary education is free and compulsory, primary school enrollment is about 65%. Overall, only about 56% of children are enrolled in primary and secondary schools, with less than 15% graduating from secondary school (U.S. Department of State, 2001). In rural areas, there are virtually no schools. The literacy rate in Haiti is about 45% (Arthur, 2002).

In America, Haitian immigrants with enough resources continue to send their children to Catholic schools or other private schools. Low-income families (whose children did not attend school in Haiti or who had limited schooling) rely on the public school system. Parents are concerned about placing students in classes based on age rather than on educational experience and abilities. Without special considerations, they sense that the gaps in their children's education will never be filled.

Regardless of social class, Haitian parents share a perspective on education that differs from what is expected in the United States. Haitian parents trust schools and teachers completely. They do not believe that they have a role in their children's education. They tend not to ask questions of people in authority. They are not accustomed to being proactive regarding their child's schooling and may not understand requests to attend meetings with teachers or administrators unless their child is in trouble. From the Haitian parents' perspective, education is the responsibility of the school, while discipline and moral development are the responsibility of the parents. In general, Haitian parents place a high value on education and have very high expectations of schools. Many immigrate to the United States in order to give their children a chance at a good education.

COMMUNICATION

Within Haitian culture, oral forms of communication are preferred over written. Communication often takes place on audiotape rather than through letters. Word of mouth (*teledjòl* in Kreyòl) is used to disseminate a wide range of information from gossip to political analysis. There are a limited number of televisions in Haiti; radio is the most important medium. Stations broadcasting in Kreyòl provide a way for Haitians to stay informed about national and international news. There are a few hundred private radio stations with programs varying from music and entertainment to talk shows. Political constraints on speech mean that talk shows allow Haitians to express themselves in ways that they might not in interpersonal settings. This use of media has continued in the United States. Cities with large Haitian populations have a number of radio stations. Cities such as New York, Boston, and Miami also have Haitian-related programs on local community access television stations.

History of Immigration to the United States

Although Haitians are often thought of as one of the United States' newer immigrant communities, Haitian immigration to the United States began almost as soon as the United States became a country. Haitians also played a key role in early American history. A small group of Haitians (the *Chasseurs Volontaires*) saw action in Georgia during the American Revolution. Jean-Baptiste DuSable, a Haitian explorer, was the founder of the settlement that became Chicago. By the early 1800s, there were significant Haitian communities in Louisiana, Baltimore, and Philadelphia. These communities helped elect Haitian immigrants to the United States Congress and created social clubs in each of these places.

From 1804 to 1898, Haiti was an immigrant-receiving nation (Fouron, 1983). In the early 19th century, runaway slaves from other colonies made their way to Haiti. At the end of the century, approximately 15,000 immigrants from the Middle East settled in Haiti (Arthur, 2002). However, as the 20th century brought continued economic and political violence, Haiti's emigration increased. In fact, 15% of the population left between 1957 and 1984 (Glick-Schiller et al., 1987). From the 1950s to the 1960s, Haitian immigrants to the United States were mainly mulatto elites and rural landowners. Because they were escaping what they thought was short-term political turmoil in Haiti, they did not think of themselves as permanent residents of the United States. Because the situation in Haiti did not improve, they were forced to remain here. For the most part, they have been completely subsumed into American society (Fouron, 1983).

The mid-1960s saw a large-scale revision in immigration laws in the United States, resulting in increased immigration from all over the globe. Encouraged by employers in the United States who had lost their low-wage workforce to the Vietnam War, many Haitians made their way to the United States. This wave of immigration was a demographically mixed population of

Haitians. On the whole, they were less skilled than individuals in the previous exodus (Fouron, 1983).

In the early 1980s, the exodus of the "boat people" began. Once they reached the shores of the United States, these unwanted and unpopular immigrants were put into detainment camps, often for long periods of time. Some of these camps were located in upstate New York and Texas, far away from family and friends. In 1982, 10,000 people marched in Washington, D.C., to protest U.S. government policy and to ask for the release of the "boat people."

When news of Duvalier's retreat from Haiti reached America, 25,000 Haitians gathered in the streets of New York City and sang in Kreyòl (Glick-Schiller et al., 1987). Most Haitians, however, did not return to their homeland. Although they can travel back to Haiti, most cannot stay there permanently. Life in Haiti is still difficult. With no money or credentials, many members of the diaspora remain trapped outside Haiti. These Haitians have built lives in the United States while remaining in touch with Haiti. Rather than having a single identity, Haitians in the United States have a dual focus—a transnational identity.

For many Haitian immigrants, ethnic identity within the United States is not the defining element of their lives. At times, they identify as an ethnic minority (Haitian), and at other times they identify as black. In Waters's (1996) study of immigrants from Haiti and the Caribbean, Haitian informants thought of themselves as hardworking, ambitious, militant about racial identity but not oversensitive about race, and committed to education and to the family. Immigrants in this study saw black Americans as lazy, disorganized, and obsessed with racial slights and barriers (Waters, 1996). Life might be hard here, but in many ways, it is better than anything they could expect in Haiti. A deep sense of relative deprivation serves to mitigate some of the oppression they experience. In this way, Haitian immigrants compare their current position to the economic situation in Haiti, rather than to that of their peers in the United States (Woldemikael, 1989).

Although subjects in Waters's study identified positive aspects of Haitian identity, for example "hardworking," some Haitian immigrants do not self-identify as Haitians. In reaction to prejudicial attitudes toward Haitians, some have become "undercover Haitians" who identify as anything (e.g., Canadian, French, Jamaican) other than Haitian (Zephir, 2001). Although this is the experience of a small portion of the Haitian immigrant population, it is significant. Outreach efforts aimed at Haitians may not reach all of the intended population. Some individuals and families may not want to seek service at a center defined as a "Haitian" center.

A current concern are differences in treatment of Haitian refugees in comparison to that received by others from their region, such as Cuban refugees.

Cubans who reach American shores are granted the status of political refugees. This is not the case for Haitians. Currently, Haitian refugees who come to the United States without documentation are kept in Immigration and Naturalization Services facilities while awaiting their hearings. Most are sent home at the end of the legal process. This difference in treatment is a key concern of the Haitian community in the United States.

Haitian Concepts of Disability

The stress inflicted on me by society is compounded by the stress I am already experiencing on a daily basis at home in dealing with my child's behavior.

—Haitian parent of a child
with a disability (January 2003)

It is rare for people in Haiti to discuss disabilities, whether acquired or lifelong. Disabilities are thought of as mysterious and dangerous. Typically, disabilities are perceived as having origins in the interaction of the natural and supernatural worlds, rather than being a medical issue. For example, a disability may be the result of a curse from a *lwa* (spirit) who is upset. Disability is a punishment—a sign that a *lwa* was not obeyed. Although *lwa* are voodoo in nature, the same type of explanation holds true within the framework of Christianity. Haitian Christians believe that going against God is the same as going against the *lwa*. God punishes those who do not obey. Disability may also be the result of a spell cast by an enemy. In this case, a disability may be a sign that the disabled individual mistreated someone else. Again, disability is a punishment. Although Protestants have campaigned against voodoo and belief in *lwa*, many still believe in spells. For this reason, regardless of religious orientation, disabilities are seen as supernatural in origin.

THE CONCEPT OF INDEPENDENCE

Haitians with disabilities want to lead independent lives. They value the same things other Haitians value, such as children, religion, and work; however, the path to independence is sometimes blocked by their families. Haitian parents have been described as overprotective with regard to both typical children and those with special needs. Even though they love their children dearly, parents view children with disability as "worthless." Parents may feel that these children cannot do anything and that they must do everything for them. This is especially the case with physical disabilities.

Many Haitian parents do not feel comfortable when their children turn 18 and are described as adults who are capable and responsible for their own lives. This feeling is more intense for parents of children with disabilities. Many Haitian parents who have children with mental disabilities choose to become their children's legal guardians so they can continue to make decisions for them.

Acquired and Lifelong Disabilities

The belief in supernatural origins holds true for both physical and mental disabilities, and for lifelong as well as acquired disabilities. Even when a traffic accident leads to a physical disability, it may be that an offended spirit caused the accident. It could also be the result of a spell. In this case, it was not really an accident, because someone set it upon the person. If there is a rumor about an individual's misbehavior, a disabling accident is taken as confirmation. This framework applies to both children and adults. If a baby is born with a disability, it is believed that someone in that baby's family, most likely a parent, did something wrong to a *lwa* or to another person. The child is innocent but must pay the price for their family member's transgression. Innocent adults may also acquire a disability because of a family member's misdeeds.

Most Haitians are afraid of disabilities and are uneasy around people with disabilities, who may be called "crazy," "stupid," or "possessed." They may also be labeled "nonfunctional" or "worthless." Because the disability may have been caused by an angry spirit, there is always the chance that the spirit may come after anyone who makes contact with a person with a disability. Similarly, people may be reluctant to touch an individual with a disability because the spell may transfer to them. Disabilities are treated as if they are contagious. Epilepsy is believed to be contagious, and people may be reluctant to come to the aid of a person having a seizure. A swimming pool will be considered contagious if someone with a disability goes in. Parents may not want their child socializing with a child who has a mental disability for fear that their child may develop the same condition.

Because people are afraid of disabilities and believe them to be a type of supernatural punishment, many parents keep their disabled children away from the public view. They do not want to expose their children to public ridicule, mocking, or teasing. This is true for both mental and physical disabilities, though perhaps it is a bit worse for mental conditions. They also do not want to expose their family to unwelcome questions. Evelyn Milorin, an activist for disability rights in Massachusetts, reports that her son Reggie was called an "animal" when she took him to her local church (personal communication, May 2002). They were soon forced to leave. She remembers clearly the words of the parishioners: "When you have an animal like this, you don't come to church." In response to these attacks, families may keep a child at home. Some even go as far as keeping the child inside a closet inside the home. This happens across social classes because both the elite and the working class have the same ideas about disabilities. For Christians, people with disability have sinned against God. Within voodoo, a *lwa* has been upset. These associations mean that there is always a reason for a disability: It is never just an accident or just genetic. Disabilities are part of the overall balance between the natural and the supernatural.

Haitian parents who have children with mental disabilities may be devastated by the fact that their high expectations about their children's education probably will not be met. They may think that their child will be a failure for life and not see the point of education or rehabilitation. Their frustration and disappointment may make it hard for them to consider any options. On the other hand, parents who reject that way of thinking may find themselves setting high expectations that most likely will not be met. These types of parents also end up dealing with disappointment and must struggle to determine the right set of expectations for their child.

What may be considered a disability in the United States may not be thought of that way in Haiti. For example, a child with an emotional disability would be thought of as willfully misbehaving, rather than dealing with a psychological condition. Gina Compère, a mother and community worker, explained that "as Haitian parents raised in a rigidly disciplined environment back home, we tend to interpret such child's behavior as rebellion or lack of submission. This is because disciplining a child in our culture is often perceived as complete submission of the child, and there is often no communication taking place to understand the reasons behind the child's behavior" (personal communication, January 2003). Similarly, a person with learning disabilities would not be recognized as needing supports but would be dismissed as "slow" or "stupid."

The Role of Family, Community, and Religion

FAMILY STRUCTURE AND ROLE OF THE COMMUNITY

In Haiti, households often consist of multiple generations. Adult siblings (and their families) may live together in a common space. The Haitian *lakay* (home) is geared toward the needs and strengths of the extended family. Usually, individuals do not dream of owning a house that is separate from their family. This preference for extended families living together causes problems for Haitian immigrants in the United States who cannot replicate their Haitian living arrangements because of economic pressures. It is not always possible for Haitian families to find places where they can all live together under one roof.

Haitian communities often consist of a dozen or so *lakay* grouped together to form a *lakou*. These families work together to complete their daily life tasks, such as farming or building new houses. This communal sharing of work is known as *konbit*. For many grassroots organizations, the *konbit* is the best way to accomplish their goals. Once a task has been defined as one that is shared by all, it is much easier to find people who are willing to work. There is a Haitian saying, "Ayisyen se krab," which translates to "Haitians are crabs." As with crabs in a bucket, when one person looks like he is going to escape, the others pull him back down. Haitian community life is complicated and sometimes contradictory. On one hand, there are communal efforts like *konbit*, and on the other hand, there is the idea that people will pull each other down.

The Haitian family and community have been described as transnational (Laguerre, 1998). The suggestion is that Haitians in the United States do not identify themselves solely as residents of America or of Haiti, but instead live a life that bridges both countries. This transnationality functions at a metaphorical or psychological level in terms of how Haitians think about their affiliations and concerns. It is true in a physical sense as well, because many Haitians make frequent trips between the two countries. Families are transnational in this sense, because family members will shift back and forth between the two countries. Children may have one parent in each country. Haitian parents in the United States may send their children to Haiti during difficult times, or if they feel that the child is misbehaving or picking up bad behavioral habits in the United States.

GENDER DIFFERENCES

Within the family, there is a traditional patriarchal dynamic (Bell, 2001). Men are considered to be the breadwinners. Their responsibility is to find paying work to support the family. At home, men typically do not get involved in child care. For this reason, men do not usually interact with the school system regarding their children's education. Both parents may consider education to be the job of schools and not the parents.

In Haiti, there are men who live with many women. These men may maintain more than one household. This type of polygamy is unsanctioned but not unusual. This pattern is particularly important to note when it comes to families containing individuals with disabilities. After a woman gives birth to a child with a disability, the father of the child may intentionally go out and impregnate another woman. He believes that if the second woman gives birth to a "normal" child, this provides evidence that the first child's disability is related to the child's mother rather than to himself. In these cases, the mother of the child with a disability is left on her own. In fact, many Haitian children with disabilities are cared for by single mothers. This behavior takes place in the United States as well. During community meetings for Haitian families that have children with disabilities, the vast majority of the participants will most likely be women.

RELIGION AND TABOOS

Like language, religion in Haiti is a very complex and sensitive topic. Most people would describe themselves as very religious, and religion affects almost every aspect of Haitian society. Although 90% of the country is Catholic and 10% is Protestant, Haiti is most famous (or infamous) for voodoo. Voodoo exists side by side with Christian faiths. Many Haitians see no contradiction in calling themselves Christians while engaging in voodoo practices. This is more often the case with Catholics. Catholicism in Haiti is very ritualistic and has adapted itself to local ritual. It is less likely that Protestants would describe themselves as believers in voodoo. There have been some Protestant-led attempts to diminish the role that voodoo plays in Haitian society.

Voodoo is a mixture of African and Haitian beliefs. It has a complex cosmology made up of a large number of spirits. These spirits are believed to have great influence on human beings, and for that reason, they must be respected. The term in Kreyòl for a spirit is *lwa*. Each family has a *lwa* associated with it. Daily life is conducted according to what would make these spirits happy. Voodoo practitioners believe *lwa* make their desires clear by possessing someone and speaking through them. *Lwa* also make their presence known in dreams. Often, *lwa* will ask a mother to dedicate her newborn or unborn child to them. If the *lwa*'s request is not honored, the *lwa* may possibly punish the mother or child by giving them a disability. Nobody wants to make a spirit angry, for the *lwa* will punish those who do not obey and respect them.

Voodoo has played a key role in Haitian history. Slave uprisings began with a secret voodoo ceremony. Voodoo helped provide some unity for the rebellious slaves. When Duvalier came to power in the late 1950s on a nativist platform, he used voodoo to support his position and power. The close association between the Duvaliers and voodoo continued throughout both men's regimes and complicates attitudes toward the religion now. The word "voodoo" conjures up Hollywood images of zombies and bizarre ceremonies. Many Haitians, particularly in America, are sensitive to being seen as voodoo worshippers, yet the practice continues in the United States.

Interactions With Service Providers

BELIEFS ABOUT REHABILITATION

When an individual has a disability, any decisions about rehabilitation are made by the family as a whole. Each member of the extended family is consulted. The preference is to address the needs of the individual with the disability through a support system within the family itself. There are times when individuals do not go beyond the family support system to explore other options for rehabilitation. They remain solely in the care of the family. If they seek help outside the family structure, they typically choose from two options: religious or institution-based rehabilitation.

Because disabilities typically are believed to be the result of an angry God or *lwa* or of a spell cast by an enemy, one option for rehabilitation is to turn to religion. Individuals or family may turn to Catholic priests or Protestant ministers to talk about their situation and condition. Becoming correct with God may cause the curse or spell to be lifted. This is also the case with voodoo-related beliefs. The individual or family may go to a *bōkō*, a traditional healer, or a *oungan*, somebody who knows about spirits. With the *bōkō* or *oungan*'s advice, they will use traditional medicines (such as herbal mixtures) to treat the disability.

If the family cannot provide support and the religious approach is not successful, individuals or family may turn to institutions that provide rehabilitation. For the most part, this means working with Westerners who staff and fund the few voluntary institutions that exist in Haiti. As part of the legacy of colonialism, many Haitians put faith in foreign-based nongovernmental organizations (NGOs), particularly if staffed by whites. Often, there is the expectation that these institutions will provide miracles. Friends pass along stories of quick and complete recoveries at NGO centers. These miraculous recoveries are the result of taking medication, so there is a belief that any medication that does not bring an immediate result is not worth taking. There is no understanding of rehabilitation as a process. This attitude may make it difficult to convince a Haitian client to follow a medicinal regimen.

A Haitian client who is taking medicine prescribed by a Western doctor may also be using traditional medicines prescribed by a *bōkō* or an *oungan* or given by the family. Depending on the medicines being taken, this doubling up may create harmful interactions.

PATTERNS IN THE UTILIZATION OF DISABILITY SERVICES

Five key themes emerge when thinking about the interaction of Haitians with the rehabilitation service system, as described below.

1. Haitians in the United States Do Not Fully
Utilize the Existing Rehabilitation System

Recent immigrants focus on the survival issues of money, food, and work. Health and disabilities are not viewed as priorities. Because of time constraints, parents cannot utilize the system. They may work two or three jobs and do not have time to go to meetings, or to explore the system. The extended family that exists in Haiti is not necessarily replicated in the United States. There are many single parents (especially mothers), with limited time and resources. For those who do have the support of their family, parents may still not interact with the system because of their preference to try to work through the family first. People may not go outside the family at all to look for support and rehabilitation.

Certain problems arise when individuals are not aware of their rights or responsibilities. For example, many Haitian parents find it difficult to understand the legal ramifications of their child turning 18. They believe that, regardless of their children's age, they are still the parents and have the right to make decisions on their children's behalf. This is especially true when the child has a disability, because parents may believe that the child is totally nonfunctional. It is difficult for them to grasp the legal aspects of independence. Parents who are acting as their child's guardian are confused by the idea that their status has to be recognized by authorities. They think that because they are already acting as a guardian, there is no need to make it official. Problems arise when these parents try to sign financial documents for their adult children.

2. Institutions Are Used as a Refuge From Stigma

For many people in Haiti, institutions that provide rehabilitation are important because they provide refuge. Because of the stigma of disability, some parents send their children to institutions to protect them from abuse by society. This could be seen as isolation. Placing children in an institution serves to hide them from the rest of society. In addition, parents view such a placement as creating a space for themselves. Although they would be happy if their child made progress toward rehabilitation or independent living, that may not be first and foremost in their minds. As one Haitian parent explains, "I tend to carry the negative feeling of isolation and shame, because of the way my child's behavior is regarded by society, which presses me to look at my child as a burden, rather than as any normal human being" (personal communication, October 2002).

3. Parents May Expect Immediate Results

For many Haitian parents, rehabilitation is not perceived as a long-term process that is achieved in incremental steps. Rehabilitation is seen more as a miraculous, instantaneous cure of what has plagued the individual (because of the supernatural origin of disabilities). This is true whether service is being provided by a religious figure (such as a priest or an *oungan*) or by doctors and teachers in a hospital or school. Parents have complete faith in Westerners and expect outside experts to be able to diagnose and cure their child quickly. With physical conditions, it may be possible to see progress such as walking. More abstract concepts like mental functions are harder to grasp, and measuring progress is difficult.

4. The Role of Consumers and Family in Rehabilitation Is Not Recognized

Josette Beaubrun, a Haitian disability rights advocate, believes that "Our Haitian parents need to be able to understand how to help their children and themselves and not to rely solely on the professionals to solve their problems for them. They need to learn to be involved and to be more confident and independent in the choices they will have to make for their children" (personal communication, May 2000). This is one of the greatest cultural differences Haitian families face. Haitians who receive rehabilitation are not proactive about their therapy. Because they have utter faith in the service provider, they do not ask questions. They will not ask the provider institution or the school questions about services. Self-advocacy is not traditionally practiced. Gina Compère notes that Haitian parents are not accustomed to "a system that expects constant direct interactions with the provider" (personal communication, January 2003). Haitian parents have no experience with a system that allows the right to disagree and to seek a second opinion.

Individuals or parents have no idea what they can offer as part of the rehabilitation process. They do not see themselves as possessing the resources or knowledge to participate and make a difference. This is less true of the rehabilitation of physical disabilities, because individuals may see that they can help in terms of motor skills, such as walking. However, if rehabilitation involves mental disabilities, most individuals do not see how they can participate. They may not view their attendance at a planning meeting for their child as crucial or even relevant.

5. Cross-Cultural Tensions Often Impede Service Provision

There may be cross-cultural miscommunication between a rehabilitation provider and a client. Two possible issues need to be addressed. First, because of their preference for oral communication and the rather high illiteracy rate,

Haitian clients may not have the experience with documentation that providers expect. They may not be used to obtaining and submitting official documents or keeping certain records. This can frustrate providers who cannot provide service without complete records. Second is the existence of what Haitians call "Haitian time." This refers to Haitians' sense of time management, which does not emphasize punctuality. It is not uncommon for a client to arrive 30 minutes after an appointment is scheduled. A Haitian client may not see this as an issue. Failure to be on time can cause many problems when dealing with service providers in the United States. As Dr. Renald Raphael notes, "Haitians often do not take time to plan, and so timing becomes an issue" (personal communication, December 2002). He also states that Haitian clients are likely to drop in without having made an appointment and will expect to be seen by the service provider.

Recommendations for Service Providers

It takes me so much resiliency and patience dealing with such a complex system, foreign to my language and my culture. And this journey never ends, because you face it every day at every corner of the system unless you find an appropriate place where you can pause and share your daily emotional and psychological struggles with those experiencing the same issues and sharing the same culture.

—Haitian parent (personal communication,
November 2002)

Places where individuals and families share the same culture can be positive, supportive, and healing. There will always be times when people in need of rehabilitation will be in places where service providers do not share their culture. However, it is possible for non-Haitian rehabilitation service providers to create places and programs responsive to Haitians' needs. A few recommendations are listed below.

OUTREACH

• Service providers need to recognize that outreach is necessary to get Haitian clients to come in for service. It is not enough to advertise a program and expect Haitian clients to attend. Haitians may not even be aware of rehabilitation programs. They may be relying upon a close family network to provide support. By receiving such services, clients and their families are admitting that a disability exists. Given the Haitian perception of the nature of disabilities, the decision to receive rehabilitation may be associated with fear of being shunned by the community.

- The best places for outreach may be places that need to be educated about disabilities. Because most Haitians attend church at least weekly, churches are perfectly positioned to promote a program or service to the Haitian community. Given the prejudice that exists within the church membership, it is not an easy task to conduct outreach in this manner. The difficulty makes it necessary to raise the consciousness of the community.

- To be most effective, outreach efforts should be done orally (such as radio or announcements at meeting places) rather than through flyers or brochures. Whenever possible, Kreyòl should be used, with English as a second choice.

ENCOURAGING AND SUSTAINING PARTICIPATION

- Given the lack of rehabilitation programs in Haiti, clients and their families may have limited understanding of what the possibilities are for rehabilitation. They may need to be convinced that a mental disability does not mean "permanent failure" (as one Haitian parent put it). Clients and their families need to be informed about programs and supports.

- Potential clients and their families need to be introduced to new ways of looking at disability. For example, the nature of emotional or behavioral disabilities needs to be explained to clients or their families before they agree to start rehabilitation.

- Clients and their families will have to be encouraged to be proactive during the rehabilitation process. Providers should be explicit about being asked questions. It may be necessary to model asking the kinds of questions that make for better service.

- Consumers and their families may expect quick results and benefits. They will discontinue a program if they think that it is a failure. If results are not what the consumers expect, they will feel deceived and not provided for. From the first meeting, it should be emphasized that rehabilitation is not quick. The results of the program, and how these results can be recognized, should be explained.

- Take time to review the documentation that will be necessary for clients and their families to have and maintain. Read the list of required documents with the clients and families, rather than suggesting that they read it at home on their own. Explain the need for each document and stress that service may be impaired if proper documentation is not provided when requested.

- Be aware of issues related to the prestige of French within the Haitian community. For example, a request for a French interpreter does not necessarily indicate fluency in French. At the same time, a client may be offended if you begin by offering a Kreyòl interpreter. Understanding a client's true linguistic background and current needs is necessary.

- If a Haitian client arrives late, it is appropriate to provide service at that time. However, it should be stressed that the expectation is that they arrive on time. Although some accommodation may be made, providers should be explicit about their policies. This is also true about unscheduled visits.

INTERPERSONAL INTERACTIONS

- As with all consumers, trust is a key issue. One way to establish trust is to sympathize with the pressures that Haitian immigrants are facing. Acknowledging the specific stressors that exist (language issues, being separated from extended family, etc.) calms a Haitian consumer's fears. Just listening without saying anything brings positive benefits.

- Be sensitive to the specifics of Haitian identity. Recognize Haitians as distinct from other Caribbean people and as distinct from African Americans. Note that all creoles are not alike. Do not confuse Haitian Creole (a French-based Creole) with Capeverdean Criolu (a Portuguese-based Creole). Many Haitians report being frustrated with service providers who do not have a clear sense of who they are and where they come from.

- Be sensitive to religious topics, and be aware that religion may arise in any conversation. Consumers may expect you to share their views about God's role in rehabilitation ("God willing") and the value of prayer. For this reason, you will need to be comfortable talking about religious issues, regardless of how you feel. At the same time, do not preface your comments with thoughts about religion. Wait for the consumer to introduce the topic. Remind yourself not to assume or generalize. This is particularly true regarding voodoo. Although some Haitians embrace voodoo history and faith, it is a sensitive topic. It is best not to ask questions about it with clients whom you do not know very well. You may come across as yet another non-Haitian who wants to find out about zombies.

Conclusion

One goal of this chapter was to encourage research on disability issues within the Haitian context (both in the United States and in Haiti). More intensive ethnographic studies and assessments of Haitian clients' responses to current service provision methodologies would provide a solid foundation for future work with this community. However, this call for research also applies to individual service providers. Cultural overviews, such as this one, are by necessity general in nature and often do not capture the rich, complex, and at times contradictory nature of communities and individuals as they go about living their everyday lives. Indeed, it may be the case that unreported specificities are the most important thing for understanding the needs of clients. For this reason, service providers are encouraged to begin to develop their own theories about disabilities within the Haitian community by going to the source and dialoguing with Haitian clients, their families, and their peers.

This chapter provides some guidelines for entering into such a dialogue. First and foremost, disabilities may be seen as supernatural in origin. Ideas about rehabilitation, inclusion, or development must all be understood in a context that is framed by a belief that accidents or disabilities don't "just happen." In addition, Haitian clients and their families tend to cede authority over medical or educational issues to professionals (such as teachers and doctors). They may be unused to being asked their opinions, and they may not exhibit the same sort of proactive behavior to which service providers in the United States tend to respond. For this reason, do not expect the dialogue to happen overnight. With time and patience, trust can be developed, and Haitians and non-Haitians can come together to have frank, productive conversations about the nature of disabilities as well as the process and promise of rehabilitation.

References

Arthur, C. (2002). *In focus: Haiti.* New York: Interlink Books.

Bell, B.(2001). *Walking on fire.* Ithaca, NY: Cornell University Press.

Dash, J. M. (2001). *Culture and customs of Haiti.* Westport, CT: Greenwood.

Farmer, P. (2003). *The uses of Haiti.* Monroe, ME: Common Courage Press.

Fouron, G. (1983). Black immigrant dilemma in the United States: The Haitian experience. *Journal of Caribbean Studies, 3*(3), 242-265.

Glick-Schiller, N., DeWind, J., Brutus, M. L., Charles, C., Fouron, G., & Thomas, A. (1987). All in the same boat? Unity and diversity in Haitian organizing in New York. In C. R. Sutton & E. M. Chaney (Eds.), *Caribbean life in New York City: Sociocultural dimensions* (pp. 182-201). New York: The Center for Migration Studies of New York.

James, C.L.R.J. (1989). *The Black Jacobins.* New York: Vintage.

Laguerre, M. S. (1998). *Diasporic citizenship.* New York: St. Martin's.

Ros, M. (1994). *Night of fire.* New York: Sarpedon.

Smith, J. M. (2001). *When the hands are many.* Ithaca, NY: Cornell University Press.

U.S. Department of State. (2001). *Haiti: Country reports on human rights practices—2001.* Available at www.state.gov/g/drl/rls/hrrpt/2001/wha/8332.htm

Valdman, A. (1984). The linguistic situation of Haiti. In C. R. Foster & A. Valdman (Eds.), *Haiti—today and tomorrow: An interdisciplinary study* (pp. 77-99). New York: University Press of America.

Waters, M. (1996). Ethnic and racial identities of second-generation Black immigrants in New York City. In A. Portes (Ed.), *The new second generation* (pp. 171-196). New York: Russell Sage Foundation.

Woldemikael, T. (1989). A case study of race consciousness among Haitian immigrants. *Journal of Black Studies, 20*(2), 224-239.

Zephir, F. (2001). *Trends in ethnic identification among second-generation Haitian immigrants in New York City.* Westport, CT: Bergin and Garvey.

8

An Introduction to Mexican Culture for Service Providers

Sandra Santana-Martin

Felipe O. Santana

Introduction

My (Felipe) left arm felt like a dead branch hanging from a tree, and I thought I would never be able to move it again. My shoulder was frozen from my diabetes; I had too many calcifications. When I tried to move it, excruciating pain resulted. My right arm was beginning to feel the same way. I recall feeling fearful, thinking I was going to be without movement in my arms. My doctor referred me to the best physical therapist in the city. The following morning, my wife, Delia, drove me to my appointment. In the Latino culture, having a relative go with the patient to see a doctor for the initial assessment as moral support is the norm. Once it is time for the patient to undress, the relative will normally wait in the waiting room and later return to the exam room to be with the patient, but this time my wife was not allowed to come in at all. The physical therapist asked me all the pertinent questions and then told me that he was going "to see if it was true that the Latinos were as macho as we claimed to be." While he was manipulating my shoulder and throughout the remaining procedures, the physical therapist kept commenting on my Latino origin and my lack of machismo because I was screaming from pain. I never returned for my second appointment—not because of his skills, but because of his lack of cultural competency.

I was diagnosed with Type II diabetes 20 years ago and was treated at the Samsun Clinic in Santa Barbara, one of the best diabetes treatment centers in the nation. My endocrinologist was an Argentine physician. I chose her because of her reputation, not because she was Latina. The same week that I went to physical therapy for my frozen shoulder, my wife drove me to my regular appointment with my endocrinologist. My wife and I went into her office, and after she saw my arm and I explained to her what happened, she called in one of the orthopedists, who happened to be Caucasian. After a brief examination, he asked if my wife was with me. I responded, "Yes." He said, "Tell her to come in."

My wife came into the room, where the doctor explained to both of us that an intervention needed to be done immediately. He was going to put me under anesthesia and "windmill" my left arm to break the adhesions in my shoulder. We agreed to the intervention. He went out of his way to make us feel comfortable.

Immediately after the procedure, while still under the influence of anesthesia, I was taken to the rehabilitation center, where I received a massage and did some exercises. When the procedure was completed, I left the clinic relieved and was able to move my shoulder. That night, I slept solidly. That was a big difference between both providers: One was culturally competent, and the other was not. I recovered, with few limitations, in a culturally competent environment.

This experience is not uncommon. Many health care professionals have not been exposed to other cultures, nor have they been trained to treat individuals from other cultures. Being culturally competent is extremely important so that the patient will be properly diagnosed and treated and the desired outcome will be achieved.

How does one become culturally competent? In terms of service providers, competencies are attitudes, knowledge, and skills that health professionals must possess in order to deliver high-quality care (Coursey, 1998). Competencies are also attributes of individual providers, though it is unlikely that a single provider will have all those necessary to treat all persons of a different culture (Hartman, Young, & Forquer, 2000). Having a general understanding of particular populations, however, is the first step in achieving this goal.

The purpose of this chapter is to provide information about Mexican culture to help providers increase their competence in serving this growing population. One must keep in mind, however, that the Mexican and Mexican American cultures are complex and heterogeneous. This chapter will present the "skeleton," or the basic foundation of the Mexican culture, with emphasis on the poor and uneducated. As with any community, change occurs and cultures fluctuate under the influences of migration, acculturation, oppression, and change in socioeconomic status.

Cultural Overview

The roots of Mexican culture are mainly from the Spanish and the native Indians of Mexico. To be more specific, according to the Mexicans, these two ethnic groups are known as the *mestizo* and the *Indian*. Historically, the term *mestizo* describes someone with mixed European (mostly Spanish) and indigenous heritage. They are also known as the whites, who were themselves divided into *criollo* (those born in the New World) and *peninsular* (those born in Spain). In current society, *mestizo* has become synonymous with Mexican culture (Merrill & Miró, 1997). This cultural root is the dominant Mexican culture that we know today, which will be the subject of this chapter. It includes the importance of family, respect, trust, and community and how these cultural issues can affect the rapport between patient and service provider.

The Indian or indigenous people of Mexico use an indigenous language in daily speech, remain active in village communal affairs, and participate in religious ceremonies rooted in native traditions (Merrill & Miró, 1997). They also tend to separate themselves from the dominant *mestizo* people. Currently, about 7.5% of the Mexican population speak an Indian language and identify themselves as Indian, although 79% of them know Spanish (Merrill & Miró, 1997). Therefore, the Spanish-speaking *mestizo* culture has influenced them as well.

It is extremely important to note that this chapter makes generalized statements about Mexican culture in order to identify common themes. Mexicans, however, are a heterogeneous group with different cultures in each region of the country.

History of Immigration to the United States

The first step in understanding the culture of an immigrant group within the United States is to know its history and the conditions that led its people to immigrate to this country. It is commonly known that most of the Mexicans of today are the descendants of the native Indians of that region and the Spaniards who conquered them. Some Mexicans are also descended from the French or from Africans as well. Contrary to a popular belief that all Mexicans have brown skin, many Mexicans have white skin and others have black skin. Mexico is as diverse as the United States in terms of racial differences, dialects, and political beliefs. Mexico also has regions that have their own cultures.

The present population of Mexico is nearly 105 million, 40 million of whom live at or below the poverty line. Mexico City is the largest city in the world, having surpassed Tokyo a few years ago (*The World Factbook: Mexico*, 2003). The population of metropolitan Mexico City is 22 million ("Mexico City," 2003). The minimum wage is approximately US$5 per day, but few employers in the city pay the minimum wage.

Although factories and assembly plants raised income levels, Mexico has never really had a middle class. Approximately 20% of Mexicans live according to upper-class standards. They have heavy investments in the United States and buy goods imported from the north. Mexicans have a seasonal agricultural orientation, and each year farmworkers are employed on the land for a certain length of time before returning home. This orientation makes factory work difficult for them to accommodate (Nelson & Rubi, 1999). Many Mexicans have migrated to the United States hoping to escape poverty, but this was not always the case.

Much of the western and southwestern United States was Mexican land until the war between the United States and Mexico (1846–1848) in which Mexico lost nearly half of its territory. Mexican inhabitants of ceded lands were offered U.S. citizenship with the promise of property rights. Some 80,000 Mexicans who originally lived in the new U.S. territory were ancestors of today's fourth-, fifth-, and sixth-generation Mexican Americans (de Paula, Lagaña, & Gonzalez-Ramirez, 1996). Some assimilated the Anglo culture, while others retained their Mexican culture.

In the late 1800s, Mexican laborers were imported to build railroads in the United States. During the World War I labor shortage in the United States, Mexicans were again recruited to help in the labor force. Between 1921 and 1930, Mexico experienced endemic poverty and Christian religious persecution. As a result, many Mexicans migrated to the United States and laid the foundation for the growth of the Mexican American population. Before 1929, the movement of persons between border communities was relatively uninterrupted. After 1929, immigration policies created a divide between Mexicans and their Mexican American kin based on whether or not they were "documented." During the Great Depression, about 458,000 Mexicans living in the United States were repatriated and deported to Mexico, and by 1940, there were more U.S.-born Mexican Americans than Mexican-born.

In 1965, the Mexican government established the Border Industrialization Program (BIP), which created a zone for foreign companies on the Mexican side of the U.S.-Mexican border. These are known as the *maquiladora* districts, in which the factory owners have special privileges, such as freedom from tariffs, in-bond importation of parts and equipment, and 100% ownership of the plant (Heyman, 1991). People from all over Mexico flocked to the *maquiladoras* to find employment, but because of the large number of potential employees and a limited number of positions, a job shortage resulted, leading to an increase in undocumented immigration to the United States. The 1986 Immigration Reform and Control Act increased the likelihood of family reunification. More skilled persons settled in urban centers and competed for jobs in U.S. service industries.

Overall, between 1900 and 1990, 2.5 million Mexicans legally crossed into the United States. An undetermined number of immigrants, provoked by the political and economic instability in Mexico, have crossed without documentation.

Fortunately, many Mexican immigrants do find a better life in the United States. They have the highest labor force participation of any ethnic group because they are willing to take jobs that most Americans would not. Migrant farmworkers constitute 42% of the population employed in seasonal agricultural work in the United States. They often work six or sometimes seven days a week in the fields, their backs constantly bent for 10 hours a day on farms that often don't have bathrooms. The majority of the farmworkers (70%) are foreign-born, and 90% of those are Mexicans. In California, half of the estimated one million farmworkers are migrants, and as many as 98% are Mexican. Unfortunately, for all their hard work, they are one of the poorest segments of the population, with a median personal income of $2,500 to $5,000 a year (Alderete, Vega, Kolody, & Aguilar-Gaxiola, 2000).

There is no evidence to suggest that Latinos as a whole work any less hard than their non-Latino counterparts, yet only 11% of Latino immigrants in the United States are employed in managerial/professional positions, compared to 30% for native-born workers. In the case of Mexican-born persons in the United States, not only are they one of the poorest groups in this country, but they are also the group most likely to not have health insurance. It is estimated that 46% of Mexican-born persons in the United States are not insured (Schmidley & Campbell, 1999). Moreover, whether or not they have insurance, they are less likely to utilize health services (Trevino, Moyer, Valdez, & Stroup-Benham, 1992). The many reasons for this include language barriers, limited knowledge of systems and services, unfamiliarity with acceptable help-seeking behaviors, possible distrust of the professional service system, and perceived discrimination by agencies or service providers (Bailey et al., 1999). Some of these factors will be discussed in more detail later in the chapter.

Mexican Concepts of Disability

In general, disability is viewed in the Mexican culture as either an act of God or as punishment for something one has done. Physical disability is more accepted than a mental/psychological disability, probably because the parents, especially the mother, blame themselves if their child is not psychologically "normal." In general, a physical disability is viewed as "normal"; people with physical disabilities appear to be treated naturally.

In the United States, disability is viewed as a limitation on a person's ability to take part in economic and social life. The goal of rehabilitation is to enable the individual to be as independent as possible so that he or she can have a "normal" life.

This is in great contrast with the predominant view in Mexico. In Yucatán, Mexico, for example, the native language of Zapotec does not even have a word for "disability" (Holzer, 1999). Persons with disability contribute as much to society as anyone else. People in Yucatán do not need to work with the sole aim of making money in order to be valued by family and society. A broad range of activities earn recognition and are considered as important as work at the market, the economic center of the town. The activities include giving each other time and attention, massaging one another, paying mutual visits, taking part in festivities, helping neighbors, and simply sitting with others and exchanging views. Those who need support are supervised and cared for by the family. In Yucatán, there are no "retirement" homes, nursing homes, or homes for persons with disabilities (Holzer, 1999).

According to Holzer (1999), Western societies, in a global sense, are *patriarchal* in that work is correlated with money and the economy. In the Yucatán culture, as well as others in Mexico, the society is more *matriarchal*. What is most important is the *mother's work*—preservation and creation of life. Money and a commodity-based economy are viewed as ideals that remove one from what is most essential in life.

The patriarchal world ignores the mother's work, which makes it difficult for someone in that society to be accepted as a dependent being whose needs must be met by others. In the matriarchal world, being dependent and cared for is part of life. In addition, the women's production and distribution of food is considered "work" and "economy." Therefore, persons with disabilities in Yucatán are viewed as contributing to society, not only because of their sheer existence but also because the activities in which they can participate, including cooking, are valued. Persons with disability view themselves as part of a community. In addition, being dependent is viewed not as a negative attribute but as a way of life.

In summary, views of disability in Mexico are quite different from those held in the United States. In Mexico, people with a disability is accepted by society and the family. It is the community's and family's role to take care of them. The pressure is not for them to become more independent; it is for them to be more functional within the family.

When persons with disability are nearly nonfunctional, they are expected to stay within a family member's home until God takes them away. The following example illustrates this.

My (Felipe's) mother developed Alzheimer's disease many years ago. My father insisted that my mother stay at home so that he could take care of her. He was in his late 70s. They lived close to my wife, my daughter, and myself, and we were able to help my father take care of her. As she progressively got worse, it was more difficult for him to care for her. I convinced him that he needed to hire someone who could clean and cook, as well as someone who could bathe my mother three times a week. He was reluctant at first to have this help because it was his responsibility as a husband to take care of his wife. As time went on, however, having the helpers in the apartment became more acceptable to him—they became more familiar with the home, and my father became more familiar with them. It may also have been a mental necessity for my father to have them in the apartment for peace of mind.

When it came to placing my mother into a convalescent home, however, he refused. One night, he awoke to the smell of gas in the apartment. My mother apparently had left it on after cooking. Even after this, my father was still not convinced that my mother needed care at a convalescent hospital for Alzheimer's patients. Although my wife and I were always around to help, if necessary, my father did not want a great deal of help.

One Sunday, my wife and I went to Santa Barbara for the day. When we returned, the answering machine was filled with messages from my father. It seemed like we literally flew over to my parents' home, only to find my mother in between the toilet and the bathtub. That morning, my father had taken her to the washroom, but with her coordination faltering, she sat on an "empty object" that she thought was the toilet, and she fell to the floor. My father was 88 years of age at the time and was unable to lift my mother off the floor. He spent the majority of the day attempting to pick her up but couldn't until we arrived. That night, he asked me to place her in a convalescent hospital, where he spent every day with her, next to her bed. In his situation, it did not matter what the therapist, doctor, or nurses had to say. He needed to know on his own that she was well. She died only 3 months after being placed in the hospital.

This is an example of the family's sense of responsibility for personally taking care of other family members. In general, if there is a child in the family who is not working, the person with the disability will move to that child's home. In the Mexican and Latino culture, in general, it is expected that the parents will live with a child and be cared for by that child in old age. Of course, there are exceptions. That is why it is important that each individual be assessed individually, but with the cultural context in mind. In general, however, children do not feel as though caring for an aging parent or a family member with disability is a burden. They look upon it as a responsibility.

Illness Beliefs

For the purpose of this chapter, it is important to understand not only the Mexican cultural view of disability but also some culture-bound illness beliefs that may affect treatment. In Mexican culture, there is no clear separation of physical and mental illnesses. It is believed that there must be a balance between the individual and the environment; otherwise, one may acquire a disease. Emotional, spiritual, social, and physical factors are major contributing forces to illness, in addition to the humoral theory, God, spirituality, and interpersonal relationships. The causes of illness are God's will or unacceptable behavior. Shame may be associated with genetic defects. Physical disability is usually more accepted than mental disabilities. Furthermore, illness is seen as a social crisis and is experienced by the entire group. Institutionalization is not common; more often, the family cares for persons with disability.

FOLK ILLNESSES

Empacho (intestinal obstruction) consists of abdominal pain, vomiting, constipation, loss of appetite, or bloating caused by adherence of food to intestinal walls.

Mal de ojo (evil eye) is a sudden downturn in physical or emotional health of an infant or young child (and sometimes an adult) caused by "admiration" (jealousy) of a person with powerful eyes. To admire an infant *without touching* puts the infant at increased risk for *mal de ojo*. Symptoms include fitful sleep, crying without apparent cause, diarrhea, vomiting, and fever.

Susto (fright, shock) manifests as malaise, insomnia, irritability, depression, nightmares, and wasting away. The illness is attributed to a frightening event that causes the soul to leave the body. Symptoms may appear any time from days to years after the fright is experienced. Some believe that *susto* can result in death.

Antojos (cravings) is the failure to satisfy food craving in pregnant women. It is believed to cause defect or injury to the fetus. For example, "strawberry nevus" (birthmark) may be explained by unsatisfied cravings for strawberries.

Nervios (nerves) refers both to a general state of vulnerability to stressful life events and to a syndrome brought on by difficult life circumstances. Symptoms include headaches, easy tearfulness, irritability, stomach disturbances, sleep difficulties, nervousness, inability to concentrate, trembling, tingling sensations, and *mareos* (dizziness with occasional vertigo-like exacerbations).

Ataque de nervios (attack of the nerves) is understood to occur as a direct result of a stressful event relating to the family (e.g., death, separation, divorce, conflicts, witness of trauma). Symptoms include uncontrollable shouting, attacks of crying, trembling, heat in the chest that rises into the head, and verbal and physical aggression. A general feature is a sense of being out of control. Some individuals report amnesia during the "event" but regain usual levels of functioning.

Given their holistic beliefs, some Mexicans use home and folk remedies to treat certain illnesses. *Curandismo* is the use of traditional Mexican healers who attempt to cure imbalances by using prayer, pledges to religious and supernatural forces, and rituals involving candles, artifacts, and herbal baths. The *curandera,* or female folk healer, is believed to be chosen by God to heal. *Yerbalistas* (herbalists) use herbs, usually in teas or broths, as home remedies.

Acquired and Lifelong Disabilities

In the Mexican population, some illnesses and disabilities appear to be common. The following statistics represent the Mexican and Mexican American population in the United States (Smedley, Stith, & Nelson, 2002).

- Diabetes is twice as prevalent as in the majority population in the United States.
- Hypertension is common.
- Obesity and being overweight are common, with 63.9% of Mexican American men and 65.9% of Mexican American women being obese or overweight, compared with 61% of European American men and 49.2% of European American women.
- The incidence of cervical cancer in Hispanic women is double that of non-Hispanic, European American women.
- Although Hispanic women have a lower incidence of breast, oral cavity, colorectal, and urinary bladder cancers, their mortality rates from these are similar to that of the majority population.

Some of the characteristics, such as a higher prevalence of diabetes and obesity, may be due to the Mexican diet, which includes large proportions of beans and *tortillas,* which are the staples in most meals, in addition to rice. Fresh fruits and vegetables also are common in the diet, including tomatoes, which are used widely for a variety of sauces and salsa. Meat is served sparingly because of cost and its fat content. Chicken is used most often, especially to make *caldo de pollo,* a soup given to recuperating individuals. Tamales are another staple of the Mexican meal. As one can see, most of these meals are high in carbohydrates and fat and are low in protein—a recipe for causing diabetes. Given that some of these dishes, such as tamales, have such a strong cultural tradition, once patients are diagnosed with diabetes or obesity, it is difficult for them to change their eating habits.

There are subtle differences between the different regions of Mexico and within the Mexican culture at large. For example, the people from Yucatán are mostly Aztec descendants, who are known to be very stoic, mild, pleasant, and able to handle pain. The people from Michoacán have a reputation of being very assertive and tough. The people from Chiapas will defend their rights and will never let the "White Mexican" conquer them.

If we were to focus on the individual regions, this chapter would be extremely long. For the purposes of brevity, we will discuss generic aspects of the Mexican culture. This discussion should be used as a guideline, not as a complete assessment, given that each person is an individual, and the service provider must assess each person accordingly. The provider must also keep in mind the level of acculturation of the individual. This will have a great impact on cultural views and behaviors of that individual. This chapter focuses on Mexicans who are poor, are unacculturated, and have lower levels of formal education. Such people are typical immigrants to the United States, hoping to make enough money to support themselves and their family back in Mexico. Before describing specific cultural habits, beliefs, and behaviors, one of these "influences" needs to be clarified—how acculturation affects one's culture.

Acculturation

Acculturation is the degree to which a member of a culturally diverse group—in this case, Mexicans—accepts and adheres to the values, attitudes, beliefs, and behaviors of his or her own group and those of the dominant (majority) group—in this case, Anglo Americans (Berry, Kim, Minde, & Mok, 1987). Berry and his colleagues divided acculturation, or the lack of it, into the following four categories.

1. *Integration:* The person maintains his or her own culture but also incorporates many aspects of the majority culture. Integration produces a "bicultural identity."

2. *Assimilation:* The person accepts the majority culture while relinquishing his or her own culture.

3. *Separation:* The person withdraws from the dominant culture and accepts only his or her own culture.

4. *Marginalization:* The person does not identify with either his or her own culture or the majority culture.

Knowing a client's level of acculturation is important because it may affect his or her treatment outcome. For example, those who are highly acculturated or assimilated into the Anglo culture may be more responsive to the therapeutic interventions commonly used in the United States, whereas those not highly acculturated or assimilated may require an approach more relevant to their native culture. We should note here that research has shown that Mexican Americans who try to "Americanize," or assimilate, have more psychological problems and drug use than those who retain their language, cultural ties, and rituals (Falicov, 1996). Acculturation thus may not only affect one's cultural identity but also affect one's mental and physical health.

The Role of Family, Community, and Religion

FAMILY

Possibly the most significant value of Mexicans (and those of most Latino cultures) is the value of *familismo*–family unity, welfare, and honor. The emphasis is on the group—not the individual, as in the Anglo culture—and on family commitment, obligation, and responsibility (Garcia-Preto, 1996). Mexicans have a deep sense of family and family loyalty, are reliant on extended family and social support networks, and emphasize interpersonal relatedness and mutual respect (Forehand & Kotchisk, 1996). Family comes first; therefore, if a major decision needs to be made, the immediate and extended family are involved in the process. Traditionally, the father or oldest male is head of the household and holds ultimate decision-making authority. The mother, however, holds greater influence over the children throughout their life span.

Children are raised in a protective environment and are expected to be obedient and respectful. *Respeto* is extremely important to the Mexican people. It ensures smooth interpersonal relationships through respect for a given individual (de Paula et al., 1996). Respect is given to elders, parents, and people in authority, and it is expected in return. As de Paula and her colleagues stated, "Because of the implied social power that health care providers have as healers, failure to demonstrate *respeto* to Mexican American clients could be perceived as oppressive, classist or racist" (p. 214).

Children are also expected to work hard and "do better" than the previous generation. They usually live in their home until they are ready to get married and start a family of their own. When their parents become older or sick, the children take care of them by having them move into their home (Bailey et al., 1999).

Family also provides a sense of community. Studies show that Mexican families tend to live near relatives and close friends, have frequent interactions with family members, and exchange a wide range of goods and services that include baby-sitting, temporary housing, personal advice, nursing during times of illness, and emotional support (Muller & Espenshade, 1985).

Men tend to have more power and control in the Mexican or Mexican American home than do women. The men work and provide for the family, while the women are expected to stay home and care for the children, the sick, and elders. These traditional gender roles are known as *machismo* and *marianismo*. It should be understood that gender roles and expectations may often be somewhat different from those that are described here due to differences in class, region, and acculturation. However, the conceptual distinction between *machismo* and *marianismo* may be helpful as a starting point, but not as an ending point, in understanding family dynamics.

Machismo or "macho" is a term that many non-Latinos use on a daily basis without understanding its cultural relevance. It is usually used negatively, as demonstrated earlier by one of the authors' experiences. The positive connotation of *machismo* is that the male is the provider and is responsible for the welfare and honor of his family. He protects his wife and family from all dangers, gives up his seat for women or the elderly, and will sacrifice anything for the family's benefit. He is also very sensitive, romantic, and responsible; he has a keen sense of his own dignity and is always ready to respond to any real or fancied offense (Gil & Vazquez, 1996). The men take a lot of pride in taking care of their family and making them happy. The other side to this, however, is that the male is considered superior to the female based solely on his gender. He is associated with power over women, which is expressed in romanticism and jealousy of a fiancé or wife. Within this context, boys are given greater freedom of movement, are not expected to share in domestic responsibilities, and are encouraged to be sexually aggressive. Boys are seen as strong in nature and not needful of the protection received by girls, who are seen as weak by nature. Males are expected to be strong, rational, intellectual, authoritarian, independent, and brave. As can be expected, this is a difficult role to maintain.

Marianismo is based on Catholic veneration of the Virgin Mary, who is both a virgin and a mother. The concept underlying *marianismo* is that females are spiritually superior to men and therefore capable of enduring all sufferings inflicted by men (Gil & Vazquez, 1996). In keeping with the values associated with the Virgin Mary, they are expected to remain virgins until they are married. As mothers, they are to be like the Madonna and to deny themselves on behalf of their children and husbands. In other words, they are to be like martyrs. This concept goes hand in hand with *hembriso*, characterized by a woman's devotion to home and family. It is about sacred duty, self-sacrifice, and chastity. Women must dispense care and pleasure but not receive them. When women become mothers, they gain a significant amount of respect and hold a great deal of power despite their outward submissiveness. Boyd-Franklin and Garcia-Preto (1995) identified Latinas as living "cultural paradoxes" because they are "morally and spiritually superior to men, while . . . they are expected to accept male authority" (p. 253). To add to the paradox, expression of female sexuality is considered negative. If a woman has sex before she is married or overtly talks about her enjoyment of sex, she is considered "*una mala mujer*," a bad woman, and risks social censorship and feelings of guilt and shame. This dichotomy is known as the Madonna-Whore Complex.

As mentioned earlier, acculturation greatly affects these cultural norms. Research has shown that after Mexicans arrive in this country, the more acculturated they become, the more health and mental problems they acquire, to a degree equal to that of the Anglo culture (Alderete et al., 2000). Among many hypotheses that attempt to explain this phenomenon, one is that it is difficult to maintain these traditional roles in the United States. Mexican women tend to find work in the United States easier than the men because they can use their sewing skills in factories or their "homemaker" skills in cleaning homes or hotels. The men, who traditionally work on farms, cannot use that expertise in the United States because of the scarcity of such jobs. They either have difficulty finding a job or they find employment in hard labor. As a result, the woman often works outside the home because the man is not able to provide enough for the family. Subsequently, she is exposed to the "nontraditional" female role of empowerment and independence. This often causes problems in her marriage if she becomes more assertive and demands certain rights. This exacerbates matters for the man who is unable to provide for his family like a "good man should." Alcohol usage rates among Mexican American men significantly increase with acculturation (Vega et al., 1998), and the change in roles appears to be a factor (Gloria & Peregoy, 1996).

In addition, the children of the traditional family are also exposed to the American way of life and may rebel against their parents, which in the Mexican culture is not acceptable. Therefore, while the parents are trying to maintain their cultural beliefs, the children are trying to reject them. This can cause turmoil in the house and possibly lead to mental and medical problems.

COMMUNITY

The community is more important than the "individual." The community, whether it is the family unit, the extended family, or the *pueblo*, makes the important decisions for an individual. Community members are also the ones who come together when one is in need or going through a "crisis." Because of this reliance on the community, many Mexicans who come to the United States feel alone or fearful because they are not as "independent" as their American counterparts. Hundreds of community-based organizations have emerged in America to provide that sense of community and support. A Mexican person now has access to advocates, health care, social services, and churches, all of which can provide that emotional, economic, and familial support that Mexicans are accustomed to receiving in their native land. They can also live in neighborhoods, *barrios* and *colonias* in which most people, including store clerks, speak Spanish.

RELIGION

Eighty to ninety percent of Mexicans and Mexican Americans are Roman Catholic (de Paula et al., 1996; Falicov, 1996). The Virgin of Guadalupe, who is considered to be the dark-skinned mother of Christ, is a powerful popular religious image. She is perceived as the model of motherhood, peace, faith, strength, and endurance. Many direct their religious promises and prayers to her (de Paula et al., 1996).

For many, "religion is a private affair centered around commitment to marriage and fertility, the sanctity of mothers, the condemnation of premarital sex, abortion, contraception, and homosexuality" (Falicov, 1996, p. 172). Feelings of guilt and shame for one's actions are common.

In the United States, the church in the *barrio* also provides a strong support system. It provides a sanctuary for undocumented immigrants, crisis counseling, space for activist groups, and community celebrations. The priest commands the utmost respect and officiates the life cycle celebrations such as communion, baptism, weddings, and the *quinceañera* (celebration initiating a 15-year-old girl into adulthood). It appears, however, that some parishioners are leaving the Catholic church and joining other religions, such as Pentecostalism, Jehovah's Witnesses, and Fundamentalist Protestantism (Falicov, 1996).

In general, many Mexicans believe that death and illness are the will of God, and many will incorporate a Rite of Anointing of the Sick if the prognosis of a loved one is grave. When a person is sick, some may use folk healing measures as opposed to or in addition to biomedical treatment (de Paula et al., 1996).

Interactions With Service Providers

Interacting with a consumer from a different culture can be daunting and less than fully effective if the service provider does not understand the consumer's culture or assumes that all patients from that culture are the same. As mentioned earlier, it is important to assess each patient individually, using the cultural framework as a starting point. In general, when interacting with a Mexican consumer, it is important to include the family, provide respect, be personable, and be trustworthy. A provider who does not perform in these ways may either have a noncompliant patient or lose the patient for good.

For example, it is recommended that the family be included in an interview or an assessment, if ethically viable. Traditionally, when a family member is ill, the family supports that member, not only financially and emotionally but also psychologically. As a result, it appears that the ill member recovers more quickly and subsequently becomes active in the community/family unit once again.

This improvement in health as a result of family support has been analyzed in numerous studies. One such study was conducted by the World Health Organization's International Pilot Study of Schizophrenia (IPSS), in which 1,202 patients from Nigeria, India, Colombia, Taiwan, the United Kingdom, the United States, the Soviet Union, Czechoslovakia, and Denmark were followed for 5 years. Findings at a 3-year follow-up indicated a markedly superior course of illness for patients from developing countries, relative to outcomes observed for patients residing in more industrialized nations (World Health Organization, 1979).

It was concluded that the observed difference in course and outcome could be explained by features of the sociocultural environment (Sartorius, Jablensky, & Shapiro, 1978). Additional observations have been recorded in subsequent studies. It has been suggested that familial and societal patterns of response to an ill individual may influence the course of illness. For example, it has been hypothesized that families who respond to an ill family member with tolerance and acceptance may contribute to a more benign course of the illness.

Another contributing factor to improvement in health is the level of "expressed emotion"—the criticism, hostility, or overinvolvement—shown by a family member toward a relative with disability, specifically schizophrenics (Jenkins et al., 1986). When the primary caregiver becomes too involved and protective, but is not critical, the patient can become completely dependent on family and friends. If the caregiver is critical, the patient may become angry and hostile but is unconsciously unwilling to get better because of the additional attention. Research has shown that in developed countries, expressed emotion in the families of schizophrenics is high and critical, while in underdeveloped countries it is extremely low. Jenkins et al. (1986) also showed that Mexican Americans had lower expressed emotion than Anglo Americans, resulting in significantly better clinical outcomes in Mexicans with schizophrenia. These results apply to any disability in that family support, not overprotectiveness, greatly increases the chances of a patient regaining an optimal level of function.

Including the family into the treatment process therefore not only is important in keeping the patient adherent to treatment but also may facilitate the healing process. This inclusion of family, according to Mexican culture, is also important because it demonstrates that respect was demonstrated between service provider and patient. This means that not only will consumers respect service providers because of their level of authority and expertise, but they also will expect respect back from providers. One example of respect is addressing adults by their last name, prefacing it with Señor or Señora. In addition, the Spanish language reflects the importance of respect, as demonstrated by use of the word "usted" (formal "you") instead of the informal "tú." For example, if the consumer were to ask the provider "How are you?" in Spanish, the provider would respond with "Muy bien, y usted?" ("I am fine, and you?"), using "usted" rather than the more familiar and less respectful "tú." This will greatly increase the chance of establishing a strong rapport with the patient.

When a service provider is to interact with a Mexican consumer, the provider must understand not only the importance of family and respect but also the importance of *personalismo. Personalismo* is having the ability to be personal. It emphasizes the personal quality of an interaction and is used to relate to and maintain a relationship with an individual. In other words, it is important to be warm, kind, and show some interest in the client. In general, Mexican people (and Latinos as a whole) do not respond well to people who have no sense of humor, who are cold, who act superior to them, and who have no time for them. This is illustrated by the firsthand experience of a Mexican mother whose son was permanently disabled:

> I would like for [the doctor] to really take his time to evaluate [my son] orthopedically . . . to sit him up, to touch him, to really notice what is happening. He only looks him over. I do not know. I believe he spends more time choosing a shirt he is going to buy or a pair of shoes than the time he spends on Miguel . . . Why doesn't he take the time to examine my son and give him quality care? I do not doubt his capacity as a doctor, as a specialist, but I sometimes doubt his humane qualifications. (Larson, 1998, p. 869)

Another value that is important in the Mexican culture is *confienza*—the ability to trust. Just as it is important for the provider to be "personable" to the patient, the provider must as equally provide the foundations of trust and safety. If the Mexican patient feels that the provider cannot be trusted, that patient may never return for services. This issue of trust is a pertinent topic in the medical field. The Kaiser Foundation conducted a survey in 1999 and asked a random national sample of 3,884 adults, in English and in Spanish, numerous questions about their perception and experiences of medical care (Henry J. Kaiser Family Foundation, 1999). The sample identified themselves as either Latino, white, or African American. One question asked how much trust they had in doctors and other health care providers to do what is best for patients. The results are shown in Figure 8.1.

Always + Most of the Time

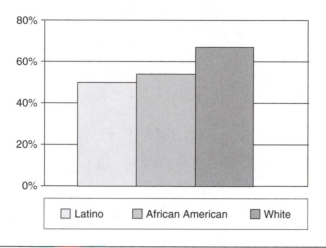

Figure 8.1   Perception of Trust in Doctors ("Always" + "Most of the Time")
SOURCE: Henry J. Kaiser Family Foundation (1999).

Perception of Trust in Doctors

According to the Kaiser Family Foundation survey (1999), 67% of white Americans trusted doctors either always or most of the time, versus 54% of African Americans and 50% of Latinos. It is believed that this difference may be a result of racial minorities having more negative experiences with their medical treatment than white Americans. For example, the Institute of Medicine found that racial and ethnic minorities tend to receive a lower quality of health care than nonminorities, even when patients' insurance status and income are controlled (Smedley et al. 2002). The same study found evidence that the health disparity between racial minorities is the result of stereotyping, biases, and uncertainty on the part of health care providers. Therefore, the lack of trust that racial minorities—in this case, Mexicans—have for providers is not unfounded. Discrimination seems to play a major role.

Discrimination

Many Mexicans do not seek professional treatment for health or emotional problems. There have been many speculations as to why. In addition to differences in cultural beliefs, one obvious factor is the discrimination that Mexicans (and, for that matter, many ethnic minorities) experience in this country.

"Healthy cultural suspicion" is a term that was initially used in reference to the attitudes of black families but has been generalized to refer to those of other ethnic minorities (Boyd-Franklin, 1989). This suspicion of intent has developed over generations in response to racism, oppression, and discrimination. It often takes the form of people's refusal to identify with and trust persons who differ from themselves in color, lifestyle, class values, and so forth.

Given that most agencies are operated and run by Caucasians, the suspicion extends to these "white institutions." As a result, minorities (in this case, Mexicans and Mexican Americans) confuse the relationship between social service agencies (e.g., welfare system, child protective services) and medical facilities (e.g., community and rehabilitation clinics). Undocumented Mexicans, in particular, fear that the system will "find them," report them to the immigration authorities, and later deport them. In fact, although Mexicans constitute only 18% of all undocumented immigrants, they constitute 86% of all Immigration and Naturalization Service (INS) detentions (Bustamante, 1995).

This lack of trust is not unfounded. Many studies have documented the health disparities between racial minorities and Caucasians in the United States. One such study reviewed medical records at a hospital's emergency room and examined how many Hispanics and whites were given anesthesia for a long-bone fracture (Todd, Samaroo, & Hoffman, 1993). The results are shown in Table 8.1.

The study found that Hispanics were less likely than white patients to receive anesthesia or a narcotic when they had similar bone fractures. Income and health insurance status were controlled in the study. The authors suspected that the results may have been the result of ethnic differences in pain expressions, in which the Latino males may not have expressed their pain as much, leading to the medical providers not prescribing analgesics. They further suspected that providers' inability to recognize the presence of pain in patients who were culturally different from themselves was a major factor, but there was no empirical evidence for this—only speculation. The reported difference in analgesic use, whatever the cause, is astonishing.

With the health disparity— as well as the discrimination that they face on a daily basis—being such a large factor in Mexican patients' lack of trust in health care, establishing that foundation of *confianza*, *personalismo*, and *respeto* is especially important.

Table 8.1   Disparities in Analgesic Use in an Emergency Medical Center (for
                isolated long bone fractures)

	White (%)	Hispanic (%)
Analgesic dose		
No analgesic	25.9	54.8
Low dose	45.4	19.4
High dose	28.7	25.8
Analgesic type		
No analgesic	25.9	54.8
Nonnarcotic	5.6	0.0
Narcotic	68.5	45.2

SOURCE: Adapted from "Ethnicity as a Risk Factor for Inadequate Emergency Department
Analgesia," *Journal of the American Medical Association, 269,* Todd, Samaroo, and Hoffman
(1993).

Language

Another factor that prevents Mexicans from entering treatment is the linguistic
barrier. How can they expect to get help when their service provider cannot
understand them? Consumers may say to themselves, "They may act like they
understand, but do they? Am I really getting the best treatment available? How
will they answer any of my questions?" Many first-generation Mexicans speak
very little English. They should not be punished for this; steps should be taken
so that language is not a barrier to treatment.

First of all, it is important to note that the word "translate" means
communicating through the *written* language, and "interpret" means communicating through the *verbal* language. It is common knowledge, however, that
much information is lost in translation and interpretation, and if family
members are the interpreters, they may tend to omit crucial information to
avoid "hurting" the consumer. In addition, research has shown that medical
interpretation is ineffective if performed mechanically or without understanding of the client's cultural background (Wardin, 1996).

Wardin (1996) performed a study in which she compared verbal evaluations of clients with limited English proficiency (LEP) and English-speaking
clients in a physical rehabilitation setting. She surveyed 200 occupational therapists and asked them about their experiences. They reported that limited
interpretation service was seen to be the most common barrier to verbal evaluation for clients with LEP, followed by cultural differences, limited time, and

limited resources. Respondents said that during the evaluations, they often misinterpreted the client's behavior because they were unaware of its cultural importance. In addition, they had difficulty understanding the role of family members who performed activities for the client instead of encouraging the client's independence. They found that this "help" and lack of will to return to work inhibited therapy.

They also noticed that when family members were used to interpret, they were perceived as not being able to accurately interpret rehabilitation information or as not sharing the informant's goals for the client. When an interpreter was not available, some of the respondents said they used gestural communication or body language to communicate, but the emphasis was on the client understanding the therapist, not the therapist understanding the client. The respondents said that picture books and language-free videos seemed to aid in communication.

In contrast, bilingual therapists reported understanding the clients' needs better. They not only used the client's primary language and met with the family but also understood the culture-specific role performances of each member. Overall, results indicate that the most effective way of understanding the client with limited or no English skills is to know the language and the culture. The next most effective strategy is to use a medically trained interpreter and to keep the culture of the client in mind so that cultural gestures or expressions will be noticed. When using an interpreter who is not medically trained, the provider should explain expectations to him or her ahead of time (for example, keeping a distance between the provider and the patient so the conversation flows naturally, avoid side conversations, don't omit anything). The last resort is to use other tools, such as videos and books, to facilitate the treatment process. The use of family members as interpreters is not recommended.

In using assessment tools for a non-English speaker or even for a patient who is Latino and speaks some English, it is most important to use an instrument that has been culturally validated. Some service providers directly translate instruments with which to assess their Spanish-speaking clientele. The problem is that these instruments are usually normed on the white American population, with a resulting likelihood of error and misinterpretation. It is important to produce or find an instrument that is validated for and normed on the Mexican community or the Latino community as a whole.

Given the heterogeneity of the Latino culture as a whole, the instrument should (a) be written in grammatically correct, simple language; (b) contain vocabulary in common usage across all reference groups; (c) be translated to retain the meaning and intent of the original instrument; and (d) be culturally relevant (Cella et al., 1998). The provider should explain to the consumer why the assessment tool is being used and what the expectations are of the consumer. Many consumers are not used to "taking tests" such as those taken in the United States and may become quite anxious when being assessed.

In summary, the interaction between consumer and service provider should be relaxed, safe, and comfortable for the consumer. If the provider shows Mexican consumers respect by including the family and by trying to understand their culture, the provider has then established a strong foundation for treatment compliance. If, during the treatment process, providers use the patient's language—either themselves or through an interpreter—and have used culturally normed assessment tools, the diagnosis and subsequent treatment should flow much easier.

Recommendations for Service Providers

The most important recommendation is to be aware of biases about ethnic minorities and, more specifically, Mexicans. This recommendation is for *all* providers, including Latinos. Racism and classism can also occur within ones' own culture, so it is important to be aware of these prejudices and biases when interacting with someone from your own race or culture. It is also important to wear your "cultural" lenses when speaking to a person from a different culture but then to "fine tune" or "focus" them to the individual. Remember that Mexican culture is diverse within itself, and that when acculturation is stirred into the mix, your knowledge of Mexican culture may not be relevant.

In general, when providing service to consumers of Mexican origin, be respectful, personable, trustworthy, warm, and humble. Try to learn Spanish, or at least the medical terminology. Respect the way Mexicans express pain and try to understand the cultural meaning behind these expressions. Use Kleinman's (Kleinman, Eisenberg, & Good, 1978) questions to help facilitate the assessment process, as described in Chapter 3.

Sometimes, when Mexican consumers appreciate all you have done for them, they may bring you a gift. Ethically, a service provider most likely is not supposed to accept most gifts. If consumers give you a gift, however, graciously accept it as a small token of appreciation and place it in your office; they may look for it later and become offended if it is not there. Pride is very important in the Mexican culture; sometimes, that is all Mexicans have left once they leave Mexico to live in the United States. Try not to offend them.

Overall, it is important to be culturally sensitive to your clients' culture and background, but be careful with halfhearted efforts, because they can be just as damaging. Sergio Aguilar-Gaxiola (2000), one of the principal investigators for a large study known as the Mexican American Prevalence and Services Study (MAPPS), presented the overall results of the study at a local training seminar. In his presentation, he provided examples of well-intentioned efforts in cultural sensitivity that were not effective.

- When General Motors introduced the Chevy Nova in South America, it was apparently unaware that "no va" means "it won't go." After the company figured out why it was not selling any cars, it renamed the car "Caribe" in its Spanish markets.
- When Parker Pen marketed a ballpoint pen in Mexico, its ads were supposed to say "It won't leak in your pocket and embarrass you." However, the company mistakenly thought that the Spanish word "embarazar" meant "embarrass." Instead, the ads said "It won't leak in your pocket and make you pregnant."
- An American T-shirt maker in Miami printed shirts for the Spanish market to promote the pope's visit. Instead of the desired "I saw the Pope" (el Papa), the shirts proclaimed "I saw the Potato" (la papa).

Conclusion

Culture is a society's style, its way of living and dying. It embraces the erotic and the culinary arts; dancing and burial; courtesy and cures; work and leisure; rituals and festivals; punishments and rewards . . . [It is] dealing with the dead and with the ghosts who people our dreams; attitudes toward women, children, old people and strangers, enemies, and allies; eternity and the present; the here and now and the beyond.

—Octavio Paz (as quoted
in Hayes-Bautista & Chiprut, 1999, p. 1)

The purpose of this chapter is to describe Mexican culture. We focused on the less acculturated, who tend to be less educated and less sophisticated and who often are immigrants who work in menial jobs, doing what other groups choose not to do. The nature of their jobs means they are more likely to have incidents that render them either temporarily or permanently disabled. Because of their need to work, they may not enter a doctor's office until their pain or disability has become exacerbated to a point at which they can no longer function. What they most need at this point is understanding.

Below is a summary of some of the key points from this chapter.

- Mexican culture is heterogenous.
- When it comes to treatment, the family may use other resources, such as *curanderos*, or *sobadores*, or use herbal remedies for their folk illnesses. Inquire about such treatments to make sure they will not interfere with any medications or cause further health problems. If the treatments are safe, allow consumers to pursue them.
- Mexicans have their own meanings for and expressions of pain.

- The roles of the immediate and extended family are important. Include family members in treatment if possible.
- Cooperation comes from empowering the family and educating them about their role in the rehabilitation of the family member.
- In Mexican and Latino cultures, it is expected that the parents will live with and be cared for by their children when they age. Children generally do not feel as though caring for the aging parent or family member with disability is a burden. They may look upon it as a responsibility.
- If the person with disability is placed in a hospital, the mother in most cases will want to stay in the hospital with the person.
- If you show respect and *personalismo*, chances are that the family will not try to sabotage or drop out of treatment.
- Shake hands and call each person by his or her last name. Use the word "usted" if using Spanish.
- Always address the father and mother first.
- Being a person with disability is "part of life" or "God's will."
- In general, count on somebody always being at home to take care of persons with disability. Relatives or close family friends may insist they can care for the injured person at home.
- Learn Spanish, or at least basic medical and cultural terms in Spanish. If you don't know Spanish, use a medically trained interpreter.
- Remember to speak at the consumer's level.
- Use culturally normed assessment tools.
- Educate the family through the use of videos, role-playing, dolls, and written material as well as oral instruction.
- In Mexican culture, a professional in the health care field is second only to a priest.
- Ethically, a therapist is not supposed to accept a gift. If offered a gift, accept it, but place it in your office. Remember the pride factor.
- Assess the level of the family's acculturation because some traditional beliefs may no longer apply. The level of acculturation may determine the family's degree of involvement and participation in the treatment and recovery process.
- Double the appointment time for your sessions with the patient and the family. You will need the extra time to apply various techniques appropriate for these consumers.
- Most important, put on your "Mexican cultural lenses" when you meet with Mexican clients and families, but focus your lenses on the individual.

We hope that this chapter will be helpful in increasing your understanding of Mexican culture. The fact that you have read this material shows that you are willing to learn and explore a new culture, but do not stop here. You may wish to take classes about Mexican language and culture, read books by Mexican authors, watch a Mexican movie, or go to museums and cultural centers. Becoming culturally aware is a lifelong process that never ends and certainly should not end with reading this chapter. Become aware of your own stereotypes and try to challenge them by finding evidence that does not support them.

It takes work and a great deal of insight, but the result is rewarding—not only for the people for whom you provide services but also for yourself.

References

Aguilar-Gaxiola, S. (2000, June). *Gaps in mental health utilization in Latinos: Capital implications for clinical practice.* Presentation at the Training and Cultural Competency Bureau, Los Angeles.

Alderete, E., Vega, W. A., Kolody, B., & Aguilar-Gaxiola, S. (2000). Lifetime prevalence of and risk factors for psychiatric disorders among Mexican migrant farmworkers in California. *American Journal of Public Health, 90,* 1-7.

Bailey, D. B., Jr., Skinner, D., Correa, V., Arcia, E., Reyes-Blanes, M. E., Rodriguez, P., et al. (1999). Needs and supports reported by Latino families of young children with developmental disabilities. *American Journal on Mental Retardation, 104,* 437-451.

Berry, J. W., Kim, U., Minde, T., & Mok, D. (1987). Comparative studies of acculturative stress. *International Migration Review, 21,* 491-511.

Boyd-Franklin, N. (1989). *Black families in therapy: A multisystems approach.* New York: Guilford.

Boyd-Franklin, N., & Garcia-Preto, N. (1995). Family therapy: The cases of African American and Hispanic women. In L. Comas-Diaz & B. Greene (Eds.), *Women of color: Integrating ethnic and gender identities in psychotherapy* (pp. 239-264). New York: Guilford.

Bustamante, J. (1995, Spring). *The socioeconomics of undocumented migration flood.* Presentation at the Center of U.S.-Mexican Studies, University of California, San Diego.

Cella, D., Hernandez, L., Bonomi, A. E., Corona, M., Vaquero, M., Shiomoto, G., et al. (1998). Spanish language translation and initial validation of the functional assessment of cancer therapy Quality of Life Instrument. *Medical Care, 36,* 1407-1418.

Coursey, R. D. (1998). *Competencies for direct service staff who work with adults with serious mental illness in public mental health services.* Rockville, MD: Center for Mental Health Services.

de Paula, T., Lagaña, K., & Gonzalez-Ramirez, L. (1996). Mexican Americans. In J. Lipson, S. Dibble, & P. Minarik (Eds.), *Culture and nursing care: A pocket guide* (pp. 203-221). San Francisco: UCSF Nursing Press.

Falicov, C. J. (1996). Mexican families. In M. McGoldrick, J. Giordano, & J. K. Pearce (Eds.), *Ethnicity and family therapy.* New York: Guilford.

Forehand, R., & Kotchisk, B. A. (1996). Cultural diversity: A wake-up call for parent training. *Behavior Therapy, 27,* 187-206.

Garcia-Preto, N. (1996). Latino families: An overview. In M. McGoldrick, J. Giordano, & J. K. Pearce (Eds.), *Ethnicity and family therapy.* New York: Guilford.

Gil, R. M., & Vazquez, C. I. (1996). *The Maria paradox.* New York: Perigee Books.

Gloria, A. M., & Peregoy, J. J. (1996). Counseling Latino alcohol and other substance users/abusers. *Journal of Substance Abuse Treatment, 13,* 119-126.

Hartman, M., Young, A., & Forquer, S. (2000). *Core competencies for practitioners providing care to individuals with severe mental illnesses.* Princeton, NJ: Center for Health Care Strategies.

Hayes-Bautista, D. E., & Chiprut, R. (Eds.). (1999). *Healing Latinos: Realidad y fantasia.* Los Angeles: Cedars-Sinai Health System.

Henry J. Kaiser Family Foundation. (1999). *Race, ethnicity & medical care: A survey of public perceptions and experiences.* Menlo Park, CA: Henry J. Kaiser Family Foundation.

Heyman, J. McC. (1991). *Life and labor on the border: Working people of northeastern Sonora, Mexico, 1886–1986.* Tucson: University of Arizona Press.

Holzer, B. (1999). Everyone has something to give. Living with disability in Juchitan, Oaxaca, Mexico. In B. Holzer, A. Vreede, & G. Weigt (Eds.), *Disability in different cultures: Reflection on local concepts* (pp. 44-57). Bielefeld, Germany: Transcript Verlag.

Jenkins, J. H., Karno, M., de la Salva, A., Santana, F., Telles, C., Lopez, S., et al. (1986). Expressed emotion of relatives, maintenance drug treatment, and relapse in schizophrenia and mania. *Psychological Bulletin, 22,* 621-627.

Kleinman, A., Eisenberg, L., & Good, B. (1978). Culture, illness, and care: Clinical lessons from anthropologic and cross-cultural research. *Annals of Internal Medicine, 88,* 251-258.

Larson, E. (1998). Reframing the meaning of disability to families: The embrace of paradox. *Social Science Medicine, 47,* 867-875.

Merrill, T., & Miró, R. (1997). *Mexico: A country study* (4th ed.). Washington, DC: Federal Research Division, Library of Congress.

Mexico City. (2003). Retrieved April 12, 2003, from www.lonelyplanet.com/destinations/north_america/mexico_city/

Muller, T., & Espenshade, T. J. (1985). *The fourth wave: California's newest immigrants.* Washington, DC: Urban Institute Press.

Nelson, C., & Rubi, M. E. (1999). Intensive treatment and problem solving to enhance rehabilitation potential in Mexico. In R. L. Leavitt (Ed.), *Cross-cultural rehabilitation* (pp. 227-232). London: W. B. Saunders.

Sartorius, N., Jablensky, A., & Shapiro, R. (1978). Cross-cultural differences in the short-term prognosis of schizophrenic psychosis. *Schizophrenia Bulletin, 4,* 102-113.

Schmidley, D., & Campbell, G. (1999). *Profile of the foreign-born population in the United States, 1997* (U.S. Census Bureau, Current Population Reports, Series P23-195). Washington, DC: Government Printing Office.

Smedley, B. D., Stith, A. Y., & Nelson, A. R. (2002). *Unequal treatment: Confronting racial and ethnic disparities in health care.* Washington, DC: National Academies Press.

Todd, K. H., Samaroo, H., & Hoffman, J. R. (1993). Ethnicity as a risk factor for inadequate emergency department analgesia. *Journal of the American Medical Association, 269,* 1537-1539.

Trevino, F. M., Moyer, M. E., Valdez, R. B., & Stroup-Benham, C. A. (1992). Health insurance coverage and utilization of health services by Mexican Americans, Puerto Ricans, and Cuban Americans. In A. Furino (Ed.), *Health policy and the Hispanic* (pp. 158-170). Boulder, CO: Westview Press.

Vega, W. A., Kolody, G., Aguilar-Gaxiola, S., Alderete, E., Catalano, R., & Caraveo-Anduaga, J. (1998). Lifetime prevalence of DSM-III-R psychiatric disorders among urban and rural Mexican Americans in California. *Archives of General Psychiatry, 55,* 771-778.

Wardin, K. (1996). A comparison of verbal evaluation of clients with limited English proficiency and English-speaking clients in physical rehabilitation settings. *The American Journal of Occupational Therapy, 50,* 816-825.

The World Factbook. (2003). Available at www.cia.gov/cia/publications/factbook/geos/mx.html

World Health Organization. (1979). *Schizophrenia: An international follow-up study.* New York: John Wiley and Sons.

9

An Introduction to the Culture of the Dominican Republic for Disability Service Providers

Ana López-De Fede
Dulce Haeussler-Fiore

Introduction

Altagracia, age 46, woke up one morning unable to move the right side of her body or to see. She refused to see a doctor, preferring to wait until her husband came home from work. As she waited, her family embarked on its own healing practices. She was rolled to her unaffected side to allow the "bad blood" to flow evenly throughout her body. Family members called their minister to start a healing prayer vigil and began to prepare a tea with properties to reverse the paralysis.

Guillermo, age 26, suffered head and spinal cord injuries from a car accident. His elderly parents are the primary caregivers, with support from siblings who live in the immediate area. They struggle with the devices provided to help him become independent, preferring to provide him with the support themselves.

Sylvia, age 20, has given birth to a child with cerebral palsy. She struggles to find the best way to tell her family in the Dominican Republic. They may suspect that drugs were involved or that the disability is the result of some evil deed or jealousy—"*mal ojo.*" The hospital staff does not seem to understand that she will return to an empty apartment. Her husband does not want anyone to see the baby.

Alicia works as a special education teacher at a local school. She often hears remarks on her patience and the many "blessings" to be bestowed by God for her labor of love with those children. She struggles to dispel these beliefs, choosing to concentrate on helping to bridge the needs of the educational system to the needs and values of the community.

Are these typical reactions for immigrants from the Dominican Republic? No single ethnic group is homogeneous in its response to illness and disability. How do providers bridge ethnicity, race, cultural beliefs, values, and practices in their efforts to provide effective disability services? The intersection between these factors and the role of providers to provide culturally competent services is the topic of this chapter. It provides a framework to explore the Dominican and Dominican American culture within the context of disabilities, chronic illness, and rehabilitation services. It is not intended to be the definitive treatise on the Dominican culture or Dominicans' experience with rehabilitation services.

Throughout this chapter, we will use case examples to illustrate key concepts, beliefs, and values. The names of the individuals and some details have been modified to protect their confidentiality. The reader is encouraged to consider the reasons for emigration, the level of acculturation, exposure to health care systems, and the socioeconomic status of the population. Dominicans comprise diverse groups of individuals. Each has a unique voice and history, a situation that calls for rehabilitation providers to be attuned to the differences as well as the common themes of their experiences. It is important to note that this chapter presents general themes about the Dominican culture in order to present service providers a point of entry. Dominicans are a heterogeneous group, and not all the experiences, beliefs, or applications apply uniformly to all individuals within this culture.

Cultural Overview

Disability service providers wishing to work most effectively with Dominicans must know the history of the country and its role in shaping the cultural framework of the population. After sailing through the Bahamas and Cuba, Christopher Columbus landed on Hispaniola on December 5, 1492, establishing the first Spanish settlements of the newly founded territory. Located in the Caribbean archipelago, the Dominican Republic occupies the eastern two thirds of the island of Hispaniola; Haiti occupies the remaining western third of the island. Situated about 600 miles southeast of Florida and 310 miles north of Colombia and Venezuela, the Dominican Republic is flanked to the north by the Atlantic Ocean and on the south by the Caribbean Sea.

Torres-Saillant and Hernandez (1998) chronicled the early history of the country, citing its prominent place in history as the center of the entire Spanish colonization of the Western Hemisphere and the first presence of "black slaves" in the colonies on the island in July 1502. These two historical precedents forever changed the history of the Americas and shaped the cultural framework of the modern-day Hispanic/Latino population. The island was home to the first settlement of Europeans, the first genocide of aborigines, and the first cohort of African slaves in the archipelago. The meeting of cultures and races, compounded later by the influx of French, German, U.S. black, West Indian, Arab, Jewish, Canary Islander, Chinese, Cuban, Puerto Rican, and Haitian immigrants, has contributed to the ethnic and cultural formation of the Dominican people. The combinations of these variables would be repeated throughout the Caribbean, forming the historical experience of the region and, to a lesser extent, Latin America.

Although race is a factor in the Dominican Republic, it is often intertwined with and confounded by social class (Charles, 1992; Wiltshire, 1992). As a people whose ancestry is a blend of European, American Indian, and African, Dominicans range in color from black, dark, medium, or light brown to white. Generally, race alone in the Dominican Republic neither restricts nor excludes an individual from a social group. A subordinate role is not assigned for individuals with African features.

History of Immigration to the United States

Early immigration to the United States occurred in four distinct groups: the "Trujillo era" (1930–1960), the "post-Trujillo era" (1961–1981), the "flotilla" group (1982–1986), and the "post-flotilla" group (1983–present) (Torres-Saillant & Hernandez, 1998). These four groups of Dominicans have unique needs and varying attitudes toward seeking help from human services professionals (Paulino, 1994). They are socially diverse, representing various social strata. As a group, the reasons for emigration have been framed by diverse socioeconomic and political situations. As an example, political dissidents constituted the largest group of the "Trujillo era" immigrants. In contrast, complex socioeconomic and political situations of the country have been the driving force for later immigration patterns. During the late 1960s and early 1970s, the improved economy of the Dominican Republic did not lead to increased employment, higher wages, or social opportunities for a large segment of the population, resulting in the expansion of migration to the United States (Bach, 1983; Georges, 1992). This economic situation resulted in the migration of the rural poor on "flotillas" of makeshift boats, seeking to enter the United States.

For a large segment of this population, immigration is viewed as temporary, which causes a circular transnational migrant network (Georges, 1990;

Grasmuck & Pessar, 1991). The results are ambivalence about their sociopolitical status in the United States and acknowledgment that the maintenance of middle-class socioeconomic lifestyle on the island is facilitated by the immigrants' dependence on the U.S. market economy (Grasmuck & Pessar, 1991, Hernandez & Torres-Saillant, 1996). Among recent Hispanic immigrants to the United States, Dominicans have been described as determined to maintain their homeland identity. Duany (1994) found that most Dominicans identified themselves as Dominicans, not American and not even Dominican American. When describing their country of origin, they often used the emotional term *mi patria* ("my fatherland"), *mi tierra* ("my land"), and *mi pais* ("my country"). It was further found that the use of the possessive adjective *mi* (my) to refer to the Dominican Republic was not extended to the United States, often referred to as *este pais* ("this country"). Duany attributed this difference to an attempt to remain emotionally attached to the Dominican Republic and unattached to the United States. Strong attachment to the Dominican Republic can undermine, complicate, and delay immigrants' adaptation to the United States and their willingness to access services (Hernandez & Torres-Saillant, 1996; Torres-Saillant & Hernandez, 1998). Thus, service providers need to explore the sociopolitical context affecting the immigration experience of Dominicans. Resistance to speaking English and adopting "foreign" health care frameworks may be associated with the fear of losing their Dominican identity (Paulino & Burgos-Servedio, 1997).

Like that of many other immigrant groups, Dominican migration has usually involved the departure of an individual family member. Children, spouses/ companions, and parents are often left behind. Separation and reunification are key family dynamics within this culture that values strong family connections, immediate and extended families, and non–blood related kin for support. The level of support garnished through family systems is an important dynamic in the delivery of services to this population. Dominicans maintain strong ties to families on the island. Participation among family members in the United States and the Dominican Republic includes financial support, involvement in child care arrangements, health care, and social relationships. Thus, many families maintain social networks and support systems in two countries. Culturally competent services for Dominicans rest with the incorporation of family members into every aspect of care and the transnational nature of social networks and support mechanisms.

RACE AND ACCULTURATION

Dominican immigrants bring a history of self-identification that transcends their affiliation to a given racial group. This is not typically the experience of racial minorities in the United States. As a result, many immigrants are identified or self-identify as black, encountering the personal and institutional barriers experienced by African Americans (Bach, 1983). To affirm their independence from racial stereotypes in the United States, some "cocoon themselves in their national identity," limiting or delaying assimilation and blocking efforts to engage with systems of the mainstream culture in the United States (Wiltshire, 1992, p. 184). The conflict is expressed best by Rosa Bachleda, the Dominican founder of an interracial group of women artists in Chicago. "I was Black to White America; I was some strange Spanish-speaking person to Black America" (Bandon, 1995, p. 59). Race, and the role that it plays in accessing services and assimilation, is a crucial issue to consider for those working with Dominican immigrants.

DEMOGRAPHIC PROFILE
OF DOMINICANS IN THE UNITED STATES

Dominicans are the second largest Hispanic/Latino grouping in New York City after Puerto Ricans (Georges, 1990). People from the Dominican Republic have resided in the United States since the late 19th century; however, the numbers were not significant until the mid-1960s. Not counted by the U.S. Census until 2000, Dominicans in the United States number between 764,945 and 1.1 million; more than 65% of them reside in New York State. The Dominican population can be found throughout the United States, with the largest populations, in descending order, in the following states: New York, New Jersey, Florida, Massachusetts, Rhode Island, Pennsylvania, Connecticut, and Washington, D.C. (Mumford Center, 2001; U.S. Bureau of the Census, 2000). The population is primarily urban in origin, is occupationally diverse, and includes skilled and semiprofessional workers and persons who have completed their secondary and college education (Georges, 1990; Grasmuck & Pessar, 1991). It is a young population, with a median age of 25 years, with families largely headed by females (Georges, 1990, 1992).

Castro and Boswell (2002) applied the analysis of sociologist C. Wright Mills and colleagues in describing the Dominican population in the United States. Mills and his colleagues reflected on the growing Puerto Rican population in the United States:

> [M]any of the immigrants are women, in a society where women's economic lot is still often more difficult. Many are Negroes, in a society where color counts heavily against them; and most of the migrants are without much skill, in a society where skill is increasingly important for adequate livelihood; and all enter a society where the opportunities for advancement seem increasingly narrow for the "foreign." (Mills, Senior, & Goldsen, 1950, p. 127)

A half century later, this insight on the struggles of Puerto Rican immigrants reflects many of the challenges facing Dominicans in the United States. Castro and Boswell's (2002) analysis of the current population surveys for the years 1997–2000 documents the following:

- The Dominican population residing in the United States is 53.8% female and 46.2% male.
- Dominicans, like many of the new immigrants, are a youthful population; 44% are under the age of 20.
- Racially, 80.2% identified themselves as white, with 19.8% self-identifying as black or Asian.
- Forty-two percent graduated from high school, with approximately 10% reporting completing a college education.
- The majority of Dominicans work in blue-, gray-, and pink-collar jobs, specifically in service occupations (33.2%) or as operators, fabricators, and handlers (30.4%). Managers and professionals account for 10.9% of Dominicans holding jobs, and 25.4% are technical, sales, and administrative support workers.
- Approximately 37% of Dominicans in the United States arrived between 1990 and 2000.
- Most Dominicans are foreign-born (56.6%), with a substantial component born in the United States (43.6%).

This profile reveals a population at risk for poor health outcomes associated with their socioeconomic and educational status, as well as recent immigration to the United States. The reader, however, is cautioned not to generalize this profile to all Dominicans seeking disability services. The profile serves to highlight some of the challenges and barriers associated with accessing mainstreamed services in the United States.

Dominican Concepts of Disability

Many Hispanics believe that illness is caused by (a) psychological states such as embarrassment, envy, anger, fear, fright, excessive worry, turmoil in the family, improper behavior, or violations of moral or ethical codes; (b) environmental or natural conditions such as bad air, germs, dust, excess cold or heat, bad food, or poverty; and (c) supernatural agents such as malevolent spirits, bad luck, or the witchcraft of living enemies who are believed to cause harm out of vengeance or envy (Molina, Zambrana, & Aguirre-Molina, 1994). Disability, in the Dominican culture, is often viewed within this framework of beliefs. The belief that moral violations or supernatural causes are responsible for an individual's disability can result in feelings of guilt or shame for the family and lead to ostracizing the individual with disabilities. Conversely, ascribing environmental or natural causes to a disabling condition can facilitate the development of strategies to overcome barriers that minimize the level of independence and full inclusion of individuals into all aspects of society.

There is no officially recognized disability policy within Dominican society, nor is there a clear expectation for full participation of individuals with disabilities in the larger society. However, legislation does exist protecting the rights of individuals with disabilities through a combination of special laws that allow for due process through the courts. General legislation applies to persons with different disabilities with respect to: the right to marriage, to parenthood/family, to political rights, to privacy, and to property rights. The following benefits are guaranteed by law to persons with disabilities: training, rehabilitation and counseling, employment, health and medical care, financial security, and independent living. Much of the legislation is modeled on the beliefs of disabilities rights models, with a focus on the limitations of disabilities as "social constructs." Unfortunately, these laws are not universally applied in the Dominican Republic because of limited fiscal resources, shortages of trained personnel, accessibility barriers, costs associated with assistive devices and prescriptions, and the lack of rehabilitation facilities outside large urban centers.

Acquired and Lifelong Disabilities

Because of limited resources and the lack of advocacy, acquired physical disabilities are often seen as more acceptable than developmental disabilities, such as mental retardation. In many cases, the family can accommodate and adapt surroundings to care for an individual with a physical disability. Modified assistive devices are often made by members within the community, purchased secondhand, or provided through a nonprofit international organization. Dominican families exercise a great deal of creativity in crafting appliances that foster independence.

The same efforts are not exerted in support of individuals with mental disabilities. The root causes of mental disabilities are more closely associated with belief in supernatural and moral violations. As an example, manic and depressive symptoms can be viewed as an attack of nerves of short duration or tolerated through the period of crisis. Herbal medicines are closely associated with the treatment of mental illness. In the United States, many families will bring a variety of leaves, flowers, and roots to increase the mental stability of the individual. The cost of mainstream medicine can exceed the fiscal resources of families with limited or no health insurance. As a result, individuals with a mental illness are often isolated, pampered so as to not upset them, and cared for exclusively by family members. Hospitalization and institutional placements are viewed by the family as a failure of their ability to care for one of their own. They are options of last resort.

The Role of Family, Community, and Religion

The levels of acculturation and adaptation to the United States can compound the stressors associated with the rehabilitation process and must be explored by service providers. The following case example describes family conflict experienced by many Dominican immigrants. Mr. Baez has chronic diabetes complicated by chronic renal failure.

> Mr. Baez, age 50, born in the Dominican Republic, the father of four grown children, has been struggling with the loss of independence associated with his chronic health conditions. He is a tall man with a husky muscular build that betrays a lifetime of heavy work as a grocery store owner. Mr. Baez worked 7 days a week, marked by long hours, to provide for his family. Rarely ill, he prides himself on being independent and on his resiliency to disease, unlike his weak "American" children. He relishes the traditional foods of his homeland—a diet not compatible with his diabetes. Modifying Mr. Baez's diet proves to be challenging for the family. Mrs. Baez is reluctant to go against his dietary wishes, choosing instead to provide smaller portions. He does not like to routinely check blood levels, preferring not to expose his employees to his condition. Nor does he perceive the need for exercise beyond the manual labor associated with running the store, and he ignores the recommendations of his doctors. Instead, the family focuses on home remedies and a reliance on prayers.
>
> Mr. Baez's condition deteriorated. Within 2 years, he underwent a kidney transplant and suffered both a decline in vision and nerve damage that eliminated his ability to work. Mrs. Baez became the chief operator of the grocery store, relying on family support for the care of her husband and the household. Mr. Baez was resentful of his wife and frequently "blamed" God for his bad luck.

In the Baez example, the level of assimilation and identification with health care practices in the United States was viewed as contradictory to cultural norms. The role of the male in the family structure, coupled with the lack of realistic dietary options, made the recommendations of the health care provider untenable for this family. Even at the risk of her husband's declining health, Mrs. Baez did not feel empowered to challenge her husband's diet preferences, citing that many of the recommended changes contradicted traditional cures for diabetes. Many Dominicans believe in a "hot-cold" theory of disease, which is similar to that held in some Asian cultures. For example, it is believed that cold illnesses should be treated with hot medications (penicillin, for example) or hot foods (for example, chicken soup or hot tea), not with orange juice, fruit, or other "cold" remedies that are commonly recommended by mainstream health care providers (Molina et al., 1994). An awareness that their recommendations may not fit with traditional remedies will help providers prevent poor compliance.

Traditionally, men in the society are viewed as the breadwinners, with any threats perceived as challenging their role as head of the household (Georges, 1992). Issues of independence, control, and the perception of masculinity associated with monitoring diabetes within the work setting need exploring with Mr. Baez. His perception of "losing respect" and being perceived as "weak" by his employees and family complicate his health status. Incorporating exercise into his daily routine is perceived as "frivolous" and taking time away from work. Therapists might explore the work environment or his sponsorship of a neighborhood baseball team as vehicles to incorporate exercise into his daily routine.

In the care of a disabled individual, the interaction of the two sexes is very clearly established by custom. As an example, a male never takes a female to the bathroom or helps her with her physical needs. In the Dominican culture, a woman is helped by another woman, and a man by another man. Fathers do not help with infants. The male parent has a very different role from the female parent.

The employment shift in the household was perceived by Mr. Baez as demeaning. He frequently cited a plot among his wife, children, and former employees to take away "his business." The growing levels of independence of women and children in Dominican households can result in marital problems and divorce. Many service providers point to the shift in gender roles as contributing to rising numbers of female-headed Dominican households. The complexities of gender and parenting roles have significant impacts on the care, prognosis, and treatment of family members with chronic conditions or disabilities.

RELIGION AND SPIRITUALITY

Roman Catholicism is the official religion of the Dominican Republic. Dominicans are greatly influenced by religion as a governing aspect of their culture and way of life. Approximately 95% of the population self-identifies as Catholic. However, many believe, especially in the context of healing, that the best way to connect to God is through intermediaries (the clergy and the saints). The saints play an important role in popular devotion and the connection to well-being. Duany (1994) commented that many Dominican homes have small shrines with images of Catholic saints and the Virgin Mary in a corner of the hall or in a private room. The altars are usually surrounded by flowers and lighted candles. Although the most popular figures are the Virgin of Altagracia (the patron saint of the country) and Saint Lazarus, the altars represent a wide range of religious images, including Saint Claire and Saint Anthony of Padua among others. The *santos* (saints) cults merge the characteristics of Christian saints with those of African deities. This is a legacy from the period of slavery when Africans were converted to Christianity. They made sense of Christianity by equating their traditional beliefs in many different spirits with the Catholic practice of venerating many different saints. Worshipers are expected to perform a *promesa* (promise or obligation). This is an act of devotion performed by the worshipper in return for favors granted by the saint. Many Dominicans hold firmly to the power of a *promesa* to cure illness and eliminate disabling conditions.

The spiritual dimension of religion and its connection to the causation of illness and healing practices must be examined by practitioners working with Dominicans. Similarly, practitioners must become cognizant of alternative health care practices. Knowledge of these practices is essential in order to (a) understand that supernatural forces and spirituality affect perceptions of illness, causes, and curative method; (b) develop cross-cultural frameworks allowing interventions that acknowledge the role of indigenous belief systems; and (c) develop linkages with community systems that support the individual's behavior and attitudes regarding cultural norms that can influence their participation in mainstream services in the United States (Paulino, 1995). As an example, Spiritism (*espiritismo*) is a folk healing tradition utilized by at least one third of the largely Roman Catholic population in the Caribbean (Delgado, 1988).

Although many ethnic groups and cultures believe in spirits and supernatural powers, the Roman Catholic church has often referred to these belief systems as superstitious and evil. The result is the disguise or incorporation of many of the indigenous beliefs within the practice and rites of the Catholic faith. Spiritism (*espiritismo*), *Santeria,* witches (brujos), and curers (curanderos) are similar in their emphasis on beliefs about the nature and causes of illness and other problems, treatment techniques, and diagnostic classifications (Paulino, 1995). As an example, *curanderos* consult the saints to ascertain which herbs, roots, and various home cures to employ. Witches (brujos) also cure by driving out possessive spirits that sometimes seize an individual. The spiritist can work in conjunction with physicians and other providers by using "spiritual" power on behalf of the individual. For many Dominicans, seeking the support of indigenous healers, combined with traditional Roman Catholic practices of prayer, allows them to cope with illness within the family unit and reaffirm God's will (*Que sea lo que Dios quiera!*). For mainstream practitioners, these belief systems have implications regarding the individual's confidence, independence, self-determination, and level of empowerment associated with decision making regarding health care practices.

The following case study illustrates the role of religion and indigenous health care practices in addressing the spiritual needs of the family.

> Sylvia, age 20, gave birth to a child with cerebral palsy. She struggled to find the best way to tell her family in the Dominican Republic. She feared that they would suspect that the use of illegal drugs or that her insistence on leaving for the United States contributed to illness (*mal ojo*). Upon learning about their grandchild, Sylvia's parents contacted a spiritist (*espiritista*) to help them remove the witching spell (*brujeria*) that resulted in the illness (*mal ojo*). In this case, the spiritist was able to help the family understand the origins of cerebral palsy by bringing in mainstream health care providers to explain the origins, treatment, and life course of the condition.

In this case, the involvement of an indigenous healer with the family validated the need to incorporate mainstream health care providers with the care of the child. As a result, the efforts of the family shifted from blaming themselves to providing Sylvia with the support needed to raise her child. Although the family continued to look for herbal supplements to ease the severity of the child's condition, they no longer prayed for a reversal of the evil spirit that resulted in the illness.

Families react differently to disability depending on their social status and educational background. In one case, a woman with four children who had varying degrees of mental retardation spent more than 25 years praying and making religious sacrifices, such as going to church every Tuesday and Thursday without eating or drinking, all to bring about the complete recovery of her children. She spoke with faith and assurance of the day the miracle would occur. When one of her sons went to jail, accused of having sexually assaulted an employee at his residential program, his mother prayed every day that her son be released from jail as soon as possible. After he was released, she never stopped telling people that it was due to her prayers and that this was only part of the great miracle that was going to occur when all her children would to be completely cured.

Interactions With Service Providers

Dominican immigrants are commonly unfamiliar with the system of referrals to specialists that is widespread in the United States. They are accustomed to going directly to the kind of doctor who deals with their particular ailment rather than going first to a primary care physician. The "medical specialist"–driven system, coupled with multiple choices of providers, is unfamiliar, confusing, and costly for families caring for an individual with a disability. The employment situation, coupled with the lack of familiarity with health services in the United States, present barriers to accessing needed disability services. As an example, in the Dominican Republic, prescriptions are not required for most medications, including contraception and antibiotics. A family may have only enough money either to go to the doctor or for the prescription, not for both. Thus, the concepts inherent in the American health care system affect how Dominicans utilize health care services in the United States.

The transnational nature of Dominican families increases levels of stress and those conditions associated with feelings of abandonment, shifting parenting and gender roles, unstable work environment, and language and racial barriers. Dominicans, like many immigrant groups, are at risk for disabilities associated with these variables (i.e., high blood pressure, obesity, diabetes, mental illness, family violence, and substance abuse). Females, as the primary caregivers for family members with disabilities, will often exhibit symptoms associated with burnout, such as insomnia, depression, and fatalistic attitudes toward themselves and their family. Successful rehabilitation services must focus on helping Dominican immigrants adapt to disabling conditions by incorporating into treatment modalities the unique features of the culture and its expression in the experiences of individuals. Not all Dominicans will react in the same fashion, nor do all the themes explored in this chapter apply equally to everyone. They serve as a guidepost for practitioners.

Recommendations for Service Providers

In a single chapter, it is impossible to incorporate all the cultural dimensions of the Dominican culture that influence access to and use of rehabilitation services. The focus of this chapter has been on the cultural characteristics and themes most closely associated with recent immigrants and those with minimum exposure to service systems within the United States. It is our hope that readers will take the opportunity to expand their knowledge of the Dominican culture and embrace opportunities to interact with Dominican immigrants outside the provision of rehabilitation services. Culturally competent rehabilitation services for Dominicans must be guided by an understanding of the following:

- Recognition of diversity within the culture and the role that immigration plays in the identity and assimilation of Dominican immigrants. The reasons for and timing associated with immigration can influence levels of acculturation and assimilation within the mainstream culture in the United States and the acceptance of rehabilitation services.

- Acknowledgment of the importance of immediate and extended families in support networks. Families must be active participants whenever possible in formulating and implementing choices associated with care. Families are almost exclusively the caregivers for individuals with disabilities. Hospitalization or institutional placements are rarely seen as viable options for families.

- Religion is an essential component in working with Dominican families. The integration of indigenous beliefs into everyday life is essential for an understanding of health, disabilities, and treatment options. Do not assume that all individuals share the same beliefs. Whenever possible, avoid stereotypes and assumptions about nonmainstream health care practices.

- The use of indigenous healers, herbal medicine, and the invocation of support from the supernatural are common practices associated with illness and disabilities. It is important to differentiate between those practices that may interfere with mainstream prescriptions (e.g., herbal medicine) and the support of indigenous healers that will not interfere with the care of the individual. Include them if possible.

- Providers must establish trust with clients. The purpose of the intervention and the approach must be clearly explained, with an emphasis on responding to questions and clarifying the role of the providers. Individuals will differ in their ability to understand the requirements for program eligibility. This is often complicated by misinformation and the fear of the possible removal of "loved ones" from their care.

- Racial tensions within the United States pose major obstacles for many Dominican immigrants subjected to barriers similar to those facing African Americans. Language further complicates the ability of new immigrants to easily assimilate outside their own group.

- The strong connections to the Dominican Republic result in a transnational community with equal ties to the United States and their homeland. This can lead to the use of health care services in both countries, which will then require practitioners to be aware of complimentary, duplicative, or contradictory practices. As an example, the U.S. rehabilitation system is unfamiliar to most Dominicans, requiring provision of information and exposure to many different services.

- Acknowledge the level of "power" attributed to health care professionals. Recognize that this does not always translate into an understanding of recommended practices, need for dietary changes, and use of assistive devices or therapy.

- Avoid standardized tests not validated with this population. Because they are such recent immigrants, limited research exists on the health care practices and needs of this population. Err on the side of caution.

- Pride is an important element in the culture. Explore options that allow individuals to maintain their pride. Do not use children or members of the community as translators without making sure that the individual does not object to sharing information with those individuals. Acknowledge that words may have different meanings based on the region of the country. Interpreters should be familiar with the Dominican culture.

- Provide information to families using cultural brokers within the community. Recent immigrants tend to reside in communities exclusively populated by Dominicans. Seek the support of community social and advocacy organizations to disseminate information, and expand your knowledge of the community.

Conclusion

The concept of culture goes beyond groups of people who can be distinguished by a common geography, bloodline, language, and set of customs. Culture is not a characteristic: It is a process that is fluid and constantly evolving. Culture can act as a unifying influence. It combines the different aspects of life into a logical whole. Culture is shaped by life experiences, migration, assimilation, psychological characteristics, socioeconomic and political status, gender roles, sexual preferences, race, health status, and environmental factors.

It is safe to say that education, information, patience, and the goodwill to serve these families will awaken in them a desire to assimilate into their culture new services and regulations. They will do anything to help their families experience a different and better way of life. Finally, language and culture play a major role in this educational approach. The clients need to hear information in their own language, preferably conveyed by a provider of the same background and race. The family needs to be reassured that their customs, culture, roots, and beliefs are understood and respected. It is our hope that this chapter has provided the opportunity to learn more about the Dominican culture. It is only a beginning. The challenge is to continue learning.

References

Bach, R. (1983). Emigration from the Spanish-speaking Caribbean. In M. Kritz (Ed.), *U.S. immigration and refugee policy* (pp. 133–153). Lexington, MA: Lexington Books.

Bandon, A. (1995). *Dominican Americans* (Footsteps to America Series). Parsippany, NJ: New Discovery Press.

Castro, M., & Boswell, T. (2002). *The Dominican diaspora revisited: Dominicans and Dominican-Americans in a new century.* Miami, FL: The North-South Center of the University of Miami.

Charles, C. (1992). Transnationalism in the construct of Haitian immigrants' racial categories of identity in New York City. In N. Glick-Schiller, L. Basch, & C. Blanc-Szanton (Eds.), *Towards a transnational perspective on migration: Race, class, ethnicity and nationalism reconsidered* (pp. 101–123). New York: New York Academy of Sciences.

Delgado, M. (1988). Groups in Spiritism: Implications for clinicians. In C. Jacobs & B. Bowles (Eds.), *Ethnicity and race: Critical concepts on social work.* Silver Spring, MD: National Association of Social Work.

Duany, J. (1994). *Quisqueya on the Hudson: The transnational identity of Dominicans in Washington Heights* (Dominican Research Monographs). New York: CUNY Dominican Studies Institute.

Georges, E. (1990). *The making of a transnational community: Migration development and cultural change in the Dominican Republic.* New York: Columbia University Press.

Georges, E. (1992). Gender, class and migration in the Dominican Republic: Women's experience in a transnational community. In N. Glick-Schiller, L. Basch, & C. Blanc-Szanton (Eds.), *Towards a transnational perspective on migration: Race, class, ethnicity and nationalism reconsidered* (pp. 81–100). New York: New York Academy of Sciences.

Grasmuck, S., & Pessar, P. (1991). *Between two islands: Dominican international migration.* Berkeley: University of California Press.

Hernandez, R., & Torres-Saillant, S. (1996). Dominicans in New York: Men, women, and prospects. In G. Haslip-Viera & S. L. Baker (Eds.), *Latinos in New York: Communities in transition.* Notre Dame, Indiana: University of Notre Dame Press.

Mills, C. W., Senior, C., & Goldsen, R. K (1950). *The Puerto Rican journey: New York's newest immigrants.* New York: Harper & Brothers.

Molina, C., Zambrana, R. E., & Aguirre-Molina, M. (1994). The influence of culture, class, and environment on health care. In C. Molina & M. Aguirre-Molina (Eds.), *Latino health in the U.S.: A growing challenge.* Washington, DC: American Public Health Association.

Mumford Center. (2001). *The new Latinos: Who they are, where they are.* Albany, NY: Lewis Mumford Center for Comparative Urban and Regional Research.

Paulino, A. (1994). Dominicans in the United States: Implications for practice and policies in human services. *A Journal of Multicultural Social Work, 3*(2), 53–65.

Paulino, A. (1995). Spiritism, Santeria, Brujeria, and Voodooism: A comparative view of indigenous healing systems. *Journal of Teaching in Social Work, 12*(1/2), 105–124.

Paulino, A., & Burgos-Servedio, J. (1997). Working with immigrant families in transition. In E. P. Congress (Ed.), *Multicultural perspectives in working with families* (pp. 125–141). New York: Springer.

Torres-Saillant, S., & Hernandez, R. (1998). *The Dominican Americans.* Westport, CT: Greenwood Press.

U.S. Bureau of the Census. (2000). *The Hispanic population in the United States.* Washington, DC: Government Printing Office.

Wiltshire, R. (1992). Implications of transnational migration for nationalism: The Caribbean example. In N. Glick-Schiller, L. Basch, & C. Blanc-Szanton (Eds.), *Towards a transnational perspective on migration: Race, class, ethnicity and nationalism reconsidered* (pp. 175–188). New York: New York Academy of Sciences.

10

An Introduction to Vietnamese Culture for Rehabilitation Service Providers in the United States

Peter Cody Hunt

Introduction

To many Americans, the word "Vietnam" conjures images of the devastating war that took place in remote villages of Southeast Asia some 30 years ago. The media portrayal of Vietnam suggested it was made up of only scattered thatched-hut villages amid the burning fire of jungle warfare. Few Americans, especially those in the post–Vietnam War generation, are aware of the rich culture and history of Vietnam.

Vietnam nestles on the eastern shore of the Indochinese peninsula, and paradise-like beaches stretch from one end of the country to another. The land is fertile and abundant with untapped natural resources. Its people are gentle and blessed with an expansive civilization and affluent culture. These are the reasons why Vietnam has been much coveted by foreign invaders over the centuries.

The aim of this chapter is to provide rehabilitation providers in the United States with basic information on Vietnam's history, culture, people, and disability issues so that they can better serve Vietnamese with disabilities in the United States.

Cultural Overview

HISTORICAL BACKGROUND

Civil warfare and battles against foreign invaders are not unknown to the Vietnamese people. Their 4,000 years of history are filled with tales of the battlefield.

The saga began when the earliest settlers migrated from the Chinese province of Kwang Si into the peninsula we now call "Indochina." They were known as the Lac and the Tay Au. In the 5th century B.C., the Viet and Yue people from the coastal provinces of China joined the earlier migrants and expanded their settlements southward. Along the way, these early Vietnamese also assimilated the people of Champa (Chiêm Thành) and Kmer (Thủy Chân Lạp) and adopted some of their culture and traditions. This migration continued southward for more than 15 centuries.

The Chinese ruled Vietnam for the next 1,000 years and instilled in the Vietnamese China's Confucian philosophy and political culture. These, however, were unsettling years. Constant rebellions emerged as the Vietnamese tried to reclaim their land. They succeeded in A.D. 939. With their hard-won independence, the Vietnamese continued to extend their settlements south to the Mekong Delta (Viets With a Mission, 2002).

In 1858, Vietnam fell prey to another foreign invader, the French. The French began their conquest in the south and by 1885 had occupied all of Vietnam. In the early 20th century, anticolonial sentiment again began to fuel a nationalist movement. This was the genesis of the modern-day communist movement led by Ho Chi Minh. In March of 1945, Japan invaded Vietnam and stripped the French of all power. Ho Chi Minh seized the opportunity and declared the independence of the Democratic Republic of Vietnam on September 2, 1945.

After World War II, the French refused to relinquish their colonial reign over Vietnam. War broke out between the communist-led Viet Minh (predecessors of modern-day Viet Cong) and the anticommunist Vietnamese, who sided with the French. The defeat of the French at Dien Bien Phu in May 1954 ended this 8-year war and led to the first Geneva peace talks. The Geneva agreement was a temporary division of Vietnam at the 17th parallel. The north was given to the communists, and the south was allocated to the noncommunists. The two sides were to reconvene in 1956 for a general election that would bring the two provisional zones together as a unified country. Instead, on October 26, 1955, South Vietnam declared itself the Republic of Vietnam.

Determined to unify the country, northern communists aggressively recruited new members and reconnected with former networks in the south.

This new force became known as Viet Cong, which led an underground, armed campaign against anyone who refused to support the cause of reunification. In 1961, in the face of internal political turmoil, South Vietnamese President Ngo Dinh Diem requested the aid of the United States. President Kennedy sent military advisers. They were followed by U.S. combat forces sent by President Johnson to help crush the Viet Cong campaign, thus initiating the Vietnam War.

The war reached its turning point on the Vietnamese New Year's Day in 1968, an effort known as the Tet Offensive. The north and south again agreed to hold peace talks in Paris. The talks dragged on at an agonizing pace while the war continued to take its toll. A peace agreement was finally reached on January 27, 1973. The United States agreed to withdraw its troops from Vietnam, but military advisers remained behind. On April 30, 1975, the communists finally took over Saigon and completed their mission to reunify the country.

Even after reunification, war continued to break out on the borders of Vietnam. In December of 1978, Vietnam declared war against its western neighbor, Cambodia. China, a longtime supporter of Cambodia's Khmer Rouge regime, retaliated against Vietnam by attacking its northern border.

In the mid-1980s, there was a drastic change in the communist party agenda, with a new focus on economic reform. The result was impressive. Vietnam became one of the fastest-growing economies in the world, with an 8% annual GDP growth from 1990 to 1997. Vietnam's inflation rate fell from 300% in 1987 to 4% in 1997. Per capita income rose from $220 in 1994 to $372 in 1999.

The 1990s was a decade of growth and prosperity. Vietnam became a member of the World Bank, the International Monetary Fund, the Asian Development Bank, the Association of South-East nations, and the Asia-Pacific Economic Cooperation Forum. The United States normalized its relationship with Vietnam in 1994. The country currently has observer status in the World Trade Organization and is applying for membership. Vietnam expanded trade with neighboring countries and European markets. The culmination was the signing of the Bilateral Trade Agreement between the United States and Vietnam in July 2000, granting normal trade relations status for Vietnamese goods in the U.S. market (Bureau of East Asian and Pacific Affairs, 2001).

CULTURE

Over the centuries, although the Vietnamese culture has been influenced by many foreign invaders, one can recognize the distinctive core values of the Vietnamese. Vietnamese cultural values rest on the principles of Confucianism. Contrary to the Western idea of individualism, Vietnamese culture emphasizes the importance of family and community, and its core values are harmony, duty, honor, respect, education, and allegiance to the family.

Harmony

The concept of harmony is based largely on the teachings of Confucianism, Buddhism, and Taoism. Total harmony is achieved by creating harmony within oneself and one's family, as well as in the outer world of humanity and nature. To produce harmony, an individual must observe moderation and avoid extremes. Moderation is practiced in verbal communication, daily life activities, consumption of food and drink, and social interaction. These measures are undertaken to ensure physical safety and to adhere to the moral imperative to keep one's dignity unimpaired.

Duty and Honor

Duty and honor are among the highest cultural values. Individuals are instilled from childhood with the values of honor, hard work, and loyalty to the family. Individuals have the ultimate duty to carry themselves with the utmost dignity in all circumstances so as to not bring shame to oneself and the family. To lose face dishonors oneself and one's family. The duty and role of each immediate and extended family member are well defined. These duties and roles govern the actions of the individual and are the sacrifices one makes to one's family. For example, the role of parents is to raise their children properly. Their duties are not limited to providing food and shelter but also require them to educate and instill the children with moral values. The children, in turn, have the duties to obey their parents and never to question their authority or teaching. When the parents get older, it is the duty of the children to take care of them.

Respect

Respect is the foundation of Confucius's teaching, and it is the guiding principle of interpersonal relationships in Vietnamese society. At home, one is expected to show respect to parents and family members. Outside the home, respect is shown to elderly people, teachers, and other authority figures. Respect is conveyed through language and demeanor. By showing respect to others, individuals indicate their expectation that they will be treated with the respect due their age, social status, or authoritative position. Respect is earned by leading a virtuous life, fulfilling one's filial and social duties, accomplishing heroic deeds, and attaining a high degree of intellectuality.

Education

Education is the pillar of Vietnamese culture. This is evidenced in its literacy rate of 94% (Central Intelligence Agency, 2003). Education begins at home. In fact, it is the duty of parents to educate their children. Education is valued more than material wealth and success. A rich person who is uneducated will be looked down upon and regarded as inferior to a learned person who is poor. In the traditional Vietnamese social system, the scholar ranks first in value, then the farmer, the artisan, and the tradesman. The driving force to be educated is fueled by a desire for social respect, prestige, and the prospect of vertical mobility in Vietnamese society.

Allegiance to Family

Vietnamese are taught as children to forsake the ego and make individual sacrifices to ensure the family's welfare and harmony. Allegiance to one's family is absolute and includes fulfilling one's responsibilities, obligations, familial role, duties, and proper conduct. "Improper conduct" brings shame and dishonor to self and family. The most feared criticism is the allegation of "ill-breeding," which can do significant damage to the ego and disgrace the family's honor. Moderation, modesty, moral probity, and self-control demonstrate allegiance to the family.

It is important to emphasize that in the past few decades, the traditional Vietnamese family has been deteriorating as an institution as a result of communist ideology, an impoverished economy, migration, and assimilation of Western culture. The communist regime mandated that the state replace parents as the ultimate authority in every household. Loyalty and allegiance to the communist party was expected to take precedence over family loyalties. In fact, children were trained to spy on their parents and report any "subversive behaviors" to the party.

Decades of war annihilated homes and villages in the countryside. After the war, many abandoned their native villages and moved to big cities in search of jobs. This often caused the breakup of the immediate as well as the extended family unit. The mass exodus of refugees since the late 1970s sent Vietnamese to countries all over the world. As children of these families assimilate Western culture and embrace the ideology of individualism, the cohesiveness of the traditional Vietnamese family institution is further jeopardized.

FAMILY

Family is the cornerstone of the Vietnamese society. As opposed to the American nuclear family, the Vietnamese family follows the extended multigenerational pattern. It is not uncommon for a Vietnamese household to include the parents, the sons and their wives (in some instances, daughters and their husbands), grandchildren, and unmarried siblings. Everyone in the immediate family has a distinctive role.

The concept of family extends to close relatives and beyond. In fact, the Vietnamese perceive society as one big extended family. This is demonstrated by the way Vietnamese greet one another. Even among strangers, kinship pronouns are often used as a way to show respect and to reinforce the importance of kinship in Vietnamese culture.

In a typical Vietnamese family household, the father is the central figure and is responsible for the well-being of every member of his family. He is usually the ultimate decision maker and provider. However, grandparents and elder relatives within the immediate household often share the authority with the father. Hierarchy of authority also exists among siblings. The oldest son of the family has the most authority, and it is his duty to look after all the siblings if the parents are deceased. Familial duties and obligations extend beyond the immediate family to the extended family and, in some cases, beyond the living. Ancestor worship is a form of filial piety. Children are responsible for the maintenance of the ancestral tombs and pay homage to ancestors' spirits at home. Beyond the extended family, familial obligations also involve the physical setting in which the family resides, the native village. The attachment and obligation to the native village stem from the concept of harmony.

COMMUNICATION

Vietnamese children are taught at a very young age to adhere to the cultural practice of harmony and to be modest and reserved in both speech and mannerism. Children are encouraged to think deeply before they speak. It is believed that useless and excessive verbal expressions can have dire consequences and create discord and animosity. Hasty words and slips of the tongue are considered to be as detrimental as hasty actions and bad deeds. Because of these values, Vietnamese often appear to be reserved, nonresponsive, or nonassertive by American standards.

Vietnamese society values formality and tradition. The Vietnamese language is perhaps one of the most formal and sophisticated of languages. Proper usage of language is considered a way to convey respect and create harmonious relationships with others. Because society as a whole is viewed as an extended family, Vietnamese use many kinship phrases to greet strangers and nonrelatives. For example, the pronoun *con*, meaning child, is used when speaking to an older person to convey respect and honor the cultural significance of social cohesiveness. Table 10.1 illustrates the usage of two common pronouns.

Nonverbal communications are equally important in conveying respect and are often used to reinforce linguistic expressions. As in many cultures, these nonverbal gestures are unique and may have meanings that are different

Table 10.1   Common Pronoun Usage

English Pronoun	Vietnamese Equivalents	Literary Meaning When Used
I	Con	Child: when speaking to an elderly or authority
	Em	Younger sibling: when speaking with an elder peer
	Tôi	Self: when speaking to your peer
	Tao	Self: use to express superiority over another person in quarrels
You	Cô	"Miss": when speaking to a young lady in general
	Em	"Miss" or "girl": when speaking to someone younger than you
	Anh	"Mister" or "brother": when speaking to a young man or a man older than you
	Chị	"Miss" or "Mrs.": in formal address
	Ông	"Mister," "gentleman," "husband": when speaking to a man or older man
	Bà	"Mrs." and "lady": when speaking to an older woman
	Mây	"You": informal use or use to express contempt

from the meanings that Americans attach to the same gestures. A few nonverbal expressions deserve attention because they may often be misinterpreted by Americans.

- As children, Americans are taught to make direct eye contact with the speaker as a sign of respect. Vietnamese children, however, are taught that direct eye contact with parents, teachers, or authority figures (a health care provider is considered an authority figure) means a challenge and should be avoided.
- In conversing with the opposite sex, direct eye contact can be interpreted as deep passion and should be discouraged, especially in public settings.
- Vietnamese children are taught to remain silent and listen attentively when speaking to someone older or an authority figure and not to talk back or ask questions. Asking questions or disagreeing with an authoritative speaker is like challenging the senior person's social status. Therefore, most Vietnamese conduct themselves in a passive or nonresponsive manner according to American standards.
- A smile can convey many different meanings as well:
  - It is used as an expression of an apology for committing minor offenses.
  - It is an expression of embarrassment that follows a blunder or a request to reveal personal information. For example, when asked about the death of a

family member, Americans would typically respond with a sad expression. It is not uncommon for a Vietnamese person to respond to the same question with a smile as a sign of being embarrassed for having to reveal such personal information.

- A smile is also an appropriate response to expressions such as "Thank you," "Hi," or "I am sorry." It is not customary for older persons, parents, and authoritative figures to thank subordinates for favors or deeds. A smile will suffice. When a person pays a compliment to another person, a "thank you" is not expected in return. Instead, the recipient will acknowledge it with a smile. Saying "Thank you" in this case would be considered arrogant or immodest.

Table 10.2 provides examples of common everyday gestures.

Table 10.2   Common Gestures

Nonverbal gesture	Meaning in Vietnamese Culture
Nodding	Greeting, affirmative reply, agreement
Bowing	Greeting, great respect
Avoiding eye contact	Showing respect to people senior in age or status or of opposite sex
Winking	Not decent, especially when directed at a person of the opposite sex
Smiling	Agreement, embarrassment, disbelief, mild disagreement, appreciation, apology
Shaking hands	Friendly greeting between men (but not the elderly), not customary between women or between a man and a woman, acceptable between a Vietnamese woman and a non-Vietnamese man
Gesture of beckoning with index finger	Offensive to adults, threatening to children
Holding hands with or putting an arm over the shoulder of a person of the same sex	Friendly gesture, no sexual connotation
Crossing arms	Sign of respect
Putting one or both hands in the pockets or on the hips while talking	Arrogance, lack of respect

Nonverbal gesture	Meaning in Vietnamese Culture
Patting a person's back, especially those senior in age or status	Disrespectful
Pointing to other people while talking	Disrespectful
Whistling at performers	Displeasure
Putting one's feet on a table or sitting on a desk while talking	Rude

PEOPLE

As a people, Vietnamese are strong, resilient, gentle, kind, and mild in nature. They maintain a social disposition of grace, reservation, and shyness. Approximately 85–90% of the population of Vietnam is of Vietnamese ethnicity, but various minority groups inhabit all parts of the country. Most of these minorities have assimilated the Vietnamese culture well but retain their ethnic identity. For the most part, these minority groups have coexisted well with the indigenous Vietnamese. Tensions and discrimination, however, have flared up at times, as they did after the Vietnam War.

After the fall of Saigon, the new regime, fueled by nationalistic sentiment and border conflicts with China, intended to expel its Chinese merchant class. Chinese people are the largest minority group living in South Vietnam. Many Chinese immigrated to Vietnam as a result of the Japanese invasion in the 1930s. Most of them still live within their own communities, send their children to private Chinese-speaking schools, and celebrate Chinese holidays and traditions. In fact, it is not uncommon for some Chinese to speak only Chinese and have no understanding of the language and culture of Vietnam. Although these Chinese are of Vietnamese nationality, many claim to be Chinese rather than Vietnamese.

Significant numbers of Hmong, Cham, Thai, and mountain people reside in the countryside. Another minority worth mentioning are the "Amerasians" born in Vietnam to Vietnamese mothers and American fathers during the war. They are referred to as *con lai* or *my lai* (biracial child or Amerasian, respectively). They are usually teased and bullied by other children, and their mothers are shunned and shamed by society. The Amerasians are treated well in the United States, however, even within Vietnamese immigrant communities.

RELIGIONS

Religion has a profound impact on Vietnamese culture. Buddhism is the dominant form of religion in Vietnam, followed by Confucianism, Taoism,

Christianity (mainly Roman Catholic), *Caodaism, Hoa Hao,* animism, and Islam.

Vietnamese practice the branch of Buddhism called Theravada Buddhism. The Chinese introduced Buddhism to Vietnam during their early years of conquest, and it appealed to the Vietnamese for many reasons. The central tenet of Buddhism is that man was born into this world to suffer as a result of his craving for wealth, fame, power, and material goods. To be rid of this suffering, man must suppress his cravings. Given the long history of suffering of the Vietnamese people from continual warfare, this aspect of the religion is appealing. Also, Buddhism mandates that man must live a life of virtue based on these principles: the right view, right thought, right conduct, right speech, right livelihood, right effort, right mindfulness, and right meditation. These virtues are congruent with Vietnamese cultural values.

Confucianism and Taoism are also Chinese imports. Again, these religions or philosophies emphasize the importance of family life, social virtues, and harmony, which are the foundations of Vietnamese culture. These two religions have coexisted along with Buddhism in Vietnam for a very long time.

Christianity was introduced to Vietnam in the second half of the 16th century by Portuguese, Spanish, and French missionaries but does not play a major role in Vietnamese culture. The number of Christians, especially Catholics, has increased since the migration of refugees from the north in 1954 and the arrival of the Americans. Many renowned figures, such as former president Ngo Dihn Diem and much of the leadership in South Vietnam from 1954 to 75, were Catholic.

Cao Dai and *Hoa Hao* are two newly established religions in Vietnam. *Cao Dai* was founded in 1919 by Le Van Trung and is practiced mainly in the Southern Delta region. *Caodaism* incorporates teaching from Buddha, Jesus, Confucius, Lao Tse, Victor Hugo, and others. The number of followers is estimated at one million. *Hoa Hao* is a reformed Buddhist sect of the Theravada variety founded in 1939 by Huýnh Phu So and practiced mainly in the Mekong Delta region. Its membership is approximately two million.

Animism in Vietnam is closely related to the three major religions— Buddhism, Confucianism, and Taoism. Animism is perhaps one of the oldest forms of religion. The basis of this religion is the worship of spirits. Elements of animism are found in the common practice of ancestor worship in Vietnam. Regardless of religion, most Vietnamese practice ancestor worship as a form of filial piety. When family elders pass away, shrines are erected in the house in their honor. Ritualistic incense offerings are a way to worship and pay homage. On the anniversary of the death, the family often plans an elaborate feast and invites the extended family to commune with the spirit of the ancestor. This celebration is known as *Cúng.*

History of Immigration to the United States and Reasons for Immigration

On April 30, 1975, the day Saigon fell, thousands of Vietnamese fled with American soldiers and government employees. Most of these were ex-military, government officials, and employees of the U.S. military and their families. This was the first wave of Vietnamese immigrants to the United States. After the communists took over Saigon and renamed it as Ho Chi Minh City, an iron curtain was drawn against emigration.

The second wave of emigration began in the late 1970s. Because of political persecution, social turmoil, and dire poverty, many escaped Vietnam by boat. The fortunate ones landed in refugee camps in Thailand, Malaysia, Indonesia, the Philippines, and Hong Kong. The unfortunate ones fell prey to pirates at sea and natural forces. Those who survived became known as the "boat people." At first, they were welcomed and treated well in most refugee camps. As the number of refugees grew, they became a burden to their host countries, and many were turned away and repatriated. The last refugee camp in Hong Kong was closed on May 31, 2000. In Hong Kong alone, 200,000 boat people arrived over the span of 25 years (Vietnamese Missionaries in Taiwan, 2000).

As the horrible tales of boat people being drowned at sea and killed by pirates came to light, the United Nations High Commissioner for Refugees negotiated an agreement with the Vietnamese government to allow Vietnamese who had relatives in the United States to emigrate. Under the "Orderly Departure Program," still in operation, a small number of Vietnamese have successfully emigrated to the United States.

Under pressure from Vietnam veterans, the United States agreed to accept Amerasians as refugees. At first, the Vietnamese government refused the offer, claiming that Amerasians were not the victims of discrimination in Vietnam and so did not fit the profile of refugees. It took an act of Congress to alter the status of the Amerasians from refugees to immigrants. Some 100,000 Amerasians eventually were allowed to come to the United States under immigrant status, but they were entitled to the same benefits as refugees.

At the same time, the U.S. Department of State also made progress to allow the immigration of political prisoners. After the war, former South Vietnamese government workers, military personnel, and intellectuals were sent to "reeducation camps." The prisoners were detained for many years under harsh and inhumane conditions. In 1988, the U.S. Department of State successfully negotiated an agreement with the Vietnamese government to allow about 100,000 of these prisoners to emigrate through the Orderly Departure Program.

In total, approximately 995,000 Vietnamese refugees have immigrated to the United States. Most settled in Southern California, particularly in Los Angeles and Orange County, because of the familiar climate and support from the large Vietnamese community. Others settled in Houston, Dallas, the suburbs of Washington, D.C., and the states of Washington, Pennsylvania, Minnesota, Massachusetts, New York, and Illinois (Southeast Asia Resource Action Center, 2002).

Vietnamese Concepts of Disability

There are two general perspectives on disability in Vietnamese society. Until scientific evidence surfaced linking Agent Orange to many forms of congenital disability, Vietnamese ascribed disability to a more traditional belief that it is a punishment for sins committed by one's ancestors. The modern perspective on disability attributes almost all forms of disabilities to Agent Orange and injuries from the war. Both of these views have consequences for how society treats people with disabilities.

TRADITIONAL VIEW OF DISABILITY

The traditional view of disability in Vietnam is significantly influenced by its religious beliefs and cultural values and attributes disability to be bad deeds or sins committed by one's ancestors. This belief stems from the concept of reincarnation, which holds that from birth to death to the afterlife, a person assumes the same identity, in physical or spiritual form. Whereas Western religion views life as a linear continuum, in Buddhism, life is seen as cyclical. The soul of a person never perishes; instead, it reincarnates into another existence and identity with each life cycle. The cycle of life has its hierarchy of significance. Humans rank highest, and insects are at the lowest level. The ultimate goal of a Buddhist is to be free from this cycle of reincarnation and reach Nirvana, a state of complete redemption and supreme happiness. Humans need to live a life of virtue in order to reach Nirvana. Persons who committed evil deeds not only will be punished by being reincarnated as a less significant form of life, but their descendants also will suffer similar consequences. Disability is associated with imperfection of the self. Hence, to be disabled is to be regarded as a less significant life-form caused by sins or evil deeds committed by one's ancestors.

NEW PERSPECTIVE ON DISABILITY

There is, however, a new perspective on disability that has emerged since the Vietnam War. This new perspective is more pragmatic and scientifically relevant. As more and more evidence emerges linking Agent Orange to a host of diseases, debilitating conditions, and disabilities, Vietnamese attribute many birth defects and congenital disabilities to the chemical agent. The American scientific community shares this view. A 1998 report by the National Academy of Sciences attributed the high incidence of Vietnamese children with spina bifida to the effects of Agent Orange.

Agent Orange was an herbicide developed by the U.S. military in the 1940s. During the Vietnam War, the U.S. military used 19 million gallons of Agent Orange to destroy all trees, vegetation, and crops in jungles and farmlands where the enemy could hide. Agent Orange is harmful to humans and contains TCDD, which causes a variety of diseases, many of which are fatal to animals in laboratory testing (Agent Orange Website, 2002). In addition to Agent Orange, other causes of disabilities are injuries from land mines, casualties from the war, and industrial labor and traffic accidents.

With this new perspective on Agent Orange, most people with disabilities are viewed as victims of the war. In the past decade, the government of Vietnam has used a paternalistic approach to address the needs of this population. Adopting measures similar to those in the United States, the Vietnamese government enacted the "Ordinance on Disabled Persons" to provide a legal basis for protecting people with disabilities in Vietnam.

Concept of Independence

Vietnamese cultural values are based on the teachings of Confucius, which emphasize the importance of family cohesiveness and social harmony. Western cultures encourage individual freedom and independence. These cultural values are instilled in children at a very young age. For example, in the United States, children may be asked what they would like to be when they grow up. In Vietnam, children are asked what they will do to contribute to society when they are grown. Children in the United States are expected to establish their own identities and to leave home once they become of age. Vietnamese children are expected to grow old with their immediate families, married or not. Typically, when a man is married, his wife will move in and live with him and his family. However, there are occasions in which a man is married into his wife's family, but the concept of generational independence is almost nonexistent in Vietnamese culture.

Confucianism also stresses the importance of reverence for the elderly and caring for the vulnerable. Vietnamese elders live among their immediate family until their death and are cared for and well respected. After death, shrines will be built at home to continue to honor them.

Similarly, people with disabilities are deemed vulnerable, and it is the immediate family's responsibility to care for them. To expect an elderly person or a person with disabilities to live alone and to be independent is considered cruel. The family in such a case would be shamed and chided by society for neglecting familial duties. This contrasts with the American concept of independence and the philosophy behind the disability rights movement.

Acquired Disabilities and Lifelong Disabilities

The traditional view attributes disability to be a punishment for the sins committed by one's ancestors. Within this context, disability, whether acquired or congenital, is associated with shame and pity. Because of the fear of public humiliation, family members usually take extraordinary measures to keep the person with disabilities out of the public eye.

People with mental disabilities are regarded differently from those with physical disabilities. Because of the influence of Buddhism and animism, mental illness is believed to represent possession by evil spirits, and exorcism is considered the remedy. Affluent families usually hire monks or fortune-tellers to conduct elaborate exorcisms in the hope of driving the evil spirit out of the inflicted. Those whose family cannot afford such treatment often end up homeless on the street.

One form of congenital disability is given special social status; however. People who are blind at birth are, in certain social circles, revered as psychics and fortune-tellers. It is believed that these persons have special vision and power that can see beyond the present life into the past and the future. They often work at a temple, in their own shop, or in the open market. For a small fee, these "psychics" can reveal to clients their past and future and what the present life will hold.

The newer perspective regards people with disabilities as victims of the war. Society in general pities, yet sympathizes, with these "victims." Because Agent Orange is believed to cause both acquired and congenital disabilities, there is no differential treatment between these two categories of disability, especially in the postwar generation. They are all regarded as victims of the war.

Interactions With Service Providers

In the United States, a major problem in providing rehabilitation services to Vietnamese with disabilities is the lack of culturally and linguistically competent professionals and appropriate programs. Outside Southern California, many states and cities have no Vietnamese staff in rehabilitation services programs. This makes it difficult for Vietnamese to obtain adequate services. Furthermore, conflicts in cultural values may deter some Vietnamese from seeking appropriate care. The following are examples of challenges posed by these barriers.

PERSON-CENTERED APPROACH

The person-centered approach in rehabilitation services emphasizes maximum participation of the consumers. Individuals with disabilities are encouraged to take an active role in guiding their course of rehabilitation. Although this approach is appropriate and adheres to the Western ideology of consumerism, it may pose considerable conflict for the Vietnamese, who are accustomed to a more paternalistic approach to health care delivery. It must be clarified that "paternalism" does not imply servitude, but instead respect for tradition. In Vietnamese society, health care professionals are authority figures who are well respected. The culture dictates that authority figures have the obligation to care for and protect all their constituents. Vietnamese not only will expect absolute guidance from health care professionals but also will comply without contesting or questioning their decisions. The following is an example of how cultural differences may play a role in rehabilitation services.

Case #1

Truc is a 40-year-old, highly educated Vietnamese immigrant who arrived in the United States less than 2 years ago. Formerly a teacher, Truc is fluent in English. However, because of his lack of professional credentials, he could not find a teaching position and works as a delivery person.

Truc was struck by a car and sustained a spinal cord injury. Upon his discharge from the hospital, Truc met with a social worker and a vocational rehabilitation counselor to discuss his future plans. When they asked how they could help him and what he would like to do after his discharge, Truc was completely dumbfounded. He expected the social worker and counselor to already have a plan for him.

When asked whether he wanted to return to his former job as a delivery person or to pursue other career avenues, Truc was even more taken aback and amazed. He expected these professionals to give him answers, not questions. After all, they were the experts, so they ought to know what he should do and provide him with the appropriate solutions. To conceal his disappointment, Truc smiled and said nothing. Baffled by Truc's nonverbal response and without pressuring him further, the social worker and counselor decided to follow up with him at a later date. In the meantime, they asked him to contact his local Office of Vocational Rehabilitation (OVR) when he was ready to be helped. Because of his initial disappointment with the professionals and the system, Truc never contacted the OVR.

THE CONCEPT OF INDEPENDENCE

In rehabilitation, the emphasis on independence creates another cultural conflict for Vietnamese. Both the traditional and the new perspective of disability in Vietnam considers persons with disabilities to be vulnerable and helpless. As previously mentioned, people with disabilities, regardless of age or social status, live with immediate family members who have the ultimate responsibility to care for these individuals. Those who neglect such responsibilities will be condemned by society. As noted, the concept of independence is non-existent in Vietnamese culture. In contrast, rehabilitation in the United States focuses on restoring function *and* independence. This might be a difficult concept for Vietnamese to accept. The following is an example of this cultural conflict.

Case #2

Thanh is a 29-year-old Vietnamese woman suffering from paranoid schizophrenia. Though able to manage her daily activities without supervision, she needs constant encouragement to see her psychiatrist and therapist and to take her medication. Thanh lived at home with her immediate family. Her mother decided to stay home to take care of Thanh full time, and her father struggled to support the family of four by working as a cook in a Chinese restaurant. The burden of care and the economic hardship created a tremendous amount of tension and stress among the family members.

Thanh's therapist suggested that she apply for disability benefits and find a place to live on her own. The case manager at the clinic was willing to help the family with the necessary paperwork. The therapist explained further that living alone would help Thanh to be more independent. She would not be on her own completely; the case manager would make sure she kept her doctor appointments and took her medication. This would help to relieve the family's burden of care. Allowing the mother to return to work would help to ease the family's economic hardship.

At first, bound by cultural tradition, the family was not willing to challenge or disagree with the therapist. However, when the case manager approached the family to begin the paperwork, the family was forced to admit it was in complete disagreement with the therapist. The parents felt that Thanh should be taken care of at home by the family. They acknowledged that it was difficult, but that it is the family's obligation to take care of Thanh, and it would continue to do so. Allowing Thanh to live alone would mean abandoning her and neglecting their family duties. The family would be shamed by relatives and other Vietnamese in their community.

LINGUISTIC BARRIERS

The lack of Vietnamese-speaking staff in most U.S. rehabilitation programs and hospitals limits the ability of Vietnamese to get adequate and appropriate care, as well as posing financial hardships and burdens of care on the family. Finding a professional Vietnamese translator in a small town or city is not easy. Persons with disabilities tend to rely on family members (often young children), friends, relatives, and immigrants in the local community for translation when dealing with health care professionals.

This means that family members, friends, and relatives need to take time off from school and jobs to help the individual in need, which may create difficulties for some families, especially when translation services are needed on a continuing basis. More important, some of these translators are neither professionally trained in medical terminology or proficient in English. Therefore, the quality of the information they provide is compromised. This can result in misunderstanding and confusion. Linguistic barriers also arise from the differences in the ways American and Vietnamese express themselves verbally and nonverbally. The following is a case in point.

Case #3

Mr. Nguyen, a 67-year-old Vietnamese man, underwent hip replacement surgery. The attending physician gave Nguyen and his daughter an update on his progress. To show respect, neither Nguyen nor his daughter made direct eye contact with the physician in the course of their conversation. The baffled physician thought the patient and his daughter did not understand fully what he was saying. To express his frustration, he put his two hands on his hips and repeated the progress report slowly and loudly. Nguyen and his daughter were surprised by the doctor's show of disrespect. Vietnamese consider putting one's hands on the hips while talking to be a sign of arrogance and lack of respect, especially when addressing an elderly person. Furthermore, because of the doctor's tone of voice, they felt they were being lectured. Nguyen took great offense to such treatment because he was much older than the physician. To conceal their anger and humiliation, they gave a polite nod to the physician. Satisfied with the response, the physician thought he had conveyed his message effectively and left the room. Both Nguyen and his daughter were so totally humiliated by the doctor's behavior that they dismissed everything the doctor had said.

ALTERNATIVE MEDICAL APPROACH

Because of the lack of access to Western medicine in Vietnam, most Vietnamese turn to folk medicine as their first line of defense when treating general maladies. It is important for U.S. service providers to be familiar with these alternative medical practices in order to prescribe treatments that are complementary and respectful of these practices. The lack of understanding of these folk medicine practices can lead to unnecessary pain and embarrassment for the family as well as the health care providers. The following case exemplifies this problem:

Case #4

A newly immigrated Vietnamese couple took their 6-year-old daughter to the emergency room at a local hospital for treatment of a protracted episode of chills and fevers. Prior to taking the girl to the hospital, the parents performed coining on her hope that what she had was a cold and could be cured. Coining involves scratching the skin on the chest with a coin applying mentholated oil and to "draw out the malady." This practice, which is common in Southeast Asia, leaves temporary marks on the body. Upon examination, the emergency doctor mistook the coining marks as marks of flogging and immediately called in social services. Because of language barriers, the couple could not explain the markings to the social worker. The couple was immediately incarcerated and charged with child abuse. A trip to the emergency room landed the parents in jail and the little girl in a foster home.

Folk medicine is an integral part of traditional Vietnamese culture, and it is still practiced widely, even among immigrants in the United States. These traditional forms of healing are strongly influenced by spirituality and homeopathy. In accordance with the practice of Buddhism and animism, many illnesses are considered to be caused by sins committed by persons in their previous life, by their ancestors, or by evil spirits or natural forces trapped inside the soul and body. Exorcism by means of chanting, holy potions, and wearing amulets are the usual remedies. Likewise, herbal medicines and homeopathic treatments are common health remedies. Table 10.3 lists common examples of treatments for general ailments:

Table 10.3   Common Treatments for General Ailments

Practice	Remedy
Coining (Cạo Gió)	Mentholated oil is applied to the back and the chest area. A coin or a spoon is used to gently scratch the skin in a prescribed pattern, down the spinal column with lines radiating to the side. On occasion, the skin is nicked with a seashell to let the bad blood out. Coining does not cause skin wounds or leave permanent marks, but it does leave mild dermabrasion that will disappear in a few days.
Cupping (Giác)	A cotton swab is used to apply isopropyl alcohol to the inside of a cup, and the same swab is used to ignite the alcohol. The cup is placed on the skin, either on the back or on the forehead. A series of six to eight hot cups is used on the back, and one

Practice	Remedy
	is used in the center of the forehead. The cups are removed once. There will be some moisture on the skin and a circular red mark that will last for a few days. The moisture is understood to be the bad force causing the malady.
Pinching (Bắt gió)	Headaches are believed to be caused by cold or hot air trapped inside the head, and it is thought that the cold or hot air can be released by the art of pinching. First, the temples are rubbed with the thumbs in circular motion, then pressure strokes are applied on the forehead in a sweeping motion from the temples to the center of the forehead. This sweeping action gathers all the air to the center of the forehead. The skin fold between the two brows is plucked by using the knuckles of the index and the middle fingers. This can be slightly painful, and the end result is a bright red mark between the brows.
Steaming (Xông)	A variety of herbs are boiled in water. The patient either inhales the steam of this broth or bathes in this herbal potion.
Balm	Brand-name balms such as Tiger Balm and a host of other medicated balms and oils are rubbed on the body to relieve muscle aches, skin rashes, small abrasions, colds, and the flu.
Acupuncture	A practice adopted from the Chinese, acupuncture is the use of small needles to relieve the pressure on certain vital points on the meridian channels. These points correspond to specific organs in the body. The practice provides healing, restores balance, and increases energy flow.
Herbs	Adopted from the Chinese. Herbs are brewed for consumption in order to treat a variety of maladies.
Packaged medicine	A variety of herbal medicines are processed and packaged into pill or liquid forms, with flavors added to ease consumption. The traditional preparation of herbal medicine requires hours. The bitter taste makes it difficult for children to consume.

Recommendations for Rehabilitation Service Providers

COMMUNICATION

- Be mindful of verbal and nonverbal communication cues.
- Do not make the mistake of speaking loudly to the person who may have few English skills.
- Do not speak in a patronizing or overly sympathetic tone, especially to the elderly.
- Anticipate evasive answers at times. Being assertive and aggressive is not encouraged in Vietnamese culture.

INDEPENDENCE

- Be prepared for "independence" to be an unacceptable goal for clients.
- Nursing homes and long-term care facilities are not acceptable solutions for many Vietnamese families.

FOLK MEDICINE

- Be familiar with some of the traditional medical practices and diets.

Conclusion

Vietnam is a country that has been ravaged by warfare throughout the centuries. In spite of it all, its people remain strong and resilient in mind, body, and spirit. The land retains its beauty, and its cultural heritage has been preserved and enriched. Having to abandon their homeland and assimilate a new culture is difficult for many Vietnamese immigrants in the United States. It is the hope of the author that this chapter sheds some light on these issues and provides basic information for rehabilitation service providers to better serve Vietnamese with disabilities.

References

Agent Orange Website. (2002). Retrieved July 16, 2002, from www.lewispublishing. com/orange.htm

Bureau of East Asian and Pacific Affairs, U.S. Department of State. (2001, July). Background note: Vietnam. Retrieved July 16, 2002, from www.state.gov/r/pa/bgn/ 4130.htm

Central Intelligence Agency. (2003). *The world factbook: Vietnam.* Retrieved April 13, 2004, from www.cia.gov/cia/publications/factbook/geos/vm.html

Southeast Asia Resource Action Center. (2002). Vietnamese refugees. Retrieved July 16, 2002, from www.searac.org/vietref.html

Vietnamese Missionaries in Taiwan. (2000, May 20). Closure of Hong Kong's last Vietnamese refugee camp ends 25-year "boat people" saga. Retrieved July 16, 2002, from www.catholic.org.tw/vntaiwan/asia/6hogkong.htm

Viets With a Mission. (2002). Viet Nam. Retrieved July 15, 2002, from www.vwam.com/vets/vietnam.html.

11

Understanding Immigrants
With Disabilities

John Stone

B y now, readers may be wondering how it is possible for service providers to work across cultures. Dozens of major cultural groups are immigrating to the United States. The cultures described in the preceding chapters are merely a sample. How can service providers possibly understand the nuances of each culture and how they relate to disability? Moreover, there are substantial differences within each culture. Individuals within the different cultural groups often hold widely differing views among themselves.

Additionally, there are differences that result from a person's socioeconomic and educational levels. Moreover, among the many factors contributing to different levels of acculturation are the length of time the person has been living in the United States and the reasons for immigration. In some cases, immigration to the United States is a long-held dream for which the immigrant has prepared for many years. In other cases, the person arrives in the United States abruptly and not entirely by choice, in order to escape from political turmoil.

Even those who have immigrated by choice probably will experience the phenomenon of culture shock to some degree. In some cases, the experience may be devastating. One of the earliest descriptions of the experience of being foreign was provided by Jack London in 1900 in his work "In a Far Country."

When a man journeys into a far country, he must be prepared to forget many of the things he has learned, and to acquire such customs as are inherent with existence in the new land; he must abandon the old ideals and the old gods, and oftentimes he must reverse the very codes by which his conduct has hitherto been shaped. To those who have the protean faculty of adaptability, the novelty of such change may even be a source of pleasure; but to those who happen to be hardened to the ruts in which they were created, the pressure of the altered environment is unbearable, and they chafe in body and in spirit under the new restrictions which they do not understand. This chafing is bound to act and react, producing diverse evils and leading to various misfortunes. It were better for the man who cannot fit himself to the new groove to return to his own country; if he delay too long, he will surely die. (Labor, 1970, p. 302)

In their introduction to the book *On Being Foreign,* Lewis and Jungman (1986) describe the phases of culture shock and acculturation. A recent immigrant may be in one of these phases and consumers of disability services may pass from one phase to another during the period in which they are receiving services.

Figure 11.1 depicts a typical reaction to a new culture. The figure shows a person's sense of emotional well-being fluctuating above or below its normal level as the person passes through certain phases of adjustment to a new culture. Although it is not possible to predict accurately when and how intensely a specific individual will react in any given period, this pattern appears to be typical.

In the first phase, during the initial contact with the new culture, there is a feeling of excitement and elation with the new environment. One is fascinated by the new surroundings and new people. Soon, however, frustrations appear when people in the new country do not behave in ways to which the immigrant is accustomed. The inability to predict or even understand behavior within the new culture creates difficulties in relating to native-born persons. This takes an emotional toll, the reactions to which may include restricting interactions as much as possible to persons from the same culture, feeling helpless and sometimes bitter, or even becoming depressed. Some

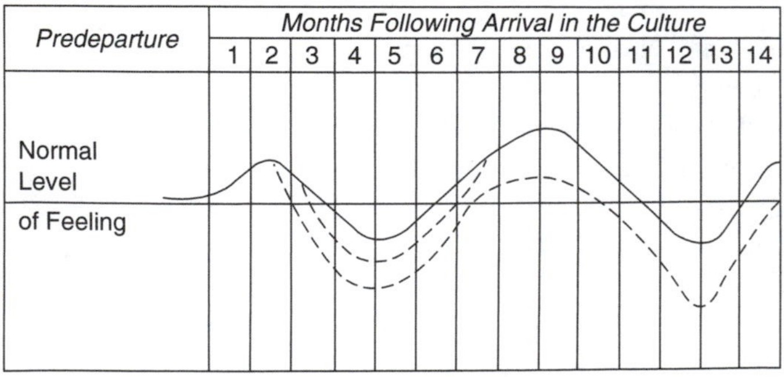

Figure 11.1   Culture Shock Cycle for a 2-Year Period

SOURCE: Kohls (1984)

NOTE: Broken lines indicate the extreme in severity with which culture shock may attack.

persons never get beyond this phase and cope with it by confining their social relationships to like-minded persons from the same country of origin.

However, most begin to understand the ways of the new culture and acquire an exhilarating sense of "making it" in that culture. Meeting the challenges of the new environment through discovery and learning provides a feeling of accomplishment and even pleasure. If learning a new language is involved, this phase is often a period of progress in language acquisition that contributes greatly to an increased understanding of the culture. Sometimes the person is fortunate enough to encounter native-born persons who are natural culture brokers. These persons may instinctively understand that the newcomer might need some explanations for things that seem obvious to the native-born.

There may be a second period of discouragement, when acceptance and progress are not as rapid as had been expected. Many people experience a series of short ups and downs, good periods and bad, as a result of successful and unsuccessful encounters with the new culture. Eventually, the curve becomes flatter, as progress becomes steadier and less a process of trial and error.

If disability service providers understand the processes of adapting to a new cultural environment, they will be in a better position to understand the consumer's frame of mind and ability to assimilate the information that the provider is attempting to communicate. Although there is no formal instrument for assessing the consumer's status regarding cultural adaptation or culture shock, a few questions during the initial conversation may provide some clues. Often, these questions can be integrated into the questions intended to elicit the consumer's explanatory model of disability that were discussed in Chapter 3.

Along with the individual's culture of origin, position within that culture, and phase of culture shock, the process of adaptation to the experience of disability is an additional element in understanding the person's psychological status at the time of the interaction with the service provider.

The degree of adaptation to the experience of disability is another factor in the panorama of elements that may help the provider understand the consumer's perspective. DeLoach and Greer (1981) describe ego defense mechanisms that enable a person to gradually adjust to disability. These include *denial, withdrawal, regression* (to a younger age), *repression* (of unacceptable thoughts), *reaction formation* (behaving in ways that are directly opposite to the way the individual wants to behave), *fantasy, rationalization* (blaming all problems on disability, or devaluing unobtainable goals), *projection* (of one's own prejudices), *identification* (achieving satisfaction through the successes of others with whom the person identifies), and *compensation* (compensating for a deficit in one area by capitalizing on strengths in other areas).

The phase of adjustment to disability and mechanisms used in each phase are important for the service provider to recognize. These mechanisms may also interact with culture, resulting in different manifestations or behaviors in different cultures.

We see, then, that a consumer from another culture will occupy positions on several continuums simultaneously, reflecting the various phases of adaptation to both culture and disability. First, there is the degree of adaptation to the new culture, which may mean that the individual may be in a state of culture shock or at some more advanced point in the process of assimilating the new culture. Second, there is the degree of adjustment to disability, which may influence the coping mechanisms that the person may be using to aid in the process of adjustment. The service provider must be attentive to the status of each client on these dimensions.

Additionally, the service provider must be aware of the specific culture of the individual and how this relates to disability. It is not realistic to expect that service providers can acquire detailed knowledge about the many different cultures of recent immigrants. There are, however, common themes and patterns that are common to many non-Western cultures, in spite of their specific nuances. In the seven chapters of this book that described specific Asian, Latin American, and Caribbean cultures, we can identify some of those common themes. We certainly do not wish to imply that non-Western cultures are identical, nor that all individuals from any particular culture hold the same beliefs and values. Nevertheless, it may be instructive for disability service providers to recognize some of the common patterns they may encounter in recent immigrants.

Health and rehabilitation professionals are respected authorities who should make the decisions regarding treatments. Consumers of disability services in the United States are accustomed to being full participants, if not the directors of their rehabilitation process, and have fought long and hard to make that wish respected. Consumers from other countries, however, may consider that the professional is the expert and may consider it odd for the service provider to be asking about their wishes. This may even cause them to doubt the technical competence of the service provider. In such cases, rather than asking consumers to express their opinions or to make decisions, the service provider may need to ascertain the values of the consumer and the family and incorporate these into treatments or plans. Gradually and subtly, the service provider may be able to increase the consumer's participation in the decision-making process.

Independence does not mean living alone or even holding a job. In many cultures, although disability is stigmatized, being cared for is not. Moreover, families who are perceived as not caring for members with disability may be viewed as irresponsible and heartless. Service providers may need to appeal to other values in the culture, such as providing the consumer satisfaction through meaningful activity or the use of talents.

The causes of disability are often attributed to nonphysical agents. Certain disabilities, especially congenital or developmental disabilities, are frequently thought to be the result of wrongdoing by parents or ancestors. Thus, disability becomes a source of shame for the family. The belief in spiritual causes may not always be fully accepted or openly expressed, but it may explain in part attitudes toward disability. Service providers may not be able to directly contradict such beliefs, but they can provide information regarding physical causes and possible interventions.

The family acts as a unit, and the individual is subordinate to the family. The family may accompany the consumer to meetings with disability service providers, and decisions may be family decisions. Service providers may be required to discuss interventions with the family and involve family members in treatments.

Interactions usually require a high degree of respect and formality. Although informality and the use of first names are often adopted by service providers in the United States as friendly gestures to make consumers more comfortable and at ease, they may have the opposite effect on consumers from Asian, Latino, and Caribbean cultures. Most of the culture-specific chapters of this book noted that consumers, especially older persons, should not be addressed by their first names.

Conclusion

Successful service provision starts with an accurate assessment of the consumers' needs and wishes. The chapter authors and I have argued that assessment of consumers' cultural perspective is necessary to provide disability services competently in a multicultural society. Disability service providers have many assessment instruments developed in their respective professions. The assessment of culture and how it interacts with disability in individual clients cannot be done with such precision. Nevertheless, service providers can obtain relevant and useful cultural insights through conversations with the consumer in light of the information provided in this volume. In the end, the caring and insightful provider will discover from the consumers themselves the information necessary to provide them with culturally competent services.

References

DeLoach, C., & Greer, B. (1981). *Adjustment to severe physical disability: A metamorphosis.* New York: McGraw-Hill.

Kohls, L. R. (1984). *Survival kit for overseas living.* Yarmouth, ME: Intercultural Press.

Labor, E. (Ed.). (1970). *Great short works of Jack London.* New York: Harper & Row.

Lewis, T. J., & Jungman, R. E. (1986). *On being foreign: Culture shock in short fiction.* Yarmouth, ME: Intercultural Press.

Index

About the Editor

John Stone, PhD, is director of the Center for International Rehabilitation Research Information and Exchange (CIRRIE), a project funded by the National Institute on Disability and Rehabilitation Research of the U.S. Department of Education. The mission of CIRRIE is to facilitate the sharing of information and expertise between rehabilitation researchers in the United States and those in other countries. As part of this project, he has served as the editor of a monograph series on the cultures of the principal countries of origin of recent immigration to the United States. He is also a clinical associate professor in the Department of Rehabilitation Science at the State University of New York at Buffalo. Prior to joining the faculty of the University of Buffalo in 1991, he worked for 17 years as a faculty member in Brazil. He also served as a Peace Corps volunteer in India from 1967 to 1969.

About the Contributors

Nora Groce, PhD, is Associate Professor, Yale University School of Public Health. She is a medical anthropologist with a focus on international health and development. Her research includes issues of disability in global health and development, violence as a universal public health problem, and health equity in ethnic and minority communities. She is a founding member of the Society for Disability Studies and the author of numerous publications on cross-cultural disability. She frequently serves as a consultant to organizations such as the World Health Organization, UNICEF, Rehabilitation International, and the World Bank.

Dulce Haeussler-Fiore came to the United States from the Dominican Republic at the age of 37. She has worked in the health field in various capacities since then, while pursuing a master's degree and later a doctoral degree in psychology. She recently completed her doctoral program with a dissertation on domestic battered and batterers. For years, she has been helping Hispanic communities as a service coordinator, a mental health clinician, and lately as a pastor of a local Massachusetts church.

Peter Cody Hunt was born and raised in Vietnam. He holds a master's of public health degree from Boston University. He has worked as a Fellow at the Center for Disease Control on research on disability among minority populations. His main interest was to study cultural influence on self-identification of disability status. He has also worked at the National Institute for Disability and Rehabilitation Research (NIDRR) as special assistant to the director. He has been an NIDRR Research Scholar and Research Fellow. He is currently enrolled in a doctoral program in rehabilitation science and technology at the University of Pittsburgh.

Erik Jacobson, EdD, is a literacy and community-based education specialist at the Center for World Cultures and Languages, University of Massachusetts in Boston. He has worked with the Haitian community of Boston for 9 years in a variety of capacities. Most recently, he has coordinated collaborative activities between the Center and three community service agencies (the Haitian

American Public Health Initiative, the Somali Development Center, and the Capeverdean Association of Brockton). He is currently working with the Haitian Family Support Program to develop outreach materials, such as videos in Haitian Creole, to raise awareness of disability issues within the Haitian community.

Mary Ann Jezewski, PhD, RN, FAAN, is an associate professor and associate dean for research in the School of Nursing at the University of Buffalo, State University of New York. She is an anthropologist who developed a model of culture brokering in the health professions. She has recently adapted it for use by persons providing disability services. She has also led research projects related to end-of-life issues.

Weol Soon Kim-Rupnow, PhD, was born in Korea but did her graduate work at the University of Hawaii. She is currently a member of the faculty of the University of Hawaii Center on Disability Studies and codirector of a federally funded research project to assist children with reading difficulties. She also works at the university's National Technical Assistance Center for Asians and Pacific Islanders with Disabilities and its National Center for the Study of Educational Supports for Persons with Disabilities.

Gloria Zhang Liu, a first-generation immigrant from the People's Republic of China, holds a master's degree in special education with a major in rehabilitation science. Since 1993, she has been working in New York City with people with disabilities in various capacities, such as counselor, bilingual case manager, and coordinator and director of traumatic brain injury projects. Part of her responsibilities in these roles has been developing and translating culturally competent education and outreach materials for use by rehabilitation professionals, consumers, and family members. She has also worked to establish support networks for consumers and their families from ethnically and culturally diverse communities.

Ana López-De Fede, PhD, holds a doctorate in health services research/health policy and master's degrees in vocational rehabilitation counseling and counseling psychology. She is a research associate professor at the Institute for Families in Society, adjunct faculty in the Department of Pediatrics, and affiliated faculty member with the Department of Special Education in the Educational Psychology Department at the University of South Carolina. She currently directs the Division of Health and Family Studies, an interdisciplinary unit that explores the links between health and family well-being. She is actively involved in consulting on programs that address the needs of individuals from the Caribbean basin.

Doreen Miller, PhD, received her undergraduate and graduate education in the United States, including a master's degree in guidance counseling from

Washington State University and an RhD in rehabilitation counseling from Southern Illinois University at Carbondale. She is currently a professor in the Department of Psychology and Rehabilitation Programs at Southern University in Baton Rouge, Louisiana, where she has worked since 1977.

Felipe O. Santana, PhD, has worked for 24 years as a senior psychologist in mental health and senior program administrator for the Ventura County, California, Department of Drugs and Alcohol. The former director of Golden State Community Mental Health, he has written on health care for Latinos, including a chapter in *Healing Latinos* titled "Dolor de Cabeza: Depression or Martyrdom." He also worked for 10 years at the University of California at Los Angeles in research projects comparing benefits of treatment programs between Mexican and Anglo populations.

Sandra Santana-Martin, PsyD, received her doctorate in clinical psychology from Rutgers University and wrote her doctoral dissertation on a community-based program aimed at Latino teenage mothers, the goal of which was prevention of childhood abuse and neglect. She has worked at the Kessler Institute for Rehabilitation in Chester, New Jersey, and the Kaiser Permanente Medical Center in Los Angeles. She is currently working in a community health center in central California as a behavioral health consultant and psychologist using a model in which primary care is integrated with mental health services. The community health center serves predominantly the Mexican farmworking community.

Paula Sotnik has over twenty years of experience working as a curriculum developer and trainer, diversity and disability specialist, and project director. She currently coordinates Community Capacity Building Projects, which includes federal and state initiatives designed to support individuals with disabilities from diverse ethnic, cultural, and linguistic backgrounds for the Institute for Community Inclusion at the University of Massachusetts—Boston and Boston Children's Hospital. She assisted in the adaptation of the culture brokering model for use by rehabilitation professionals and coauthored on this topic for CIRRIE at the University at Buffalo at SUNY. She also worked on projects examining the relationship of diverse cultures in employment for persons with HIV/AIDS, using Person-Centered Planning Processes with unserved communities and responses to the use of assistive technology by individuals with disabilities from diverse cultures. Ms. Sotnik provides consultation to a variety of public agencies and private organizations on outreach and provision of responsive disability services to people from diverse cultural backgrounds. She is the author of several publications on culturally responsive outreach strategies and the capacity development of diverse grassroots community and faith-based organizations.